Gay Fathers,
Twin Sons

Gay Fathers, Twin Sons

The Citizenship Case That Captured the World

Nancy L. Segal

ROWMAN & LITTLEFIELD
Lanham • Boulder • New York • London

Published by Rowman & Littlefield
An imprint of The Rowman & Littlefield Publishing Group, Inc.
4501 Forbes Boulevard, Suite 200, Lanham, Maryland 20706
www.rowman.com

86-90 Paul Street, London EC2A 4NE

British Library Cataloguing in Publication Information Available

Library of Congress Cataloging-in-Publication Data Available

ISBN: 978-1-5381-7125-7 (cloth)
ISBN: 978-1-5381-7126-4 (electronic)

For transnational couples
whose twin and non-twin children were delivered abroad—
may America welcome you

Contents

Preface

$\mathcal{I}$deas for my books usually come from other people. *Someone Else's Twin* was inspired by a colleague who sent me a captivating newspaper article about switched-at-birth twins in the Canary Islands. *Deliberately Divided* was the product of a conversation I had with a filmmaker whose documentary film featured the most controversial twin study I had ever encountered. *Accidental Brothers* came from a call with a social work administrator who told me about a double identical twin switch in Colombia, South America. And my first book, *Entwined Lives*, was proposed by a literary agent who sensed correctly that a general but highly informative popular science book on a range of twin-related topics was missing from bookstore shelves. These unplanned, unexpected ventures were completely irresistible and always thrilling, but that pattern changed in January 2018. A headline story in the *Los Angeles Times* first caught *my* attention.[1] I knew with complete certainty that my next book—one that combined gay marriage, twinship, egg donation, surrogacy, and citizenship—was begging to be written. Here is what I learned at that time.

Andrew Banks, a citizen of the United States, and Elad Dvash, a citizen of Israel, were married in Canada in 2010. The Defense of Marriage Act (DOMA) was the reason they married outside the United States.[2] Signed into law by former president Bill Clinton in 1996, the ruling did not allow Andrew to sponsor Elad for a United States visa, since federal recognition of same-sex marriage was lacking.[3] Consequently, Canada was their next best choice for marrying and establishing residency; Andrew had dual citizenship as a Canadian, since his parents had been born there. As a citizen of Canada, he could also sponsor Elad's application for permanent residency in that country.[4]

Several years later, the couple—now Andrew and Elad Dvash-Banks—conceived fraternal twin sons, Aiden and Ethan, with a gestational surrogate. Both men had contributed sperm that were mixed with donated eggs to create embryos for implantation in the uterus of a Canadian woman. But there was no guarantee that both men would become fathers, because not all embryos survive the recommended three- to five-day window prior to implantation, or implant successfully after that.[5]

Happily, it turned out that two embryos did implant, and two baby boys were born—Andrew had contributed his sperm to one newborn (Aiden) and Elad had contributed his sperm to the other (Ethan). The twins were born just minutes apart on September 16, 2016. It was a celebration of family ties that promised years of joy, nurturance, and love, not to mention bar mitzvahs, swimming lessons, and school graduations.

Several months later, in 2017, Andrew and Elad prepared to relocate to Los Angeles where Andrew had been raised. The move would allow them and their then-four-month-old twins to be close to Andrew's sisters and brothers. Andrew's mother, Ann, despite living in Florida, traveled frequently to the Los Angeles area to visit family and friends. Leaving the frigid winters of Toronto for the mild climate of Southern California was another incentive for Andrew and Elad to head southward.

But there were unanticipated hurdles and heartbreak waiting for Andrew and Elad when they arrived at the United States consulate in Toronto. After being directed by security to Consular Services, they took a number and waited their turn. Consular officials completely upended the couple's plans—hardly the routine visit that Andrew and Elad had envisioned. The fabric of this young family was suddenly and severely threatened as one of their twin sons was denied US citizenship. What happened next was four years of legal filings, media exposure, and constant fear that they would be unable to live together in the United States.

In 2018 I could not write about this extraordinary case, nor could I speak with any of the Dvash-Banks family members. Legal proceedings were in play, and the couple's attorneys warned them not to discuss their situation with anyone to avoid jeopardizing their hoped-for outcome. Still, I persisted discreetly. As someone who had studied reared-apart twins (and is a same-sex fraternal twin herself), I wanted to prevent an impending twin separation—I had seen the heartache and regret that twins experience when they reunite and mourn the loss of growing up together. And in all honesty, I worried that another author and/or film-maker might secure the couple's story ahead of me, and, in my mind, I was committed to doing it.

In July 2018 I contacted journalist Brian Melley, who had covered the case for the *Orange County Register* in southern California. Melley had interviewed the couple, prompting me to ask him for their contact information, even knowing he would decline. (I never release personal information about the twins I study without their permission.) Melley said his call to Andrew and Elad had been facilitated by Jackie Yodash-kin, then public affairs director at Immigration Equality,[6] a New York City–based nonprofit organization that supports immigrants and mem-bers of the LGBTQ and HIV-positive communities facing discrimina-tion. Melley provided the contact information for Jackie Yodashkin (also posted on the organization's website) and the telephone number and website address for Andrew's sister, Ashli Shapiro.

I reached Ashli by telephone in late July 2018 and was delighted at her enthusiasm for a book about her brother, brother-in-law, and the two young nephews she adored. I also learned that Ashli was the mother of then ten-year-old fraternal twin boys, Liam and Wesley, and that she was a gifted photographer. Ashli graciously offered to provide her best family photographs for the book when the time came—and she has fulfilled that promise, as you will see throughout the chapters. Our somewhat stilted conversation did not last long since we both knew—and regretted—that we were forbidden from speaking. She wrote:

> Nancy—thank you for your message—I hate not being able to dis-cuss(!). Off the record—personally I love your book idea! And please know that I would love to be considered as a contributing photogra-pher should you be looking for one . . . :)

Jackie Yodashkin was also favorable toward my idea of a book about the Dvash-Banks case—mine was the only book proposal she had received, but there had been interest from documentary filmmakers. She also explained why Ashli had not returned my last call. "I asked her to hold off on calling you back pending our conversation, which is why she hasn't responded." However, Jackie agreed to pose my book idea to Andrew and Elad following the trial portion of the case. I told her I understood that reporters were not allowed to be present at trial, but that as an academic, perhaps I could be admitted. I was wrong.

I also confessed to Jackie that, several months earlier, I had exchanged e-mails with Alexa M. Lawson-Remer, special counsel at the international law firm of Sullivan & Cromwell, in Los Angeles, who was working on the case pro bono. I felt I could be helpful, having been an expert witness on twin cases involving wrongful death, injury, custody, classroom placement, and cheating accusations. Ms. Lawson-Remer replied that if I were needed, I would be notified. Jackie agreed to pass on my portfolio to Alexa and to others on the legal team. I had plenty to do while waiting to see what the court would decide.

At the time, I was hard at work on a proposal for a book about the 1960s–1970s New York City twin study in which newborn identical twins were intentionally placed apart by Louise Wise Services and studied for twelve years by a team of psychiatrists, physicians, psychologists, and assistants associated with the Jewish Board of Guardians. The adoptive parents were never told they were raising a "singleton twin." The twin study became headline news with the accidental reunion of separated identical triplets, the focus of a 2018 documentary film, *Three Identical Strangers*. In February 2019 I was offered a contract for a book—*Deliberately Divided: Inside the Controversial Study of Twins and Triplets Adopted Apart*—with Rowman & Littlefield,[7] but I still followed the Dvash-Banks case whenever a new legal development was reported in the press.

Still hopeful of breaking the impasse, I tried my luck with Spencer Tilger, then public affairs manager at Immigration Equality.[8] Spencer was interested and courteous but insisted on my maintaining silence. Importantly, by May 2019 the US government had appealed the district court's decision to grant US citizenship to Ethan to the circuit court. Spencer explained: "Unfortunately, it means that their [Andrew and Elad's] legal team is going to advise them against any book deals until the case is truly resolved." I updated Ashli by e-mail and was gratified by her reply (I will say more about our memorable back-and-forth in a later chapter).

Gay Fathers, Twin Sons is a book that needed to be written. In addition to revealing events surrounding the family's emotional upheaval, Aiden and Ethan's blossoming twinship, the legal proceedings, and the wide-reaching implications of decisions by attorneys and judges, I wanted to humanize the people involved. I was (and am) struck by how ordinary citizens trying to do ordinary things can be foiled by outdated expectations, legal misunderstandings, and antiquated legislation—and how Andrew and Elad's love for their twins sustained their fighting spirit and unwavering dedication to what they believed was right.

Unanticipated circumstances can put anyone's life on hold. Thus, after a brief introduction, I will follow Andrew, who was raised in Beverly Hills, California, but who explains that he was really from the "less affluent" southern section of that exclusive neighborhood. Next, I will profile Elad, whose childhood bridged a comfortable residential area of Tel Aviv and the upscale community of Givatayim. Following that, I will track the couple's three-and-a-half-year courtship, marital decision, and reproductive choices—and the citizenship policies that provoked their legal battles, ushering them into a limelight they did not seek.

Introduction

$\mathcal{I}$ was introduced to Andrew by telephone in November 2020 and to the couple via Zoom a month later. I didn't meet them in person until a year later, in December 2021, because of COVID pandemic restrictions and ongoing legal challenges. Revealing these events chronologically preserves the process by which I came to know these two men, their family, and their friends. Of course, we would have met sooner had the legal obstacles and the COVID-19 pandemic not intervened.

Our first two contacts in 2020 were really social visits, meant to get us acquainted. I conducted my first serious interview on the third visit, in 2021.

TALKING WITH ANDREW

When I called Andrew at our prearranged time, he was in his car having just dropped his young sons off at nursery school. He was enjoying a few peaceful moments that he admitted are becoming more infrequent. The lawsuit against the State Department had not reached a final settlement, but we were able to talk because, as Andrew explained, his lawyers were "waiting out the sixty-day appeal process—it's a different kind of appeal, because [the government] already appealed. So, this would be like an appeal of the appeal." Given that Donald Trump had been voted out of office in 2020, there was optimism among Andrew's legal team that the Trump administration would not resurrect the case during the final weeks of his presidency—and virtual certainty that president-elect

Biden's judicial appointments would support the Ninth Circuit Court judge's decision, granting US citizenship to Ethan.

We discussed the substance of the book. I listed the themes I wanted to address, namely twinship, gay marriage, citizenship policy, and reproductive surrogacy. Andrew replied, "I think—I mean, it might be a little cliché—but the theme of just, like, family and love and bonding." He added, "And a parent's will and desire and necessity to do whatever they can to protect their child." I assured Andrew that I would give plenty of attention to these concerns.

I also told Andrew who I wanted to speak with for a comprehensive portrait of their story. He was certain that the staff at Immigration Equality would be willing to share their thoughts. However, he noted that the lawyers who handled the bulk of the litigation, in Los Angeles and New York, preferred to stay in the background. "They focus on protecting their clients, and [are] uninterested in earning accolades for working pro bono," although Andrew was willing to approach the attorneys when the time was right. I also mentioned that it was important for me to contact the Canadian surrogate who bore the twins. "She's always said from the beginning, during our case, if you need me to talk to anybody, I'll do whatever."

Andrew's large assortment of brothers and sisters promised a rich source of reflections on their brother and the events of the last four years. Andrew is close with all five of them—Ashli, James, Jennifer, Brian, and Jonathan (Jon). He was certain that they, and his mother, Ann Banks, who had retired to Florida, would be excited to talk. I had also read in a newspaper article that the two fathers (but mostly Elad) were compiling a digital diary about their circuitous journey from Canada to the United States. This project was intended for the twins, so they could learn about their story when they were old enough "to understand kind of where we were in the world when they were four years old." Andrew promised to share portions of the record with me as my book progressed.

As our conversation ended, I mentioned to Andrew that it was great to be working again with people who wanted to talk with me. It was a familiar feeling, one that I had enjoyed throughout the writing of my first six books about twins. Everyone—twins, those who know them, and those who know of them—is captivated by the similarities and contrasts, friendship and support, that variously characterize identical, same-sex fraternal, and male-female pairs. I reminded Andrew that the heated debates surrounding my seventh book—*Deliberately Divided: Inside the Controversial Study of Twins and Triplets Adopted Apart*—made writing it a constant challenge. Many people refused to speak, did so only if not identified, or participated reluctantly. But ultimately, the end product was rewarding because the ethical offenses made by the investigators who purposely separated twins and secretly studied them needed to be revealed, and the twins' life stories needed to be told. *Gay Fathers, Twin Sons* is not a pleasant tale in all respects, but the hoped-for outcome is vital to countless families and children seeking the freedom to thrive. "Yeah, this will be a different experience," Andrew concluded.

ZOOMING WITH ANDREW AND ELAD

I scheduled a Zoom session one month later with Andrew and Elad together. I could see that both men were dressed casually in loose T-shirts and worn jeans. There was an easiness about them, both as individuals and as a couple, and a willingness to allow each partner opportunities to speak freely. The one who sat quietly for the moment nodded his assent from time to time, showing how much they were in sync about what they had endured. I spent slightly more time talking to Elad, since I had had a long conversation with Andrew just weeks before.

The two men seemed at peace—they both had good jobs, and their kids were doing well at school. Most importantly, they "detected signs" that their case would be dropped, although they remained cautious because the government could still appeal. At that time, in December 2020, they were living temporarily in a house in Westchester, an area of Los Angeles with a small-town feel, not far from the airport. They were eager to move into their new home in Hawthorne, much closer to the children's new school and to Andrew's workplace. Not surprisingly, renovations had delayed their move until July 2021.

We discussed their surrogacy experience, a financially expensive procedure without the guarantee of a healthy child, or a child at all. Andrew and Elad were equally interested in raising boys or girls, hoping only for healthy children. They understood that preimplantation genetic screening (PGS) of embryos can identify many chromosomal anomalies, such as Down syndrome (trisomy 21) and Tay-Sachs disease. That is important because embryos with detectable defects would not be chosen; however,

PGS does not test for all congenital conditions or specific diseases.[1] Andrew and Elad also told me about the pregnancy and the birth and the unexpected events that happened when their "lovely surrogate, Amanda," was in the delivery room. These are details I have saved for later.

I learned that Elad's parents, Tova (Tovi) and Mordehay (Moti), would be open to an interview as long as a Hebrew–English translator were available. He was sure that his younger sisters, Neta and Yarden, would agree to participate, and also urged me to speak with Rotem Cohen, his best friend since third grade. Rotem was living in Canada when the boys were born, but she had moved back to Israel in 2013. As I expected, nearly everyone suggested someone that I "*had* to speak with." I spoke with all of them because people recall events in slightly different ways, such that the truth lies at the intersection of their memories and reflections. I also planned to interview the twins' transitional-kindergarten teacher and swimming coach.[2]

I admit that I e-mailed Andrew in February 2021 when the government's appeal period had not elapsed, but I had good reason. I was completing the proposal for *Gay Fathers, Twin Sons*, and hoping to strengthen my case for the book, I asked Andrew if he and Elad were open to a documentary film or other media. He answered, "With the change in administration we anticipate any day now—[we hope] that the new administration will drop the appeal and we will be finally DONE with this. Our lawyers are still very wary until that happens. But as soon as the case is dropped [hopefully], we will have the freedom and flexibility to do as we please."

FIRST MEETING—AT LAST

When I was a young child living in the Bronx, I thought that the television actors and cartoon characters I saw on screen were inside the box. What a joy it would be if they were to emerge from their confinement and appear in person in our living room! I eventually understood that the figures in the programs I loved were broadcast across wires from remote studios to private homes around the country. When I met Andrew and Elad in person, it was as if they had come from "inside the box," since I had seen them so often in media images and online interviews. A childhood fantasy realized.

The Dvash-Bankses' new home, built in 1949, is one of many single-story single-family dwellings, located in the middle of a street belonging to a large grid of similar streets. The exterior was painted an attractive teal blue–medium gray color, distinguishing it from the others in the area. It's just a short drive to the lovely beaches of Hermosa and Redondo, and to Andrew's place of work at SpaceX. Important to Andrew and Elad is that the neighborhood schools received high marks from *GreatSchools Ratings and Reviews*.[3] The children's school at the time was down the block from where they live. Despite the large number of homes in the area, no restaurants or shops were in sight except for Denny's, part of a popular chain of diner-style eateries in the United States and abroad.

When I arrived, I spotted the twin boys riding bikes, their dog London, a pug-terrier mix, lounging on the front lawn. London had also made the journey from Toronto to Los Angeles with the family. I smiled, thinking that no one at the US consulate had questioned London's citizenship.

The interior of the Dvash-Bankses' three-bedroom, two-bathroom home was modern and sleek but had a homey feel. The front part was an open concept in which the kitchen, breakfast nook, dining area, and living room blended into one another; it was spacious, airy, and very "California," i.e., casual and sunny. The kitchen counter was crowded with cool-looking machines and fancy gadgets that I had no names for. Wall hangings, a menorah, mezuzahs, and various decorative objects and artifacts placed on walls and shelves reflected the Jewish identity and culture of this young family.

I was introduced to the then five-year-old twins, Aiden and Ethan, who were at ease with an unfamiliar visitor. As we shook hands, I presented each boy with an oversized, spherical lollipop made of marshmallow, chocolate, and mint. They relished the treat for about five minutes before moving on to a different pastime. There would be several interruptions during the prearranged two-hour interview, but Andrew and Elad were experts at engaging the twins in different activities and games. The boys alternately played together and apart; I sensed that Ethan was the more dominant and independent twin, an impression confirmed by his parents. Finally, the three of us moved to the living room and sat around a circular coffee table. I remembered that when we were scheduling this session, I was asked if I preferred meeting outside at a park, since their patio furniture had not yet arrived—COVID was still a worry, and the twins had not been vaccinated—but I felt comfortable being indoors. I was impressed by the couple's thoughtfulness and concern.

Because I considered this meeting to be our first "formal" session, I presented Andrew and Elad with two consent forms, one for the use of interview material and one for the publication of photographs. Both forms were standard documents provided by my publisher, Rowman & Littlefield. When signed, the forms grant permission for using information gathered from discussions with interviewees, as well as any letters, diaries, or other personal sources they provided. Andrew and Elad signed the second form (for the use of photographic images) without discussion but wanted their lawyers to review the first one prior to signing. (They still consented to proceed with the interview.)

I understood that they were accustomed to being cautious due to their history of legal traumas. Their hesitation came specifically from the idea of signing away the rights to their story and their control over how the information would be presented. I explained that I would be undertaking this book project for the thrill and honor of bringing their extraordinary story to the policy makers, politicians, administrators, and families who needed to hear it. I was pleased and relieved that they agreed with this view. And I also assured them that they could review the different chapters prior to submission, a practice I have followed to confirm the accuracy of the information and guarantee the comfort of those involved. I reminded them that I am a university professor and academic researcher whose integrity and reputation rest on getting things right. I received their signed consent forms several weeks later.

We talked about many of the same topics I had raised previously, but in greater detail—the structure of the book, who to interview, details of their courtship and marriage, family planning, the reproductive process, the pregnancy and delivery, and how the boys' names were decided. They emphasized how hard it was to find legal representation and expressed how grateful they had been to Immigration Equality for supporting their case. I told them I didn't want to overwhelm them with "assignments," but I would need a litigation timeline at some point; Elad promised to provide one.

When our two hours were nearly up, I asked if I could take a family photo. Andrew explained that they were meeting relatives in Beverly

Hills for an annual dinner excursion to Lawry's, an upscale restaurant chain famous for prime rib—and I should wait a few moments until they were dressed for the occasion. A dinner at Lawry's around the December holidays was a tradition started by Andrew's father and one that continued after his death. The large number of siblings, along with their spouses and children, often guaranteed a thirty-person party. Andrew's brother James later explained that it was a time to get together and to remember the senior James (Jim) Banks.

The two fathers managed to get the boys into crisp white shirts and dark pants, but getting them to stand still for a photograph required dispensing some pre-dinner treats. I snapped a picture of the four of them and one of Elad and Ethan, but Aiden was not willing to cooperate further. Moments before, Aiden had been visibly upset to discover that some of the twins' art supplies had been used up. He wanted to glue strips of paper onto a larger page, but Elad encouraged him to draw a picture instead.

When I saw my boyfriend's car pull up, I waved good-bye and said I'd be in touch. I felt thrilled by the interest and generosity they had shown during the visit. The next day, I sent an e-mail to Andrew and Elad, thanking them for their time and reminding them to contact their siblings about being interviewed for the book. They had also wanted to watch the riveting reunion tape of separated fraternal twins, Michele Mordkoff and Allison Kanter, who had been placed apart in the 1960s by the Louise Wise Services in New York City.[4] I forwarded the link.

Two days later, Andrew wrote to say that he had notified his siblings about the book project and would introduce me when the time came. The exhilaration I had felt at the end of our meeting returned, tempered by my belief that the future of this family, and others like it, was going to raise new challenges.

· 1 ·

Private Citizen to Global Stage:
Andrew Banks

$\mathcal{S}$ome names become headline news, but not because of an extraordinary accomplishment or exceptional skill. This can happen unexpectedly, when a person's life events do not align with what the law requires, or what society demands. Without intention, some individuals leave a lasting mark on legal interpretation, social policy, and/or public awareness, easing the lives of those who come after them. These individuals are committed to setting things right, and in doing so they elevate themselves from private citizen to the global stage, even when they do not seek recognition.

Andrew Dvash-Banks is such a person.

Andrew, now a forty-two-year-old husband, father, son, and brother, enjoys the two ingredients that someone once told me are the basis of a happy life—a secure, loving relationship and an interesting, challenging job. He and his husband, Elad, and their now six-year-old twin sons settled into their new home in Los Angeles in July 2021. Andrew's position as travel manager for Elon Musk's SpaceX, which involves establishing airline rates, hotel costs, and car rentals for the thousands of participants in the company's national and international launches, is his "dream job." But alongside this satisfaction loomed the threat that US citizenship would be denied to one of his sons—even the real possibility that young Ethan would be forcibly removed by immigration officials while he and Elad were at work.

Headline news does not neatly capture the humanity of people who achieve significant change, suffer agonizing loss, or weather grueling personal battles. Andrew's life during his growing-up years and beyond reveals wonderful moments interspersed by trying times. Some of the darker episodes most likely prepared him for his family's nightmarish attempt at leaving Canada for the United States in 2017. His circumstances and situation were uniquely his, but at a different time or in a different place, we might aspire to his actions.

ANDREW'S FAMILY MEMBERS AND FRIENDS

Elad Dvash-Banks	Andrew's husband
Aiden Dvash-Banks	Andrew and Elad's son; Ethan's twin
Ethan Dvash-Banks	Andrew's and Elad's son; Aiden's twin
James "Jim" Banks	Andrew's father
Ann "Annie" Banks	Andrew's mother
James Banks	Andrew's brother
Ashli Shapiro	Andrew's maternal half-sister
Jennifer Levinson	Andrew's paternal half-sister
Jon Banks	Andrew's paternal half-brother
Brian Banks	Andrew's paternal half-brother
Jennifer ("Jen" or "Jenni") Sikov	Andrew's high school friend
Jessica Yousem	Andrew's high school friend
Laurel Mintz	Andrew's college friend

BEVERLY HILLS, CALIFORNIA

Andrew—"Drew" to his family and friends—was born in Santa Monica, California, an upscale coastal city to the west of Los Angeles. But he was raised in nearby Beverly Hills, a city famous for its celebrity dwellers, high-end shops, and exclusive eateries. He is quick to tell you that his parents, Jim and Ann, chose a four-bedroom, three-bathroom apartment in the less desirable part of town because they had limited finances. As an infant, Andrew slept in his parents' room until Jim's burgeoning accounting business allowed him to purchase a home in a relatively affordable section of the city.

Despite his growing financial success, Jim spent his money carefully. He took advantage of the free car washes and electrical repairs offered by his clients. He didn't care about fancy cars or designer labels;

when Ann asked for a Mercedes, Jim purchased the oldest and cheapest one he could find. The only exceptions to Jim's frugality were his sons' bar mitzvahs. Andrew's celebration took place at Sony Pictures, and James's commemoration was a lavish affair held on a boat.[1] Jim also cared a great deal about his place of worship, the University Synagogue in Brentwood, serving as its president for a number of years and using his accounting skills to improve its financial status.

Andrew's mother, Ann, thinks very differently about their residences. "The apartment was a block from where John Lithgow [the actor] lived, and Andrew played occasionally with his kids, Phoebe and Nathan, before the Lithgows left for Westwood." The family's next residence was a house on Rodeo Drive, where they moved when Andrew was eleven. "It's worth four million dollars today! We had a swimming pool, a guesthouse, an inlaid paneled library, and everyone had a bedroom with en suite bath." His older half-brother Brian, who visited on weekends, remembers the house as being "really nice." Ann added, "I know this was not a ghetto, but it was just south of Olympic Boulevard [the less trendy part of town]. When you think of Beverly Hills, you're thinking of those multimillion-dollar mansions north of Sunset Boulevard; at that time, our house was not one of them."[2]

Andrew still jokes that his family's financial success probably placed them above 99 percent of most people in the United States but left them at the bottom 1 percent of Beverly Hills residents. He feels blessed to have had many comforts but believes in hard work. He is quick to say that he had no handouts.

Seeing him now, Andrew hardly fits the stereotypical image of a former Beverly Hills resident. He prefers loose-fitting, non-designer T-shirts and slacks to the fashionable attire crafted by Calvin Klein, Ralph Lauren, or others of their ilk. (However, his younger brother James claimed that Andrew was more attentive to high style during his growing-up years—"He used to have a good fashion sense.")[3]

Another sibling recalled that Andrew's "more colorful traits" were/are expressed when he becomes emotional. And another said he seemed flamboyant in his teens, suggestive of Franck Eggelhoffer, the eccentric wedding planner in the 1991 film *Father of the Bride*. Having examined a clip from the film, showing the father, mother, prospective bride, and the Eggelhoffer character (played by Martin Short), I did not see similarities between Andrew and Franck. I wondered if those qualities, if present early on, dissipated in Andrew's later years. It seemed that they had.

It never bothered Andrew that many of his classmates came from much wealthier families—the ones who lived in mansions—since it wasn't in his nature to keep up with the crowd. In fact, his parents initially chose Beverly Hills because of the high quality of its schools rather than its glamour or prestige. Education was everything to them, and they wanted the best opportunities for their children, two of whom were ten years old—Jim's daughter Jennifer, and Ann's daughter Ashli, from their previous marriages. The girls were about to enter middle school when their respective parents became a couple and moved to the United States from Canada. Their focus on education continued when it came to their sons. Ann also wanted Andrew and his brother James to receive music instruction, take swimming lessons, and play in Little League, opportunities offered in Beverly Hills.[4]

Ann insisted that Andrew learn French even though she was not from Canada's French-speaking province of Quebec. While the family was "first and foremost an American family," Ann's determination to raise a "Canadian-minded" child was largely motivated by her memories of the Vietnam War, in particular, having conscientious objectors from America among her friends. (Canada did not officially participate in that war.) By the 1980s, when Ann was living in the United States, she had two small boys and did not wish to see them serve in the military against their will. In fact, the family flew both Canadian and American flags outside their home, one at a time, depending on the holiday (e.g., Independence Day or Canada Day),[5] although the American flag took precedence.

MOTHER AND FATHER, SISTERS AND BROTHERS

During Andrew's growing-up years, Ann was director of membership at the Beverly Hills Country Club. Her success at attracting new members led to an offer from a comparable country club in Manhattan Beach. There, according to Andrew, his mother "sold herself out of a job" in 2001 when the membership reached its limit. She retired in 2012 and moved to Perth, Australia. As of 2015, Ann lives in St. Lucie West, Florida, where she remains youthful in outlook and appearance.

Andrew described his mom as a "sixteen-year-old trapped in a seventy-something-year-old body—she's got that free spirit."

When I spoke to Ann a week later over Zoom, allowing me to see and hear her, it was clear that Andrew had it right. Words like "vivacious," "enthusiastic," and "dedicated" define her. She belongs to book clubs and writing groups, and stays connected to her Beverly Hills friends, one being its mayor. Her looks are striking for a woman of any age; on the day of our Zoom call, her shoulder-length blond hair was stylishly arranged, beautifully set against a black turtleneck top and gold jewelry.

But Ann's most impressive quality is her devotion to her children, evident to me by way of her extraordinary generosity and passion for my book. Throughout the writing process and mostly on her own initiative, she forwarded insightful recollections, useful contacts, and wonderful photographs. She hopes to one day return to Southern California to live closer to her family.

Andrew's father, Jim H. Banks, grew up in Toronto, Canada, but moved to Los Angeles in the 1960s to be with his first wife, Penny. The couple had three children: the oldest, Jennifer, followed by Brian a year later, and Jon two years after that. They eventually divorced, leaving Jim to make frequent trips to Toronto to visit relatives. On one such occasion he met Ann Mason-Johns, a divorcée with a young daughter. Ann and Jim's casual association evolved into a more serious relationship, and in 1980 they married and moved to Los Angeles.

Andrew is certain he was conceived on their wedding night, because he was born exactly nine months later, on January 18, 1981. Two and a half years after that, Andrew's younger brother James was born, yielding Andrew's total of three half-siblings (via his father), one half-sibling (via his mother), and one full brother (via both parents). Andrew shared his childhood home with Ashli and James, while the other three siblings lived with their mother, Penny, in Encino, about twenty miles from Beverly Hills. I was excited to learn that Andrew's half-sister Jennifer has two sets of twins, both male and both identical, and his half-sister Ashli has a set of fraternal male twins.[6]

Andrew's father Jim started his career as an attorney for the Equity Funding Life Insurance Company, a Los Angeles–based conglomerate with offices around the country.[7] The company marketed mutual funds and life insurance to private citizens in the 1960s and 1970s. In 1973 it was revealed that Equity Funding had been involved in bogus insurance, as well as securities and mail fraud. Jim was sentenced to three years in jail but served time for one year at the Federal Correctional Institution in Lompoc, California, followed by six months "in hard-core prisons" in Chicago and Joliet, Illinois.

Upon his release, he launched his successful accounting business. It was a commendable way of turning his life around, coming out of that experience and building something back up again.[8] Of course, Jim was very embarrassed about his past, given his disbarment and jail term. His only option was to start his own accounting practice, since no one would hire someone with a felony record; such information is required on job applications. His humiliation also explains why he hid this episode from his younger sons, Andrew and James.[9]

Andrew didn't discover this family secret until he was nineteen, when it was accidentally leaked to him by his father's son, Brian. The two half-brothers were spending the day at the University of California, Santa Barbara (UCSB), where Brian had graduated ten years earlier, and Andrew was thinking of applying. It was the first time that the two were both old enough to have "real conversations."[10] According to Andrew, "Brian said that the book written about Dad is here, and he asked me if I wanted to see it. And I was like, 'Someone wrote a book about our dad?' And he's like, 'Yeah, about, you know, the time he went to jail and the fraud scandal and everything.' And I was just like, 'He went to jail?'" Andrew recalled, "I still had no idea what he [Brian] was talking about."

Brian, upset that he had inadvertently divulged this news, decided it was time to head home. But this was not the only secret revealed that day.

In an effort to end the "awkward silence" during the two-hour ride back to Beverly Hills, Andrew recalled saying, "'Well, you know what we *can* talk about?' I was like, 'I'm gay,' and it [was] just like, 'Okay, let's talk about that.' So that's how I came out to Brian."

They talked about it the rest of the way home. Brian asked a lot of questions but accepted what Andrew had to say.[11]

VERY BRIEF INTERLUDE

When I asked Andrew to describe his childhood and adolescence, he declared with considerable pride that he has a "photographic memory."

"I'm really, really good with dates and names and just the details of my life. And I'm super interested in the history of my family." I marveled at how many of my questions Andrew anticipated and how honest he is about people, places, and events. "I guess as part of being an Ashkenazi Jew, I just, I'm very open with my feelings. Elad is a little bit different, maybe that's part of being a Sephardic Jew—a little more closed with his feelings—but the two of us together are very open. And, you know, I think it's important to tell our story for other families that might find themselves in a similar situation, and for our children's sake, as well."

GROWING UP AND COMING OUT

Andrew was eleven or twelve years old when he developed a crush on a male student at Hebrew school. That's when he knew he was gay. "It was definitely before my bar mitzvah."[12]

Being gay thirty years ago was very different than it is today, something Andrew believes many people do not understand. "We were coming off the crest of the AIDS epidemic. Things had just turned a corner, but there was no general acceptance [of homosexuality], and it was still politically a dead issue. No one talked about it or wanted to deal with it." He reminded me that ABC's comedy show *Ellen* was canceled in 1998 when its lead character, played by Ellen DeGeneres, announced she was gay.[13] "That was huge," Andrew recalled. "But it was such a slap in the face for the LGBTQ [lesbian, gay, bisexual, transgender, queer or questioning] community. Here you come out and now we're going to cancel you because no one wants to see you."[14]

Despite living in one of the most liberal cities in America, Andrew was the only openly gay student at Beverly Hills High School. As a junior, he had revealed this news to several friends, but they talked, and rumors spread quickly. He was bullied by fellow students, had his car tires slashed, and was chased on the high school grounds. Administrators believed he was not safe at the school and called for measures to protect him and to educate students and staff about issues faced by gay pupils.[15] His defenders were mostly female students, many of whom he remains close to today. But according to Ann, Andrew's favorite childhood playmates were identical twins, David and Jarod Krissman; according to her, "they were inseparable." He also had lots of girls as friends because he was cute and good-looking, as well as masculine and into sports.[16] But the bullying was hard to handle. As Andrew explained, at that time there was no real term for gay discrimination; any attack on a student by another student was "bullying." Then he discovered Teen Line.

Co-founded in 1980 by clinical social worker Dr. Elaine Leader and psychiatrist Dr. Terry Lipton, Teen Line continues to be a nonprofit, national hotline of teen listeners (not counselors) trained to address the questions and concerns of teens struggling with any number of friend, family, and identity concerns. Phone calls are anonymous. Dr. Leader also organized an outreach program in which gay students, including Andrew, spoke at local schools and community centers about growing up gay.[17] Volunteering at Teen Line at age sixteen and beyond helped Andrew feel comfortable with himself by assisting teens in similar circumstances. Ann became an active board member and vice president of the organization, as well as a lifelong friend of Dr. Leader, even though Ann was unaware of Andrew's sexuality concerns at the time.

In a curious twist, Ellen DeGeneres is responsible for Andrew's coming out to his mother. Each year, Teen Line hosts a fund-raising ("Food for Thought") luncheon, at which they honor an individual who makes a significant difference in people's lives. This annual event is held at the Crystal Ballroom of the Beverly Hills Hotel. In 1998, Teen Line chose Ellen DeGeneres as their honoree. Ellen was accompanied to the fund-raiser by her significant other at the time, the late actress Anne Heche, and Ellen's mother, Betty. The three were surrounded by people taking photographs, but Andrew was undeterred. He went up to them and asked to speak with them privately for a moment. "Sure, it was ballsy of me. There was literally a line of people waiting to take a picture with them. I pulled the three of them away and said, 'Look, I'm gay, and I'm ready to come out to my mom. And she's here today.' "

Andrew said he wanted his mother to see him as he really was, and that he admired the close relationship Ellen and Betty clearly enjoyed. "They didn't even really say much to me. It was just an opportunity for me to tell them what I was going to do. But just to have that acknowledged by them [was special], and Ellen made some funny joke. I don't even remember what it was, but Betty said, 'You know, you'll be fine. Your mother will accept you and she'll love you.' "

After Andrew and Ann came home that day, they were seated alone in the kitchen when Andrew opened up to his mother. "I'll never forget

Teen Line's 1998 "Food for Thought" Luncheon, held in the Crystal Ballroom of the Beverly Hills Hotel. The theme of the event, which honored Ellen DeGeneres, was "Growing Up Gay." Ellen DeGeneres is in the center, and next to her, to the right, is her then partner, the late actress Anne Heche. Andrew is next to DeGeneres on the left, and next to him is his high school friend Jenni (Stone) Sikov. The female behind DeGeneres and Heche is Sarah Pollack, while the two males behind them are unidentified. *Source*: Photo courtesy of Elaine Leader.

it. She was super supportive and, you know, everything that I knew she would be. It was obviously such a weight off my chest. I'm sure she was sad because she didn't want me to have a difficult life or be discriminated against. But it's a funny, interesting coming-out story that Ellen DeGeneres and her mother were involved in."

Coming out to Ann "wasn't super comfortable," but it was more comfortable than coming out to Jim. Andrew was nervous because his father was a proud conservative whose political views and social values were at great odds with Andrew's. Andrew recalled his father commenting that "AIDS is a gay disease." And if the family went out to dinner, Jim would point out people who appeared to be gay. "Look at them!" he would say.

Andrew was certain his mother wouldn't tell his father about his sexuality, since relations between his parents were strained at the time. So, he decided to write about being gay in his college essay—after all, his father, unaware of Andrew's sexual orientation, had been pushing him to write it. When Andrew presented it to his father, "He didn't express any emotions or acknowledge it, he just said there were no spelling errors! He was obviously very uncomfortable, but we didn't have a real relationship anyway, so the fact that he didn't acknowledge it didn't bother me."[18] In fact, Ann recalled Jim saying that Andrew had come into "a right-handed world as a left-hander," and care should be taken to avoid elbowing people at the dinner table. "I thought [Jim's comment] was brilliant," she said, understanding that her son's life would not always be easy. But privately, Jim confided that he might have been heartbroken if Andrew were his only son to carry on the family name.[19]

Telling his sister Ashli and some of his other siblings was easier. In fact, he had told Ashli before telling his mother. Ashli is ten years older than Andrew, and he considers her "the cool mom you always wanted, that you can relate to." He added, "I wasn't really hiding it. So, it's like anyone with three brain cells could tell I was gay." Andrew's good friend from Teen Line, Jennifer (Jen) Sikov, said she "just knew"; they have remained close friends for over twenty-five years.

However, the situation got tense at school when Andrew was a sophomore. The yearbook, while focused on seniors, did include material about other classes. Next to Andrew's picture the yearbook staff had indicated that his favorite song was "I'm Every Woman"—done as a gag and without his consent. He came home distraught. Ann, who was then public relations commissioner for the school district, demanded that a longer piece about Andrew, acknowledging his many achievements, be included in the next edition, and her efforts paid off. Andrew was the outstanding junior student featured the following year. The yearbook highlighted his participation on the swim team, water polo team, AP (Advanced Placement) classes, and community service. Andrew believes this was done to compensate him for the pain they had caused him the year before.

Then it was senior year.

One of Andrew's female friends was editor of the high school newspaper, the *Beverly Hills Highlights*. She wanted to write an article about him coming out as gay, and he agreed. "I was comfortable. At this point everyone knew, and, like I said, I was the only student [who was open about it]. The paper was distributed every Friday and widely read because Internet and cell phones were unknown." The article appeared on the front page of the paper and was supportive, with reassuring quotes from teachers and friends, but that didn't matter to some students. "I got a lot of flak for it, and the harassment definitely picked up," Andrew recalled. His brother James, a sophomore, knew without being told. James is also gay but delayed coming out until he turned twenty-seven. According to James, "We [Drew and I] were kind of opposites in a lot of ways growing up. And, maybe, I feel like at least at the time, [this] gave me more justification for denying who I was."[20]

Andrew's openness about the issues in his life and his drive to resolve them would be evident again in his fight for the citizenship of his child.

ALL IN THE FAMILY

Andrew was not raised in a harmonious household, but one that was "very complicated and messy." Growing up, the various maternal and paternal half-siblings saw each other only occasionally. That was partly because Ashli lived with Ann and Jim, while Jon, Jen, and Brian lived with their mother, Jim's ex-wife Penny. Andrew's half-brother Brian observed that the two parents (Jim and Penny) put their children in the middle.[21]

Worse was the constant conflict between Jim and Ann, leading to their bitter divorce in 2000, when Andrew was a freshman at the University of California, Santa Barbara. He was not surprised when it happened, describing his father as cold, distant, and often working late into the night. "He was always yelling and was just overall unpleasant and very dominating in his demeanor." Ann was the opposite—"loving, supportive, and giving me everything I needed." The divorce, while not unexpected, was traumatizing and heartbreaking for Andrew. He worshipped his mother, believing she was infallible, before discovering her imperfections. "You see that through an adult perspective—it's important that every child learn that their parents have shortcomings." Ann remained a solid source of love and support, especially during the four years that the divorce proceedings dragged on. And despite her relocation to Florida, where the time is inconveniently three hours ahead of Los Angeles, Ann and Andrew are in almost daily contact.

Andrew and his father eventually reconciled their differences and grew close while Jim and Ann went through marital difficulties and divorce; Andrew was a college freshman at the time. His relationship with Jim deepened further when Jim was diagnosed with cancer in the early to mid-2000s and experienced an aortic rupture in 2012 that nearly killed him. Jim passed away in June 2016 at age seventy-seven. One of Andrew's greatest sorrows is that his father never knew his twin grandchildren, Aiden and Ethan.[22]

Andrew's younger brother James, a radiologist in Fort Lauderdale, lives about a two-hour drive from their mother's home. Still, the brothers remain close despite the distance between them. The paternal half-siblings became closely connected with the approach of adulthood that blurred the eight- to ten-year age difference among them. During the writing of this book, on February 19, 2022, Jennifer, Brian, and Jon lost their mother, Penny. James flew to Los Angeles so he and Andrew could offer their support.

Andrew's concern for family and individuals in need would be expressed in other unforeseen circumstances, prior to the incident at the US consulate in Canada. And he was honest when lying would have been a simpler solution. As a student at UCSB, he was threatened, even chased, causing him to be very fearful at times. These experiences, while painful, drove him to provide assistance when needed.[23]

WEST COAST TO MIDDLE EAST

"Drew has always been keenly aware of our world. He hung a huge map of the world in his bedroom and could locate obscure countries easily."

—Andrew's mother, Ann Banks, 2022

Andrew always loved and longed for international travel, language, culture, and adventure. He backpacked alone across Europe during the summer between his junior and senior years in high school and lived for a while with a family in France. When it came to college, his father insisted that he attend a public university, which is considerably less costly than a private school, but that didn't dampen Andrew's travel ambitions. He chose the University of California, Santa Barbara, with a major in global studies and a minor in Italian.[24]

Given his penchant for new and exciting places, he took part in Santa Barbara's study abroad program by enrolling in Ca'Foscari University of Venice. Founded in 1868, the school is housed in the Venetian gothic palace of Ca'Foscari and ranks third among Italian universities.[25] Andrew studied the Italian language and culture and took "really interesting classes in Italian." His interest in foreign policy led him to an internship at the Woodrow Wilson Center in Washington, DC, during the spring semester of his junior year. Upon returning to Santa Barbara for his senior year, Andrew declared Italian as a second major. He still speaks Italian, as well as Hebrew and French. During his senior year he traveled to Israel in a program for young Jewish adults, sponsored by the Birthright Israel Foundation.[26]

After graduating from college, Andrew moved to New York City with his boyfriend of the past year.[27] The journey did not start or end well. Andrew's partner was driving when they arrived in Wyoming and hit a deer in the middle of the night, destroying Andrew's car. They finally flagged down a driver to take them to the nearest town and finished the trip in the only vehicle they could get—a U-Haul. When they reached New York City, Andrew's partner "dumped him." He called his high school friend, Jessica Yousem, who was in New York with her family. Jessica was shopping, so she ignored his repeated attempts to reach her. When she finally answered, Andrew was sobbing. Jessica insisted that he meet her right away. He did, and he spent that night at the hotel with Jessica and her parents. "He was like family, and still is," Jessica reflected.[28]

Andrew stayed in New York for two and a half years—his mother had moved there, he had friends in town, and *Sex and the City* was his favorite television show. Being in New York was "so cool—exciting and dynamic." His close college friend, Laurel Mintz, was living in Philadelphia but joined Andrew on weekends. "He was the life of the party," Laurel remembers. "But we weren't just party friends, we were true friends."[29]

Andrew found an apartment and began working at Anthropologie, a retail clothing, jewelry, and furniture chain where he had worked in Santa Barbara. The money was hardly enough to live on—he had to walk several miles from his shared East Village apartment to the Midtown store because he couldn't afford public transportation. When his father occasionally came to visit, he treated Andrew to steak dinners at Smith & Wollensky's famous East Side eatery. He would eat part of his meal and take the rest home in a doggie bag.

Eventually, Andrew found a job as an account manager for a translation firm. He also applied for entry into the US Foreign Service, easily passing the competitive written exams. He was invited for an interview in Chicago, but it did not go well. After a day of individual meetings and group presentations, he was rejected. Andrew wonders if he may have come across as less than professional in this setting, perhaps too lively and colorful. He was "heartbroken."

After two and a half years, New York's attraction was starting to dim, eclipsed by the high cost of living and a gay scene that was "brutal." Andrew recalled, "I was just kind of over it, being poor and such. But I wasn't ready to come home. I really always fantasized about my time living in Italy and having the freedom to travel anywhere, learn a new language, and be exposed to a different culture. That's the kind of stuff that really motivated me and got me excited."

Foreign travel was in Andrew's future, but he was in New York City on September 11, 2001. From a friend's rooftop at 96th Street, in Spanish Harlem, he saw the airplane hit the second tower of the World Trade Center and witnessed its transformation into a "smoky pillar." This terrorist act and what happened next profoundly shaped Andrew's sense of self, sharpening his awareness of hostility toward American values and discrimination against gay men and minorities.

"How could someone hate us that much to do this?" he wondered. "I knew I was watching history and I needed to see this more and understand it." Andrew and his friend started walking toward Lower Manhattan, "the only two idiots walking downtown." They couldn't get past 14th Street, since the streets had been blocked. They saw a man holding his briefcase, dripping blood, and appearing oblivious to where he was going. Papers littered the sidewalks, "flying around like tumbleweed." Feeling helpless, but eager to help, they went to a hospital to donate blood. The lines were long, but they felt the need to do something.

Andrew was finally handed a form with the question, "Are you a gay man who's had sex with other men since 1979?" He answered honestly, and his offer to donate blood was denied.[30] He can joke about that day now, but it's a facade that masks the emotions coursing through his consciousness at that time. "I couldn't call my parents and my loved ones because cell phones weren't working. And then to be rejected for giving blood because of being gay! I didn't even know there was such a thing until it happened to me. I could have lied [about being gay], but why would I lie? Why are they discriminating against me? I was in my most vulnerable state—you feel like a second-class citizen."

He continued. "There're instances that constantly happen to you throughout your life of discrimination, all the shit I endured in high school, with people harassing me, and in college, and then that incident in New York, and just these things that keep happening. And obviously, you know, culminating in the ultimate discrimination that happened a decade and a half later with my son [Ethan]. These things keep happening and it just leaves this imprint on you. . . . I never thought about this before, but now that I'm talking about it, that emotion was retriggered in the consulate office in Toronto, because I was in an extremely vulnerable state. I was in a strange place with my twins to get my boys their citizenship, and so blindly thinking that it wasn't going to be an issue, just like I did in that [hospital] line in New York City on 9/11, blindly thinking I'm going to give blood, like, this isn't going to be an issue."

New York had lost its allure, but there was an upside to Andrew's 9/11 experience.[31] He developed a renewed fascination with the Middle East and decided to live on an Israeli kibbutz, a communal settlement, mostly agricultural but sometimes industrial, in which finances are held in common among its members.[32] The advantages are free room and board and Hebrew language instruction ("ulpan") in exchange for work. Airfare isn't covered, but Andrew's father offered him his airline miles as a birthday present. Andrew chose Kibbutz Yagur, a community to the north of Israel, near Haifa. He worked the "shittiest jobs"—cleaning bathrooms, washing clothes, vacuuming rugs—but he was happy. A discotheque on the premises offered nightly excitement, and the kibbutz's location allowed access to a culturally rich urban center. It was the "best six months. It was just so much fun, and I really fell in love with the country."

Returning to Los Angeles in 2006, Andrew began looking for a job. The year 2006 was a pivotal one in the Middle East. The war had broken out with Hezbollah in Lebanon that summer, stoking Andrew's interest and desire to return to the area.[33,34] Feeling nostalgic for Israel, he began working for Birthright, leading young people to discover (or rediscover) their Jewish roots—the same ten-day trip he took as a college senior. When each journey was completed, he would return home and start the trip again with a new group of travelers. These experiences only deepened his fascination with the region and his longing to understand it. This led ultimately to Andrew's next quest in 2007, which was to enroll in the Middle East studies program at Tel Aviv University in Israel. The program was conducted in English, but completing courses in Hebrew and Arabic and writing a one-hundred-page thesis were required for earning a master's degree. Andrew focused his attention on the topic of Israeli–Arab peace negotiations.

Andrew successfully completed the two-year master's program. He hadn't planned to spend a third year in Israel, but his personal life changed dramatically in March 2008, during the second semester of his first year: He met Elad Dvash, a second-year Israeli student working toward a bachelor's degree in comparative literature, fell in love, and the two became a couple. In recounting their romance, Andrew and Elad provided somewhat different versions of their first meeting, confirming what I said in the introduction: that the truth generally lies at the intersection of different people's memories and reflections. I will save this story for the third chapter, because there is more to say about Andrew, and I have yet to get to Elad.

IN THE EYES OF OTHERS

"Nobody could put one over on him."

—Ann Banks, 2022

When Andrew was six or seven years old, his parents Ann and Jim arranged for him to take piano lessons at their home. One day Andrew said he didn't like his teacher, complaining to his mother, "He has hair on his hands." Shortly thereafter, the piano instructor commented that Andrew's behavior was "horrible," and he would no longer be giving him lessons.

In fact, Andrew was a victim of sexual assault. According to Ann, "Andrew was the child who could get away from him [the piano teacher] by making the situation so uncomfortable that the pedophile left without being asked. He had the building blocks [to do this] which some other child might not." She continued, "I applaud Andrew for being able to stand up and point a finger and be able to say, 'This is not right.' That's why it's not a surprise that, as he has moved forward in life, he will still point a finger and say, 'This is not right; you can't do it, and I'm going to make sure you're not going to do it.' "[35]

Despite the bullying Andrew suffered from being gay, especially after his school's newspaper covered his coming-out story, he was one of three students nominated for homecoming king at Beverly Hills High School. He lost to the captain of the football team but was voted the "most popular" member of his graduating class. And as a senior he once scored the winning goal at a swim team event. According to Jen Sikov, who has known him since they were sixteen, "Andrew still has more friends than anyone I know." Jessica Yousem, who met Andrew in high school, is "proud" to be in his top group of friends. "He is a very loyal individual—and no one can mess with his girls!"[36]

In 1999, Teen Line honored Rosa Parks, a Black woman and civil rights activist from Montgomery, Alabama. Parks became famous in 1955 for refusing to give up her seat on a bus to a white man.[37] A group photograph taken at Teen Line's event shows Parks surrounded by nine of the young volunteer listeners. Andrew is seated in the center, closest to the honoree, and is helping her hold the bouquet she had been given.

In 1996, Andrew received a high school athletic award for achievement in water polo and for maintaining standards of citizenship and leadership. This recognition allowed him to wear the Beverly Hills athletic emblem. He was also given an award from the Beverly Hills Chamber of Commerce for his work with Teen Line. Ann had this certificate framed, but Andrew doesn't display it or show any of his other honors.[38] When asked to name them, he said he would have to look through boxes stored in his closet.

Why do some people resist wrongdoing, while others react passively? Why are some people at the center of an event, while others drift to the sidelines? Ann's observation that Andrew had the "building blocks" to check unwanted sexual advances captures the essence of what twin studies tell us about human behavior: our genetically based tendencies predispose us to act, and react, in certain ways.

Teen Line's 1999 "Food for Thought" Luncheon, honoring Rosa Parks. Parks is legendary for her refusal to give up her seat on a bus to a white man in 1955. The photograph displayed here, showing six volunteer listeners, is a partial reproduction of the original. Rosa Parks is on the lower left, seated next to Andrew. Andrew's brother James is at the top, with Mazier Yafeh next to him. Tim Choi is above Andrew, and next to him is Nina Boyajian. Jen Sikov is at the lower right of the picture. *Source*: Photo courtesy of Ann Banks and Elaine Leader.

"Building blocks" is a convenient metaphor for the genetically based tendencies and temperaments with which each of us are born. They affect the way we experience the people, places, and events that surround us, filtered through a unique genetic lens. Of course, genes do not work in deterministic ways; rather, they play probabilistic roles.[39] An inquisitive individual is likely to enjoy good books, museum trips, and interesting lectures, while an indifferent individual may find these opportunities boring or unnecessary. Of course, not all stimulating activities attract a curious student, and some indifferent pupils may become excited by a particular hobby or task. In addition, parent–child resemblance is never perfect. A child with biological alcoholic parents is three to four times more likely to develop alcohol use disorder (AUD) than a child with nonalcoholic parents, but the outcome cannot be definitively predicted.[40]

A wealth of twin studies, as well as family and adoption research, shows that our genetic backgrounds substantially shape our general intelligence, personality traits, interests, and attitudes.[41] Researchers find that identical twins are more alike than fraternal twins on virtually all measured traits, a difference demonstrating genetic influence. This is to be expected, since identical twins share 100 percent of their genes, while fraternal twins share 50 percent of their genes, on average. However, identical twins do not show perfect similarity, meaning that environmental effects, before and/or after birth, also shape who we become. It is striking that two children living in the same home with access to the same resources and opportunities (like Andrew and James) often differ in fundamental ways.

The words independent, intelligent, caring, passionate, friendly, well-liked, popular, "fiercely loyal," supportive, outgoing, fun, gregarious, outspoken, "honest to a fault," generous, and amazing were repeated in the many conversations I had with people who described Andrew. A few voices were slightly dissenting. Andrew's half-brother Brian observed that the younger Andrew did not always exemplify these traits, while showing "admirable maturity" as an adult. He explained Andrew's progression from "reckless and materialistic teen" to loving spouse and father by crediting his strong relationship and parental responsibilities. Sometimes siblings see the youthful sides of us that other people do not see; recall that James also observed a materialistic bent to his brother when it came to appearance and style. "He was very into

Italian fashion, but now he's focused on his work and kids." And, according to James, Andrew was not a straight-A student but had a "different kind of smarts—he understood the way that the world works. He uses his experience to raise awareness and to help others who could be going through something similar, but don't have the courage to stand up." Andrew's older half-brother Jonathan commented that "Andrew always shows concern for the little guy."

Everyone acknowledged Andrew's exemplary parenting skills—"He's in hog heaven when the kids crawl all over him"; "he has a real knack for fatherhood"[42]—but sometimes we see qualities in ourselves that might surprise others. Andrew admitted, "I'm a good parent in the sense that I hold the line. I'm firm with my kids. I'm definitely the strict parent, the one that says 'no' comfortably. But I definitely struggle a lot." He claims he was ready to become a parent at age thirty-five—he had lived, studied, and traveled in many places—but he was "not quite ready to leave the old life behind."[43] Visiting new lands is clearly his passion, one he admits is not fully replaced by caring for his boys. A partial solution has been the family vacation—Andrew, Elad, and their sons have been to Canada, Hawaii, Europe, Israel, and many locations within California and across the United States. "There's so much that you sacrifice when you become a parent. We don't have grandparents [living locally] to support us. I feel like, anthropologically speaking, that's kind of a new phenomenon—because it takes a village of grandparents, neighbors, and others, but we're raising the twins ourselves. I'm lucky to have my siblings, but they have families of their own and don't live close by."

Andrew surprised me again. He had identified science and math as his least favorite subjects in school, yet there he is, surrounded by designers and builders of rockets destined for Mars and various outer space locations. "We all have the same goal, but I go to meetings [at SpaceX] and I'm, like, the stupidest person in the room. These people have gone to Cal Tech or MIT and I'm, like, UC Santa Barbara! But they respect me because I'm an expert at what I do. . . . I'm important to the team and I'm part of changing the world." He continued, "I feel like if we're in 1492, Musk is Christopher Columbus and I'm the low-level deckhand. But I'm part of this journey." I had not expected Andrew to be so self-effacing; no one had hinted at this. I did expect

Andrew to know that Elon Musk, founder of SpaceX, is the father of twins and triplets—he did.[44]

ENTER ELAD

There was a moment in Andrew's life when the promise of an exotic trip to a faraway place could not quell another type of excitement he was experiencing at the time. It was the thrill that comes from finding the person you want to share your life with.

In 2008, shortly after Andrew and Elad met in Israel and started dating seriously, Andrew's brother James invited his brother to Nepal for a three-week visit. James was helping to run Global Heed (Health, Education, and Economic Development), a nonprofit organization in Nepal he had helped set up, and had been visiting each summer between 2005 and 2008. The flight from Tel Aviv to Kathmandu takes eleven hours, less than the fifteen hours flying time from Tel Aviv to Los Angeles. The trip appealed to Andrew—it was a chance to experience a new country and culture with a familiar local guide. But this was the first time he would be apart from Elad for more than a few days. According to James, "I remember [their separation] being really hard on Drew because they had already formed a really strong bond. I think he was really frustrated because we were in the middle of nowhere with no cell-phone service or any way for him to contact Elad. I remember Andrew being pretty emotional at that time—this was a really special relationship. It felt different, you know, seeing him so infatuated or just so into someone. I hadn't known him to be like that, so I knew Elad was special."[45]

It's now time to meet Elad. Neither he nor Andrew had ever imagined that their relationship and family plans would become the source of yet another injustice they would be compelled to battle.

Transitions and Traumas: Elad Dvash

$\mathscr{A}$ childhood event sometimes defines us, shaping our thoughts and behaviors for short periods of time, or for years. As a psychologist who has researched and identified genetic influences on ability and personality, I admit the preceding sentence may seem out of place. However, we are all a complex blend of the genetic predispositions we inherit *and* the environmental effects we experience. An upsetting event can set us off course, but we generally drift back to our characteristic ways.[1]

Something happened to Elad when he finished the third grade, derailing the happy and fulfilling existence he had enjoyed since the first grade. "It was definitely one of the most traumatizing events of my childhood," he confessed—and it was one of the first things he talked about when highlighting his childhood memories. Elad gradually

ELAD'S FAMILY MEMBERS AND FRIENDS

Andrew Dvash-Banks	Elad's husband
Aiden Dvash-Banks	Elad and Andrew's son; Ethan's twin
Ethan Dvash-Banks	Elad and Andrew's son; Aiden's twin
Mordehay "Moti" Dvash	Elad's father
Tova "Tovi" Dvash	Elad's mother
Yarden Dvash	Elad's sister
Neta Dvash	Elad's sister
Rotem Cohen	Elad's lifelong friend
Ilona Krashanny	Elad's army buddy and friend
Kari Zalik	Elad's friend from Canada

transitioned out of that disturbing time, again becoming the intelligent, confident, and creative child everyone knew. But that early experience stayed with him, affecting his later approaches to problems and how to solve them.

A FIRSTBORN SON

Elad is the firstborn child *and* the firstborn son of Israeli couple Tovi Dvash (née Abadi) and Moti Dvash, from Tel Aviv. He is also the first grandchild on his father's side of the family. And while Elad is the second grandchild on his mother's side, he is the first grandson, a distinction that also meant a great deal to his maternal grandparents.

Firstborn sons carry a certain significance in Jewish families, as written in the Torah, the five books containing the laws and principles of Jewish instruction and guidance. Fathers see their sons as continuing the family line. And, according to tradition, firstborn sons acquire a double portion of their father's inheritance, predicated on the notion that eldest sons are responsible for family affairs when their fathers pass away. Today, these arrangements are not strictly followed except in the most pious of families—but the legacy of the firstborn son lingers in the minds of many Jewish parents. Reverence for the firstborn son is also present in other faiths and societies.[2]

Without being told, Moti (as a firstborn son) knew that having a grandson was of great importance to his parents, given their adherence to the Jewish religion and culture. Tovi's family, while less religious than her husband's family, openly expressed their preference for a grandson, perhaps because Tovi has just one brother, as well as a sister—and her mother Naomi (Elad's grandmother) is one of five sisters. "Tovi prayed for a son," Moti told me. Elad's birth—*making him the firstborn son of a firstborn son*—was a joyous occasion for everyone. Elad's sister, Yarden (her name means "the Jordan River"), insisted that her older brother was always the "preferred child."[3] She stated that as a matter of fact, without bitterness or envy.

Elad's mother and father were young newlyweds when he was born on March 20, 1985. At twenty-two and twenty-three years old, they had been married for just one year. Both sides of his family have a broad, multinational heritage. Elad's grandparents are Mizrahi Jews, those from the Middle East and Africa. His paternal grandmother, Ziva, came from Fez, Morocco, and his paternal grandfather, Chaim, was from Tunis, the capital of Tunisia. His maternal grandmother, Naomi, came from Baghdad, the capital of Iraq, and his maternal grandfather, Eliyahu, was from Damascus, the capital of Syria; both are deceased.[4]

Tovi and Moti began their married life living in the home of Tovi's parents in Tel Aviv, a major city and economic center of Israel.[5] This proved to be a convenient arrangement for everyone since both of Elad's parents worked full-time. Moti, who had completed two years of college, appraised home damages for an insurance company. Tovi, who had earned a high school degree, worked as a manager in the claims department of a different insurance company, a job she still holds. Elad's maternal grandmother, a "very influential figure" in his life, essentially raised him until he turned three.

Living in his grandmother's home was a fortunate decision for another reason: according to Elad's mother, Tovi (and what Elad has been told), the "preferred child" was "terrible and horrific, the infant from hell, a nightmare."[6] He hardly ate, had trouble sleeping, and cried incessantly. Moti recalled that when Elad did fall asleep, the family stayed silent so as not to wake him up. His grandmother was the only person who could handle him.

Unlike Elad, whose birth had been planned, Tovi's pregnancy with Elad's younger sister, Yarden, was unexpected. Tovi cried for weeks at the thought of raising a second difficult child; Elad was about three years old when his mother conceived. But happily, Yarden turned out to be an even-tempered baby who ate regularly and slept soundly, "the total opposite of me—calm, shy, and quiet until her teenage years." Tovi felt that God had answered her prayers by sending her an easy child.[7]

The prospect of easier parenting, coupled with the family's improved financial situation, eventually allowed the family to move to a home of their own. When Yarden was born and Elad was nearly four, they moved to their own apartment in the modest middle-class neighborhood of Kfar Shalem ("Peaceful Village") in east Tel Aviv.[8] Their new residence was "nice, but small," one of many units in a huge building that was noisy and crowded. "There was little privacy, no balcony and no backyard, no nothing." But Elad's home had plenty of love and relatives around, and Elad and his sister Yarden were always very close.

MOTHER AND FATHER ("IMA" AND "ABBA")

Elad described his mother, Tovi, as very warm and loving, "almost too much so." She gave up everything for her family, nearly to the point that she was a "slave to her children." As an example, Tovi would have liked taking English classes but never had the time. She was a devoted cook, and because she prepared meals every day, the family rarely ate in restaurants, despite having the means to do so. She and her husband spent a lot of time at home—Elad's parents had few friends during his younger years, so they never went out socially or entertained.

Moti was uninterested in sports for himself or for his son, but he was "100 percent dedicated" to Elad's education. When Elad was two or three years old, and for the next few years, Moti invested nearly all his time in teaching and testing his son. He printed new vocabulary words on cards, placed them around Elad's room, and quizzed him on what they said. Moti also completed "tons of puzzles" with Elad and even bought him one of the first home computers sold in Israel. Elad could read when he turned four and write by the time he turned five. But once Moti was promoted to CEO and became part owner of his insurance company, "my dad was there, but not there," Elad recalled. Over the years Moti held several different jobs within the same company, including project manager as well as appraiser. He is still working, but some pressures have lifted.

This crack in the father-son relationship began when Elad was seven and lasted until Elad was in his late teens. "Now he's much more available and doing other things." But when Elad was growing up, Moti worked constantly, leaving for work before he and his sister were awake, and returning home as late as eight o'clock at night. Even when Moti returned earlier, he would immediately go to the dining room table, turn on his computer, and "just work, work, work, work, work." Nobody was allowed to talk to him or interrupt him for any reason. When cell phones were introduced in Israel, Moti was always on a call with someone. He and Elad argued often. "He was at home, but he wasn't there for his kids."

Moti's work schedule meant that the family never ate meals together during the week. Once Tovi made dinner, the children went to the kitchen, made a plate for themselves, and either took it to their bedroom or ate while watching television. But they celebrated Shabbat (Sabbath) together, with Friday-night dinners at Moti's parents' home and Saturday-night meals at Tovi's parents' home.[9] (The only meal Elad's family ate together in their apartment was lunch on Friday afternoons.) Many aunts, uncles, and young cousins were invited to the Friday and Saturday Shabbat dinners, since Tovi has two siblings and Moti has three. "It was literally like growing up together—it was a very warm extended family," Elad recalled.

Elad was raised in a nonreligious secular home. Shabbat evenings with extended family were important, as were some holidays and traditions noted above, but meals were not strictly kosher. Food was "kosher style," meaning that items like shrimp and pork that are forbidden in the Jewish faith were never served, while the separate preparing and eating of meat and dairy dishes was generally not followed. But like most Jewish boys, Elad had a bar mitzvah, the event recognizing the passage from boyhood to manhood at age thirteen. Tovi's parents, Naomi and Eliyahu, celebrated significant Jewish holidays but did not closely follow other rituals or regulations. In contrast, Moti's parents, Ziva and Chaim, were "Masorti Jews," descended from Arab populations that maintained many religious traditions in modern times.[10]

BECOMING ELAD

Even at the young age of four or five years, Elad transitioned easily into the role of "older sibling." He explained, "I was always at the top of my class, always tried to be the leader, always tried to be the teacher's pet. I volunteered for everything." His parents were aware that their son stood out among the other students; in fact, his kindergarten teachers told him he was "the smartest kid." Elad's recollections of his teachers' accolades were confirmed years later when he had opportunities to meet them as an adult. "They said they had seen something in me and recommended that I go to what's called in Hebrew 'the School for the Arts.'"

The School for the Arts–Arison Campus in Tel Aviv is an educational institution that offers professional programs in film, dance, fine art, drama, and photography, as well as classes in science and the humanities, to students in grades one through nine. In contrast with most Israeli schools that provide free public education, the School for the Arts is a small, semiprivate school that requires parents to pay partial tuition.[11]

Admission is highly selective—only those kindergarten students who pass a series of entrance exams and interviews (e.g., tests of IQ and emotional intelligence) are invited to attend. Elad was accepted immediately, and despite the extra expense, his parents were able to cover the cost. The only other requirement for admission was that students reside in Tel Aviv.

Elad loved everything about the school. The program was "child-led," in that students' interests and progress guided the choice of subjects they would eventually study. Classes were small, consisting of twenty students rather than the typical forty found in most Israeli public schools. The atmosphere was relaxed and informal. Teachers knew each student's name and gave each child a hug when they arrived, rather than simply saying "good morning." "It made me feel special," Elad said, sounding wistful. "As young as we were, it was like a cooperative arrangement between each student and teacher. It also helped develop certain skills, like public speaking, leadership abilities, and team cooperation. And it gave us characteristics like self-confidence and self-worth that I carry with me today." At parent-teacher conferences Moti and Tovi were told that such meetings were unnecessary, since Elad was so smart and engaging; still, the teachers were interested in meeting his parents and getting to know them.[12]

Elad's interests and talents clearly flourished in the atmosphere and opportunities provided by the School for the Arts. However, children are not born as blank slates. Each child enters the world with a unique genetic blueprint that may be expressed differently, depending upon the environments and experiences he or she encounters.[13] The School for the Arts, by screening its applicants, most likely identified students with the potential to thrive in the kind of educational setting it provided. Elad was one such student—he had the potential for productivity, inventiveness, self-confidence, and self-worth that his school desired and supported. Elad would rely on those qualities to contest the prejudice he later experienced as a gay man, a Sephardic Jew, and a devoted father whose son was denied US citizenship.

"I learned everything," Elad recalled with great enthusiasm. He danced ballet, studied drama, played musical instruments (flute and piano), sculpted figures, and painted pictures. Students were evaluated at the end of the third grade to determine the subjects they would pursue more seriously the following year. Elad was chosen for theater and ballet.

"I was really excited about it. I had dancing shoes that let you stand on your toes. And my parents were excited for me."

FIRST TRAUMA

Elad never donned those coveted dancing shoes.

At the end of Elad's third-grade year at the special school, Moti and Tovi decided to move again, not just to a better home but to a better neighborhood. Their finances had improved steadily after Moti was promoted to CEO of his insurance company. They settled into the small, upscale municipality of Givatayim ("Two Hills"), situated inside Tel Aviv, but a city unto itself.[14] Their apartment was in a "newer, nicer, fancier, semi-gated building." It had a big private park that was ideal for children to run around in. Everything felt beautiful, except for one thing: Elad could no longer attend the School for the Arts, because he now lived outside the school's district. His third-grade fees had been paid by then, but he no longer qualified for half-tuition after the move. Moreover, the free transportation that the school provided did not go beyond certain borders.

At first, Moti and Tovi tried to accommodate Elad by driving him to school, but the heavy city traffic was a "nightmare"; the trip lasted one hour each way, and Elad was too young to ride public transportation on his own. Tovi and Moti solved the situation in the only way they knew how—by enrolling Elad in a public school.[15]

Public schools in Israel offer high-quality education, but their curricula and approach to teaching were vast departures from what Elad had enjoyed at the School for the Arts. "All of a sudden I was thrown into this new place." His classroom had twice as many pupils, and the teacher didn't know his name. "No one cared about me as an individual—I was just one of forty kids. I was shocked, I was crying. I missed my friends and the special things I was doing and studying." The only subjects he was taught were math, English, literature, science, and Bible stories. There were no arts and no extracurricular activities. "It was really, really hard. My parents say that for months I didn't fit in. It was very clear that I was depressed because it was just not a good place for me. But there was nothing they could do." I wondered why Elad couldn't live in Tel

Aviv with his maternal grandparents, Naomi and Eliyahu, but Tovi and Moti wanted to keep the family together.

Once a happy and motivated student, Elad began "acting out" in the fourth and fifth grades. "I became very defiant toward my teacher and toward the other students. From the 'golden boy' and most talented child, who never had any behavioral issues, I became one of the most problematic kids in the classroom. I was called to the principal's office a number of times." Not understanding the limits of student-teacher relations at the new school, he jumped up on a teacher from behind—but he was only in search of a hug.

Looking back, Elad thinks of his first two terms in public school as "adjustment years." "Without hurting anyone's feelings or sounding like I am condescending, I had to dumb myself down and fit in with everyone else. Then in the sixth grade I went back on track, my grades improved, and I became a better-behaved student. I had a really good teacher that year."

Some experiences are completed but never fully finished. Over the years, Elad has spoken to his parents about their decision to place him in public school. Even now, thinking about his removal from the School for the Arts is emotionally upsetting. "I'm like, 'I will never forgive you. What you did to me—I was accepted at one of the most prestigious schools and you just plucked me out of there.'"

In retrospect, Tovi said it was one of the "worst decisions" they could have made, and she regrets it to this day. She realizes that to deprive Elad of a rare opportunity in a selective school was "unheard of." He had many friends there. After class the school bus would deliver him to his friends' homes where they would play together until their parents returned. Elad missed them terribly when he entered public school. Tovi recalled that during his first year Elad would dream about his friends and talk about those dreams. In the end, what "saved him" was being a very smart child.

Moti remembers that Elad kept a journal in which he recorded his thoughts and feelings about being at the new school, although Elad has no recollection of this. When I asked Moti how he felt about the decision to remove Elad from the special school, he could not say. "We do not know what the outcome would have been had he stayed at that school," Moti said. "Maybe he would have been a painter and never made a living." But he said that his son has done well in his personal life and in his career.

His school experience taught Elad that "parents might not make the best decisions for their kids, but the kids obviously have no say." His early school days would help shape him into the sensitive and protective parent he has become.

EVERY GIRL'S BOYFRIEND

With the approach of adolescence, Elad was the most popular boy in his class. Just about every female in the fifth and sixth grades wanted to be his girlfriend. In accordance with the middle school ritual of the day, each girl hoped to receive one half of Elad's heart-shaped necklace to confirm their steady relationship. Elad bestowed his half to ten different girls at different times. Rotem Cohen, Elad's close friend since third grade, when he was the "new kid," said he changed girlfriends every week. Today, they laugh about it, remembering that Rotem never received part of Elad's heart-shaped charm.[16]

During childhood and beyond, Elad's preferred playmates were the girls in his class.

"We spoke the same language. Even to this day I feel more comfortable with women. And I'm just not interested in sports." While the boys at school were on the field playing soccer, Elad was busy doing other things. In fifth grade Rotem recalls being part of "a group of about seven girls—and Elad." He was "very cute." In his first year of public school, Elad took a cooking class and officiously carried around a little suitcase with his kitchen materials. Rotem met him in this class. She also recalled starring in films Elad produced after school, using his family's video camera. "He would write scripts and give them to us to read out loud. He even paid us one shekel each so we would take it seriously, kind of like a job. He was a very creative little guy."[17]

Nothing sexual happened among the group of friends in the fifth or sixth grades. "It was just kissing," Elad recalled, "and that was the biggest deal. But by the seventh and eighth grades, maybe it wasn't."

Elad believes he was in seventh grade, age twelve or thirteen, when he felt his first attraction to males. Seated on a bench in a shopping mall, waiting for his parents, he watched as "some guys" walked by. "That was the first time I [was] thinking, 'Oh, he's really good-looking.' And then I asked myself, 'Wait, why are you saying that guy is good-looking? Do you want to look like that? Or are you attracted to them?' " These thoughts confused him.

Then, toward the end of seventh grade, Elad had his first intimate sexual experience with a male classmate. He decided he was probably attracted to men, as well as to women—but with time Elad learned that he was not attracted to women at all. "I think it was my brain trying to fool me, to say that I am bisexual, just to give my parents hope that maybe I'll marry a woman and have a family."[18]

At about the time Elad was questioning his sexuality, Tovi gave birth to her second daughter, Neta, in December 1998. Elad was nearing fourteen. Tovi had been pregnant the year before, but she had had a miscarriage, due to a severe genetic defect in the child she was carrying. She became depressed and was unable to return to work for at least a month. Perhaps these distractions prevented her from sensing the conflict and confusion that Elad was experiencing. However, Tovi had generally ignored Elad's atypical childhood behaviors, such as wearing her dresses and putting on lipstick. Instead, she rationalized away any suspicions she may have had; after all, Elad spent most of his time with girls who wanted to wear half of his heart-shaped necklace.

Wearing dresses and putting on lipstick do not necessarily signal a potentially gay male child, but according to Elad, these were "clear signs."[19] However, as a sensitive child Elad was very protective of his emotions and feelings, concealing a great deal from those around him. Tovi and Moti never knew that their son was seeing his first serious boyfriend at age seventeen, or that he visited nightclubs wearing a black mesh shirt with sparkles or a glittering pink tank top. Elad would bundle these clothing items in a bag and toss the parcel out the window to his friend who was waiting outside.

Elad hid his sexual identity from his sister Yarden for five years and from his parents for six. Elad and Yarden were out shopping when he finally confided in her. She was not at all surprised by his admission and accepted him completely. Yarden claimed that she could not fully explain her suspicions—only that her brother "didn't remind her of other straight boys because there was something different about him." She believes that her parents also accepted him but that they tried to conceal the difficult time they were going through. Yarden also insisted that

Elad's revelations did not damage his status as preferred child. "Nothing changed—he was the favorite both before and after [he told them]."[20] Of course, Yarden was only fourteen or fifteen years old at the time, possibly explaining why she did not fully perceive how her parents reacted. And Elad's youngest sister, Neta, was only four or five years old, so she would not have been aware of or even grasped her brother's revelation.

A year later, when Elad turned eighteen, he decided he no longer wanted to live a lie. He was with a new boyfriend and serving the first of his three years in the Israeli army.[21] But when he spoke to Tovi, "It was like someone told my mother she had lost her son. She was crying; she didn't understand it." He had told her he was bisexual but realized immediately that that was a mistake. "She said, 'If you're bisexual, why can't you be with a woman?' My mother took it hard for several reasons. First, she wondered what other people would think." At that time, Israeli society was not welcoming to gay men and women, and traditional Judaism equated homosexuality with sinning. "My mother asked herself how she could have a perfect family if she had a gay son. Secondly, she worried that I would have a hard life—she believed I would die alone because most gay people never got married and never had children." In 2003, when Elad was eighteen, few countries around the world either performed or recognized gay marriages.[22]

Tovi didn't speak to Elad for the next six months, other than to tell him when dinner was ready or to ask if he needed something. Their relationship was "all matter-of-fact," and it was very upsetting to him. Years later, Elad learned that his mother had entertained suspicions of his sexual leanings, but she had denied their reality until he had told her when he was eighteen.

In surprising contrast, Elad's father, Moti, was far more rational and accepting of the news. In the first of many "heart-to-heart conversations" between father and son (exchanges that were "very foreign and new to me"), Moti assured Elad that Tovi needed time to process the information. "With time I learned that my uncle (my dad's brother) is also gay, but I didn't know that at the time. My uncle never came out officially, but I think my dad and everyone [in his family] knew; for one thing, my uncle never had a girlfriend. Maybe my dad was accepting [of me] because he had gone through this realization with his brother. It was definitely a [positive] turning point in our relationship."

The different reactions of Elad's parents were "shocking" because they were so unexpected. Elad had assumed that his mother, "who loved me so much," would have supported him no matter what. But it took a long time for Tovi to come to terms with his sexuality, and even then, they never discussed his boyfriends. When Elad began dating Andrew seriously, Tovi asked him not to tell their extended family. And given his past contentious relationship with Moti, Elad had anticipated a hard time from his father, unaware at that time of his father's experience with a gay brother.

Ironically, Tovi could not have predicted that nearly twenty years later, Elad would be the only one of her three children to give her grandchildren. Neither Yarden, at age thirty-four, nor Neta, at age twenty-four, are married or in serious relationships. Yarden is a college graduate who majored in human resources and behavioral studies and owns a fitness studio for women in Tel Aviv. Neta did not complete a college degree. Instead, she takes courses in fitness and works part-time in Yarden's studio. Elad described his youngest sister as "shy and elusive" but also as someone who likes to party. I asked him to arrange an interview with her, but he wasn't encouraging. The brother and sister love each other and are in touch.

CURIOSITIES AND CONTRADICTIONS

"I was very anti-religion," Elad noted, "completely anti-religion, when I lived in Israel." Although raised in a secular home, Elad grew up in "the religious version of Israel." He explained that at the time, gay people were considered "sinners" who were rejected by society as though they had a disease—and the disease could be cured. "I decided, 'You don't want me, I don't want to be Jewish.' " He admitted that his reasoning back then was "stupid," because while he was born Jewish, he insisted that he was not. This attitude swayed certain decisions and judgments that Elad would make later in life, such as the arrangements for his wedding ceremony in 2011. (I will return to Andrew and Elad's wedding in the next chapter.)

Elad now works for IKAR (meaning "essence" in Hebrew), a very progressive, liberal Jewish community and synagogue whose membership numbers over 1,200 households in the Los Angeles area. IKAR's mission is to "reanimate Jewish life and develop a spiritual and moral foundation for a just and equitable society. . . . We are diverse and dynamic, proudly opening our doors to newbies and ringers, seekers and cynics, activists and ambivalents. All are welcome here."[23] Elad began as development manager before being promoted to director of development, then director of development and capital campaigns, and most recently, chief advancement officer responsible for fund-raising, finance, and operations. He loves analyzing numbers on the Excel spreadsheets he works with every day.

As we spoke, I found myself focused on the curiosities and contrasts in Elad's life: How did someone so rejecting of the Jewish religion come to work so enthusiastically for a Jewish establishment? And how did a former student majoring in comparative literature and global affairs—subjects that invite lively discussions, intense dialogues, and diverse opinions—end up working with sums and totals arranged neatly in rows and columns?

Elad had answers to both questions.

"I found a new way of being religious." Having lived in Canada and the United States, Elad learned for the first time that you can practice Judaism any way you like; he explained that as long as you feel part of the religion and follow certain practices, you can connect with the Jewish people. Living in Israel, he could not feel part of a religion that rejected him as a gay person. He also looked unfavorably at the Judaism he grew up with that forbade interfaith marriages and relegated women to separate, less desirable seats in the synagogue. Now, Elad and his family regularly attend prayer services and related events on weekends, and his sons go to Hebrew school. And, as I indicated in the introduction, many Jewish objects and artifacts decorate the walls of their home.

Elad's position at IKAR is his "favorite job" because it combines two areas that he most enjoys—"building meaningful relationships with people, and tracking numbers, overseeing money, and fund-raising." Still, Elad seems surprised by how his professional life has played out. "If someone had told me that I would be attending services every Shabbat, or working for a synagogue, I would have said 'You're crazy.' "

Understanding Elad's zeal for finance and fund-raising can be found in the observations of his high school literature teacher, who profoundly influenced his thinking and sense of self. "She told me I was one of the most interesting students she had had. She explained that some students are busy with math and science, while others are into humanities and history. But you [Elad] fit both categories perfectly." Elad delights in processing numbers and sums because "they add up—it's black or white." Recall that as a child, Elad loved putting puzzles together. He is also "obsessed" with the stories, languages, and art that reflect the experiences of individuals and cultures. "I have always had both of those sides in me, I guess." The duality of Elad's interests was further defined in high school and in the Israeli army.

Israeli high school students are required to complete two years of Arabic and to choose a major area of study. Elad chose Arabic as his major because of the special connection he felt to the language—not surprising, since he was surrounded by Arabic-speaking grandparents—but he also believed that peace between Israel and the Arabic states rests on building bridges between them. At the same time, he is intensely interested in literature, prompted by the pleasure he finds in people and the stories they tell. Looking back, Elad believes it was his background in Arabic that shaped the three years he spent between high school and college, when both males and females perform mandatory service in the Israeli army. His military experience deepened these interests—what he calls "the two faces of Elad."[24]

Every high school student who majors in Arabic is targeted for the army's intelligence force. Elad passed the language exams, intelligence tests, and other requirements, and was accepted into Unit 8200, Israel's elite electronic surveillance unit, which uses sophisticated technology to monitor communications. It is the single largest component of Israel's defense forces.[25] For the next three years, Elad collected information about enemy countries and organizations, giving him a sense of connection to global affairs, military intelligence, and security studies. He also headed a small team that encouraged high school students to learn Arabic to prepare them for positions in the Israeli military. One team member, Ilona Krashanny, became an "army buddy" and close friend. The two traveled to Europe together and even applied to be part of the American CBS-TV series *The Amazing Race*.[26] Based on their application video they were invited for a live audition, but their participation went no further.[27]

At the end of Elad's military service, his commanding officer, Shimon Atias, offered him a career in the army. Elad's performance had impressed him, and such positions come with benefits and prestige. Moti

Elad during his service in the Israeli army, 2004. He recalled feeling like a "big shot at the time." *Source*: Photo courtesy of Elad Dvash-Banks.

and Tovi urged him to accept the offer, but Elad was conflicted. He had loved his work in the military but had planned for months to meet and travel with Rotem and several other Israelis who were newly released from the army—he had tickets to fly to the United States the very next day. But there was more.

"I told Shimon that I am not a military guy. I dislike regimented activities. And I would want to wear civilian clothes and have normal work hours. Shimon said he would explore these things for me." For Elad it was a struggle between immediate satisfaction (to travel and have fun) and long-term commitment (to work and to make a difference). Ultimately, his desire to travel won. Thinking back to that time, he cannot say if his decision was right or wrong. He does know that working in the military would have delayed his studies—and he would not have met Andrew and been father to twin sons. Still, he says he would never know what could have happened if he had stayed in the army.

AFTER THE ARMY

It has become a tradition—Elad calls it a subculture—for young Israeli men and women to live abroad for six to twelve months during the time between leaving the army and entering college or starting a job. "It cleans your brain—you're your own master now," he said. At the time of the offer from the army, Elad might have stayed if not for his travel plans. Ilona believes Elad would have taken the job because he is rational and likes to have the pieces of his life in place. But there was another side to Elad's decision. "I wasn't an army person, that was the problem. I'm not that kind of a guy. It didn't feel like the right thing for me to do. My boss was very disappointed." Ultimately, he has had no regrets based on the decision he made.[28]

Elad loved California. He spent three months in Los Angeles (Chatsworth area) and three months in San Francisco. He had a wonderful time exploring "the land of possibilities." He also visited San Diego, Yosemite, Las Vegas, and New York. As Passover 2007 approached, Elad felt a little homesick and, with his visa expiring, chose to return to Israel and start his college career.

COLLEGE DAYS

Elad's army experience, coupled with his love of literature, triggered his internal debate over his choice of an undergraduate college major—the more "usable" political science/international relations vs. the more "artsy" literature/humanities. When he enrolled in Tel Aviv University as an undergraduate in 2007, he chose comparative literature as his major subject, with a minor in history, confident that he would eventually work toward a master's degree. "I decided to have fun by getting my bachelor's degree in something I liked [literature], and my master's degree in something more practical [global affairs], and that's what I did. I had everything planned in advance."

Even as an undergraduate student, Elad satisfied his competing interests in literature and world events. His favorite academic pursuit was analyzing stories using the intertextual approach—attempts to see how stories written years ago resonate with modern times, and how recent writings are shaped by older novels and stories.[29] For example, Jean Rhys's 1966 novel, *Wide Sargasso Sea*, is an adaptation of Charlotte Brontë's classic 1816 work, *Jane Eyre*. By modifying the characters and settings, Rhys presents an alternative story and interpretation of timeless themes, such as women's roles in society.[30] Elad was also intrigued by courses that combined feminist perspectives and comparative literature. He completed his bachelor's degree at Tel Aviv University in 2010, and as planned, he earned a master's degree in global affairs at the University of Toronto in Canada several years later. His project title was, "The Egmont Group of Financial Intelligence Units Combating Money Laundering and Terror Financing."[31]

Recall that Elad's interest in Arabic was largely motivated by his desire to improve Arab–Israeli relations. At the same time, Elad occasionally confronted different forms of prejudice, some that affected him personally.

OUTSIDE LOOKING IN

Tensions between the Jewish people from Western European nations (Ashkenazim) and those with roots in Spain (Sephardim) and the Middle East and Africa (Mizrahim) were prevalent even before Israel's 1948 establishment as an independent state.[32] Elad's paternal great-grandparents, as Mizrahi Jews, were subjected to discrimination and humiliation when they immigrated to Israel with their children (Elad's grandparents, Ziva and Chaim) in the 1950s. Living and working on a kibbutz (collective farming community), the Ashkenazi children living there tried to lift his great-grandmother's skirt to see if she really had a tail, as they had been told.[33] Such attitudes are less common today, but prejudices still exist, even though the Sephardim and Mizrahim comprise about half of Israel's Jewish population.[34] These tensions have historical roots that are both cultural and religious.[35]

When I asked Elad if he had ever encountered discrimination because of his Sephardic background, he answered, "Yes—absolutely!" He lived in the Israeli culture where it is commonly believed that Ashkenazi Jews are smarter, richer, and more successful than Sephardic Jews. Some of Elad's Ashkenazi classmates at his public school in Givatayim derogated him by calling him "black" because his skin tone was darker than theirs; he had never encountered such slander at the School for the Arts, where students and teachers were more "open, progressive, and accepting." Being gay was another source of disparagement, one that provoked bullying at times. Legislators, teachers, and other authority figures were never there to help.

"We always felt like we had to prove ourselves more than others," Elad recalled. He knows these experiences largely explain why he worked so hard in school, seizing every opportunity that came his way. His family held a similar view. As a child, he had heard his parents, Tovi and Moti, often say that "we" (Sephardim) have to show "them" (Ashkenazim) that they are wrong. Being a private person, Elad didn't express his difficulties to others, instead addressing them internally, resolving to be the best student he could become.[36] He still took pleasure in his activities and accomplishments, but that was not Elad's only motivation.

Unfortunately, other sources of discrimination were to come.

The 2001 terrorist attacks on the World Trade Center towers in New York City, the Pentagon in Washington, DC, and United Airlines Flight 93 over Somerset County, Pennsylvania, exacerbated unfavorable views and unfair treatment of people who appeared to have Arabic ancestry. Sephardic Jews were among them. Elad was profiled many times in airports because of his dark Middle Eastern skin and was taken by officials to "random" security-check areas. This happened nearly every time he flew after 9/11.

Bias of a different sort followed him to Los Angeles in 2017. Elad, Andrew, and their twin sons initially settled into a tiny apartment in the prosperous, mostly white neighborhood of Brentwood. When he took his infant twins out in their stroller, people occasionally referred to Elad as the "children's nanny." When the twins were three, they moved again, becoming homeowners in the Westchester area near the airport. In 2021, the family relocated to their new home in Hawthorne, a middle-class, diverse neighborhood, where Elad feels at ease.[37] He and Andrew know other pairs of gay fathers in the Los Angeles community.

People rarely find jobs that allow them to express their full range of talents. However, Elad's position as IKAR's chief advancement officer combines his passions for building relationships and building budgets. And he can offer support to people from a wide range of ethnicities, age groups, family structures, financial resources, sexual orientations, and interests.

OTHER PEOPLE'S PERSPECTIVES

According to the people who know him well, Elad always wants to do what is right. Feeling insulted by the United States when they did not accept his son, Elad, together with Andrew, fought back. Elad did not seek or relish the worldwide attention that the case attracted—he admits he is a more private individual than Andrew is—but he knowingly placed himself in the public eye. He refused to take the easy way out, not just for his son Ethan, but for other desperate families who fear being divided.

Elad's friend Rotem, who has known him since the third grade, followed her friend's citizenship legal ordeal very closely. "Elad is high in self-esteem, he is well-spoken, and he knows how to stand in front of a crowd," she noted. Rotem could also see what Elad's teachers had seen in their young pupil. "If you asked any teacher, she would tell you she knew that he was a trailblazer even when he was a little kid."

"[Elad] is the kind of guy who makes everyone feel on track," Rotem continued. "He keeps me grounded. He's very down-to-earth and likes people to ask questions. We haven't been in touch much lately because of COVID-19, but we did talk yesterday, and it was like a soul-to-soul connection. He's kind, sensitive, loving, and very responsible." Rotem also spoke admiringly of Elad's dream to be a father, a subject to which I will return in a later chapter.

Yarden added the perspective of a younger sister. "He is a leader. He always stood out, no matter where he was or who he was with. He was the guy [always] surrounded by everyone." Yarden stressed her brother's intelligence and successes, obvious from an early age. She was too young to clearly recall Elad's experience when he left the School for the Arts, but she knew the family stories. "That [school] was like a dream, a much better fit for him. After we moved, he was devastated."

On a personal level, Yarden sensed that Elad treated her more like a parent would than a brother would—he was authoritative and controlling, but "in a good way," which kept her steady. They were very close as children and continue to be. "We hung out together and played together. We knew everything about each other because we told each other everything." The ten-hour time difference between Los Angeles and Tel Aviv limits the frequency of their telephone calls and Zoom sessions to once a month, but they know what is happening in each other's lives. Both siblings are in touch with their parents and take advantage of the family's WhatsApp group for posting pictures.

The consensus among those who know Elad was as remarkable as the consensus I found among Andrew's family and friends. The most im-

(L) Elad's maternal grandmother, Naomi Abadi, with Elad. They are at the wedding of Elad's cousin, Shimrit, in Tel Aviv, November 2014. Naomi was the only person who could manage her difficult grandson during his early years. The two were extremely close until her death in 2015. *Source*: Photo courtesy of Elad Dvash-Banks.

pressive comments came from Andrew's side of the family. "I just love him." "He is the greatest." "Absolutely wonderful." "He's perfection." Many of them zeroed in on Elad's extraordinary culinary skills—he loves to cook and is famous for preparing memorable meals for anyone who dines at their home. Elad openly admits, "I love eating; I'm a foodie. I cook like my mother and my grandmothers. I remember as a child standing next to them and asking, 'What do you do here? How do you make this sauce? What do you put here? How long does that take?' " I couldn't help thinking about the little suitcase Elad carried so proudly to his elementary school cooking class.

When I began this book project, I was captivated by the timely themes and topics posed by Andrew and Elad and their lengthy struggle over citizenship policy, gay marriage, twinship, surrogacy, and family. But as I completed the different chapters, I found myself enjoying the people, their personalities, and the intersection of their lives in ways that felt new and fresh. Since they were born four years apart, I thought about what each one was doing at a particular point in time. When Elad was born in 1985 in Tel Aviv, Andrew was attending kindergarten in Beverly Hills, about 8,000 miles away. When Elad felt confused about his first attraction to males, Andrew had just come out to his mother and father. As Elad was entering the Israeli army's Unit 8200, Andrew was struggling to make a living in New York City. But then their lives came together, all because Elad enrolled in Tel Aviv University as a freshman, the same school Andrew had chosen for his graduate studies.

Elad began his undergraduate studies certain of the academic path he intended to follow. But as John Lennon once said, "Life is what happens when you're busy making other plans."[38] Six months into the program, in 2008, Elad took a job as an overseas student counselor at Tel Aviv University, a decision that would ultimately revise his carefully crafted academic blueprint. He could not foresee that he would be moving to Canada in 2010 with the man he would marry, and that his master's degree in global affairs would be awarded by the University of Toronto.

"A Fabulous Couple": Andrew and Elad

$\mathcal{E}$ach week, the Sunday *New York Times* prints stories about the meetings, courtships, and marriages of ordinary couples. And during the week
their "Modern Love" column publishes reader contributions that capture their "relationships, feelings, betrayals and revelations."[1] I suspect
the universal fascination with these romantic tales lies in the seeming
improbability that two individuals who ultimately fall in love find themselves in the same place at just the right time.

Some people believe that chance events best explain why certain
paths cross while others never do. While there is a likely element of
chance in some meetings, the life choices we make reflect our interests,
temperaments, and talents, increasing the probability of unions between
like-minded individuals.[2] Of course, unusual circumstances, like the
2022 war in Ukraine or the coronavirus pandemic, and minor distractions, like being shut out of a popular class or missing the six o'clock
bus, can significantly affect the way one's life unfolds. But barring extraordinary happenings and consequences, I believe chance plays less of
a role in mate selection than seems to be the case. Andrew and Elad are
exemplary in this respect.

It may seem improbable that Andrew, born in the United States
in 1981, and Elad, born in Israel in 1985, should meet in the overseas
student office of Tel Aviv University in 2008. But both young men had
a passion for Israeli culture and global affairs, and were eager to assist
anyone who needed their help. Both had been bullied for being gay and
had felt frustrated at the lack of social support. "No one knew what to
do with us," Elad complained.[3] These experiences prompted Andrew
to work for Teen Line, helping teenagers talk through their problems.

And they motivated Elad to become an overseas student counselor, eager to smooth the adjustment of international students to a new land. Part of Elad's job also involved planning parties, excursions, and other social events to acquaint the students with Israel and with each other.[4] The fact that Elad entered the office while Andrew was sitting there may have been a chance matter—*but such chance occurred within an academic landscape that attracted them both.*[5]

FIRST GLANCE AND A PURIM PARTY

I asked Elad and Andrew (independently) to tell me about their first meeting. The two stories aligned well, except for one important detail—*the first glance*—a moment Elad recounted, and Andrew omitted. But when reminded of it, Andrew said it was true. I also listened to them tell the story together.

One morning, in March 2008, Elad entered the office for international students. He was now a counselor and dormitory resident after having lived at home for the first six months of his college career. "I saw this guy sitting in a chair by the computer, totally relaxed, talking to the secretary. They were laughing. He was telling her about a trip he had just taken to Morocco and about a guy he had met there. He was very openly gay in front of everyone—he was even a little cocky—let's just say he was not lacking in self-confidence! So, he was talking about this guy, and I saw him, and I'm like, in my head, 'Oh, he's really good-looking.' Clearly, from the first sentence I heard, I figured out he was gay. That was the first time we saw each other and he's like, 'Oh, hi, I'm Andrew, who are you?' And I'm like, 'I'm Elad. I work here. I just started two months ago.' He's like, 'Oh, nice to meet you.' And that was the extent of our conversation. He left and we didn't have any other interaction until the Purim party."

The holiday of Purim is celebrated in late winter or early spring. It commemorates the Jewish people's salvation from Haman's plan to kill all Jews living in the ancient Persian Empire during the fifth century BCE. *Purim* means "lots" (pebbles or stones) in Persian; Haman threw lots to determine if he would act on his plan.[6] Purim is a joyous occasion—some people (Elad included) have labeled the day as "the Jewish Halloween." Guests come in costumes, drink wine, and consume the traditional three-cornered hamantash (triangular-shaped pastry with a sweet poppy-seed filling). Dancing is part of the celebration and may include customary folk dances, like the hora, or more contemporary styles, such as those performed at the "Boogie," one of Jerusalem's longest-running dance parties.[7]

When I spoke to Elad and Andrew in 2022, Purim had just passed. It had begun on the evening of March 16 and ended on March 17. "It was almost exactly fourteen years to the day that we met," Andrew recalled. (Despite their brief encounter in the overseas student office, both Andrew and Elad consider the Purim party to be the place where they *actually* met one another.) People often ask them how they got together—a question Andrew "really hates," especially from individuals unfamiliar with the holiday. "When we say, 'Purim party,' they hear *porn party*. They let me go on talking for ten minutes, thinking we met at a porn party, because we're gay. We have to emphasize that we met at a *Purim* party."

I wanted to know how the two of them found one another at this gathering, since it's easy to miss people in a crowded room. According to Elad, Andrew went up to one of the student counselors to ask her if this guy (Elad) she worked with was gay. "What's his deal?" he wanted to know. And she said, "Why don't you ask him yourself?" At this point in the conversation, Andrew interrupted to say, "That's not what she said. She said, 'Yeah, he's gay, and he's been asking about you.' And I'm like, 'Oh, that's all I need. I don't need you anymore. I got it. I can take it from here." Elad did not recall this particular exchange, but he found it "believable."

He remembers Andrew approaching him on the dance floor, where they talked to one another and exchanged telephone numbers. They immediately connected when Elad told Andrew he had lived in Southern California for six months, part of that time in Chatsworth, a city in the San Fernando Valley. Andrew pronounced Chatsworth "the worst place to live," but they both knew this comment didn't matter, because they had already bonded. They also knew that a romantic relationship between a staff member and a student was "taboo"—but later on, Elad's supervisor understood that the relationship was serious and did not interfere. "The rest is history."

Whenever I watch twins, romantic partners, or news anchors and their guests in conversation, I keep a watchful eye on the person who is not talking at the time. Their facial expressions and body language tell me whether they agree and are happy with what their partner is saying, or if they disagree and seem impatient to jump in. A relaxed look, a nod, or a smile reflect pleasure and pride, while a grimace, a fidget, or a roll of the eyes suggest otherwise. Andrew and Elad were both leaning back and grinning while the other was speaking, eyes fastened on their partner's face, and accepting corrections and additions with a laugh or a nod of the head. At one point they went back and forth over when Elad had finished his army service—2005? 2006? It was hilarious. And they debated over the year Elad had started college—2006? 2007? More hilarity. Their pleasure and satisfaction with one another were palpable. They are "a fabulous couple" in the minds of everyone who knows them.

Andrew's older brother, Jon, and his wife, Julie, often discuss the couples they know, focusing on whether the respective partners make each other "better" or "worse." Jon is adamant that Andrew and Elad make each other better. "No one has had the effect on Andrew that Elad has had," Jon insisted. [8]

The couple's complementarity is an asset that was emphasized by many of their family and friends. According to Elad's Canadian friend, Kari Zalik, "They have different personalities that fit." I was told that where Elad is calm, Andrew is excitable; Elad is practical, Andrew is emotional; Elad is conforming, while Andrew is untraditional; Elad is imaginative, Andrew is detailed; Elad is the grown-up, Andrew, the child in the room; Elad focuses on single activities, while Andrew tackles a hundred things at once; and whereas Elad is financially carefree, Andrew is financially cautious.

Elad's friend Kari, who launched the music publicity company Bad Parade, is aware of Elad and Andrew's different styles of involvement in popular culture.[9] Kari's suggestion that they attend a John Mayer concert met with a green-colored emoji (indicating "puke") from Andrew. Elad asked, "Who's that?" Elad and Andrew also acknowledge their contrasting sides. Elad knows he is more reserved about family matters than Andrew, who is more open. When it comes to religion, Andrew says Elad "calls all the shots in this house." Both have settled happily and comfortably into these roles.

Interestingly, research on mate selection has convincingly shown that similarities, especially in attitudes and values—not differences—are what draw people together.[10] I found many meaningful ways in which

Andrew and Elad are alike—both are intelligent, altruistic, politically aware, family-oriented, and travel-obsessed—not to mention gay and Jewish. The divergences that other people named seemed to be more a matter of degree, rather than genuine differences. Andrew and Elad concur on most big questions but hold somewhat varied views on others. One of their shared priorities is finding the best intervention plan for one of their twins, who had shown behavioral problems, a topic I will address in another chapter. They disagreed over how much to involve their family members, but they are open to the other's perspective. When Ethan was denied US citizenship, both fathers were strongly committed to doing what was right but were somewhat at odds over the best solution. In the end their decision was consensual, and they are confident now, as they were then, that they made the right choice. Of course, Andrew and Elad have also had some contentious times, just like other couples.

THEY LOVED EACH OTHER

"There is no chance these two are going to make it."

These words from an anonymous speaker appear to clash with the heading of this section, and with the observations of so many people close to Andrew and Elad, but they don't—because despite some early arguments, they found a way to be together. In fact, the same person insisted that "they loved each other, and their connection was so strong. After two years, it was as if the fighting stopped." In the beginning, Elad's army friend Ilona, who lived nearby and spent a lot of time with Andrew and Elad, also had doubts. "How can it last?" she wondered. But her doubts came from knowing the couple's cultural differences (e.g., Israelis are more direct in conversation; Americans are more formal in manner of dress[11]). "Perhaps I am old-fashioned?" she asked herself. Andrew also tied the couple's clashes to cultural norms and practices— "Israelis push ahead in line and yell at each other," he complained. Nonetheless, he was "madly in love."

In the weeks and months following the Purim party, Andrew and Elad's relationship flourished. In the beginning, Andrew was living in an apartment with a roommate in Tel Aviv and Elad was living in a student dormitory. Andrew moved into Elad's dorm room in mid-2009

Andrew Banks (L) and Elad Dvash on vacation in Herceg Novi, a coastal town in Montenegro, September 2009. This photograph was included in the thank-you notes sent to their wedding guests in 2011. *Source*: Photo courtesy of Andrew and Elad Dvash-Banks.

until they rented an apartment together in downtown Tel Aviv, on Rupin Street, close to Gordon Beach. By then, Andrew had earned his master's degree, but he chose to stay in Israel another year so Elad could complete his undergraduate education. Once their relationship had become serious, they both understood that they would eventually move to California. Elad had always been excited about living abroad, and Andrew was eager to be close to his family in Los Angeles. Part of this understanding was that they would eventually get married. "It's really an inspiring story," observed Elad's friend Rotem.[12]

I heard different takes on the status of their Tel Aviv apartment. Andrew said it was "nice," noting that it was a former bomb shelter that had been converted into a studio apartment. Elad's friend Ilona called it a clean and tidy flat on the ground-floor level of an old building, next to an elevator. Rotem had other thoughts. "They started out in a tiny apartment and the three of us would go to the beach, come back, and

Andrew's mother, Ann Banks (L), meeting Elad for the first time. Andrew is seated in the center with Elad in the right of the picture. The setting is a Carrows restaurant in Los Angeles, California, during Andrew and Elad's visit in July 2009. "LOVED Elad at first sight," Ann wrote when she sent me this picture. *Source*: Photo courtesy of Andrew and Elad Dvash-Banks.

wash off in their little shower. It was a really shitty place with cockroaches and whatever." Elad agreed with Rotem, likening the apartment to a converted basement with very little light coming in through its three windows, two of which didn't even open. Nevertheless, he and Andrew loved living there, insisting that the incredible location and low rent overcame the downsides.

One of Andrew and Elad's early arguments happened at the apartment—a situation in which they took opposing sides. Andrew, Elad, and Rotem had been out drinking one night, and when they returned, they discovered they had lost the key to the apartment. They went back and forth at each other until Andrew sat outside and announced that they were all going to sleep on the street. But Elad climbed into the apartment through a window and opened the front door two minutes later. Neither Andrew, nor Elad, clearly recalls that evening, but Rotem does.

Reflecting back on that incident, Rotem says they complete each other. "It's amazing to see. I saw all the nuances because I really lived with them. And it's amazing—they're an example to me of how people that are so different can love each other so much, you know, be on the same team and fight for the same cause. I think their children [Aiden and Ethan] are going to be really proud of them when they are old enough to understand it all."

Understanding it all means knowing the legal status of gay marriage, not just in the state of California, but in the United States.

CHANGE IN PLAN: CANADA

In 1996, then-president Bill Clinton signed the Defense of Marriage Act (DOMA) that defined marriage as the union of a man and a woman. It gave states the right to not recognize same-sex marriages performed in states where they were allowed. Among other things, DOMA had the effect of denying federal benefits to same-sex partners and preventing a nonbiological parent from having a legal relationship with a biological child of the other parent.[13]

On May 15, 2008, the California Supreme Court ruled that same-sex marriage was legal in California. However, the following year, Proposition 8 was approved by a majority of voters in that state, reversing the 2008 ruling. Proposition 8 was upheld under state law, but it was not federal law. Vaughn Walker, a US district court judge, ruled that the proposition violated the Constitution; however, the decision stayed on appeal to the Ninth Circuit Court of Appeals and the US Supreme Court. It was not until June 26, 2015, that same-sex marriage was ruled to be a protected right under the US Constitution; thus, the states could not ban it. Same-sex couples were granted the same rights as heterosexual couples under the law.[14]

It was 2010, and the timing could not have been worse for Andrew and Elad, whose long-term plans were to move, marry, and raise a family in California. Israel was not an option for them because that nation does not allow gay marriage, although it recognizes such marriages if performed abroad. Moreover, living in Israel was not part of the plan—both young men were eager to relocate to the United States.

"[DOMA meant that] I couldn't marry him [Elad] and have him immigrate and get a green card like we could if we were a heterosexual couple. We discovered that in 2009, and it was really heartbreaking for me," Andrew recalled. Gay marriage had, however, been legal in Canada since 2005, and Andrew held a Canadian passport, since his parents had been born there. He had never lived in Toronto, but he had spent a lot of time there on family vacations. Andrew and Elad decided to visit Toronto to see if it was a city where they could both be happy.

They loved it. Andrew recalled the elation they both felt when they returned from their trip. "We're going to move to Toronto, where we're equal citizens and where we can get married!"[15]

Andrew's father Jim Banks (center), meeting Elad for the second time, in October 2009. Elad is to the left of the picture, and Andrew is to the right. They are standing outside an Outback Steakhouse restaurant in Burbank, California. Jim first met Elad at the Brasserie restaurant in Tel Aviv, May 2009. When Elad reached into his pocket for his wallet, Jim warned him that he would "chop off your hand" if he tried to pay for his meal. *Source*: Photo courtesy of Andrew and Elad Dvash-Banks.

DOWN ON ONE KNEE

During the nearly two and a half years that Andrew and Elad were a dating couple, they talked often about moving, marriage, and family. But they never really discussed an engagement, perhaps because proposals often come unexpectedly with some fanfare, even as couples knowingly move closer to lifetime commitment. "It wasn't like [it would have been] a surprise if he proposed or a surprise if I proposed. We kind of knew it was going to happen," Elad said. He admitted, "I wanted to be the one who did it, but I got cold feet every time I tried to plan something." He suspects that Andrew finally proposed in July 2010 because, by then, they had bought their one-way tickets to Toronto and were scheduled to leave Israel the following month.

Andrew planned the proposal with Rotem's help. They chose a good wine, three different types of cheese, and other delicacies for a picnic that took place on a cliff overlooking the Mediterranean Sea in Tel Aviv. Rotem brought along her guitar and a camera, and Andrew (in a break from tradition) fastened an engagement bracelet—not a ring—on their dog's neck. Andrew and Elad had bought their dog together, a black pug-terrier mix—the kind that Andrew had always wanted—and named him London. Elad recalled, "We walked our dog as the sun was setting and, all of a sudden, Andrew asked, 'Did you see what London has on his neck?' I looked and thought I saw a weird collar. I took it off, and then Andrew went down on one knee and proposed. It was very special."

LONG WAY AROUND: TORONTO

Andrew and Elad hosted a going-away party at a Mexican restaurant in Tel Aviv to say good-bye to their friends. Then, armed with "four suitcases, their dog, and one thousand dollars in the bank," Elad and Andrew exited Israel for Canada in August 2010. The excitement and anticipation of a new life in Toronto helped Andrew manage his regret at not moving to California, but resentment lingered. "It's not something I paid much attention to at the time because it was just kind of matter-of-fact. It's, like, 'Okay, well, the United States has these laws on the books. They won't allow us to marry. But I have to choose between being with my family and being with the man I love, which is not really a fair place to put anybody.' "

Andrew's Canadian relatives found them an apartment, but he needed a job to pay the rent. Taking advantage of the free Wi-Fi offered at the nearby Starbucks coffee shop, Andrew searched the Internet, landing a job with Gogo Worldwide Vacations. Desperate for money, he convinced the agency to let him begin working immediately, rather than wait a week. He sold land products for travel—hotels, flights, excursions, and rental cars. Elad did not have permanent residency status, so he volunteered at the University of Toronto's Hillel House. He also planned the couple's wedding gala to take place the following year, visiting floral shops, clothing stores, and wedding venues. Meanwhile, Andrew and Elad were legally married by a justice of the peace on August 19, 2010, but they had a real wedding celebration to look forward to one year later.[16]

WEDDING BELLS

On August 14, 2011, one hundred and twenty guests gathered just outside Toronto to witness Andrew and Elad getting married. The ceremony took place on a sunny Sunday afternoon in the garden of the Sunnybrook Estates.[17] The couple's parents, nieces and nephews, and Andrew's brothers led the procession. Next, Elad was escorted down the aisle by his sisters, Yarden and Neta; Andrew followed, accompanied by his sisters, Ashli and Jennifer. The lunch that followed the ceremony was a "classy" affair, with flowers on display everywhere. Held at the Elizabethan-style Vaughan House located on the estate, the celebration was "beautiful, with music and dancing." Andrew's mother Ann was struck by the multinational quality of the affair—"The rabbi came from Wales, one groom came from Israel, the other groom came from California, and the wedding was in Canada."[18] It was the first and only gay wedding that most guests had attended, but it was the tone and feeling that set it apart from other nuptials.

Andrew's brother Jon described the wedding as "a truly fantastic, wonderful event. It had meaning in that it could only have been done in Canada at that time. That was unfortunate—but it also didn't feel like it should have been anywhere other than where they lived. Our daughters [Cara and Sydney] were flower girls, and James, Brian, and I [the three brothers] stood up with them." Ilona likened the wedding to a "fairy tale." Andrew's college friend, Laurel Mintz, who delivered a speech, described the wedding as an "extremely emotional" event. "I was so honored to be asked to share in that special moment. I had traveled with both and known them for years and seen the incredible life they were going to build together."

Also in attendance were Andrew's celebrity identical twin cousins from Canada, Caillianne (Cailli) and Samantha (Sam) Beckerman. The twins are fashion bloggers and the 2017 winners of the Digital Fashion Creator Award, given annually by the Canadian Arts and Fashion Awards (CAFA).[19] The wedding was "unforgettable"; both twins were thrilled and touched to "feel the love and support that Andrew and Elad had for each other."

When asked for a childhood memory, Cailli and Sam, who are just six months older than Andrew, described his bar mitzvah invitation, calling their cousin "the coolest." The invitation was a poster showing the cast of the popular TV show *Beverly Hills, 90210*, in which Andrew's image had been added.[20] "That was amazing in the days before Photoshop!" The twins didn't attend the event, but they "kept the poster forever." Andrew never mentioned the invitation when he described his bar mitzvah to me.

Ann also told me that the wedding was "magic," explaining that "they're in love, and everybody was feeling it in every little detail. We all helped. Ashli [Andrew's sister, a photographer] had an incredible book printed up that people could write in, and there were photos of them [Andrew and Elad] through the years." She added, "I had a friend make a gown for me. It was really beautiful. And she kept saying, 'Look at it this way, Annie, you're not going to upstage the bride.' So it was our little joke."

True to their shared zest for seeing new sights, Andrew and Elad chose "travel" as their wedding theme. Guests learned their table and seating assignments from a "boarding pass." It turned out that Elad's Israeli family and friends accounted for only eight of the one hundred and twenty wedding guests. Seated at the single "Israeli table" were his parents (Moti and Tovi), two sisters (Yarden and Neta), an aunt (Shuli), a cousin (Orel), and two friends (Rotem and Ilona). Elad explained,

Andrew and Elad's wedding, August 14, 2011, at Sunnybrook Estates outside of Toronto. The ceremony was performed by licensed wedding officiant Jeremy Citron. *Photo credit*: Paul Cheney, 360 Photography in Toronto.

"I never brought boyfriends home. Even when Andrew and I started dating, she [my mother] asked me not to tell anyone in the extended family. My grandparents didn't know, and [most of my] my aunts and uncles didn't know."

Elad's mother finally agreed to invite her sister Shuli, Elad's aunt. He admits it was difficult seeing just one table with people from his home. "It was hard for me not to have my grandparents there, and not to have my other aunts and uncles there. They all know now, and I feel like I had to apologize that I had a wedding and didn't invite them. They say they understood, but I feel like they were hurt, especially my cousins, who said, 'You should have told us—we would have been the most supportive [people] in the world. We would have flown to Toronto to be at your wedding, to celebrate and support you.' But I didn't know. I was scared to come out fully." Elad's relations with his parents, especially his mother, have changed dramatically since he revealed his sexual orientation when he was eighteen. Tovi and Moti both called the wedding "special and beautiful."

Elad's Israeli friends, Ilona and Rotem, arrived in Toronto several weeks before the wedding to help with preparations. Ilona recalled that Andrew and Elad presented the different tasks to her in a way that she found very inspiring. Rotem saw herself as "kind of a best man." During the ceremony and celebration, she sat with the other Israeli guests to translate the vows and toast and deliver a speech on their behalf. In contrast with most Israeli weddings Elad had attended, which typically take place in a large indoor hall and are unscripted and casual, the Dvash-Banks affair was held outdoors and was highly scheduled and formal.[21] Selected guests delivered speeches at preassigned times.

Andrew wore a white tuxedo jacket over a black dress shirt and pale yellow tie; Elad's complementary attire consisted of a dark gray jacket, white dress shirt, and purple tie. Both had a yellow boutonniere fastened to their lapel. And recall that Andrew's mother's gown had been specially designed for the occasion.

A cocktail reception followed the ceremony, and then guests entered the ballroom for the festive meal. Elad, a self-identified "foodie," recalled the menu: three entree choices—halibut, chicken breast, and an "eggplant tower" for vegetarians. But the wedding cake was Elad's greatest pleasure—a red velvet and cream cheese creation with vanilla butterscotch sauce, surrounded by white chocolate shavings. A huge dessert bar offering a variety of different candies was also available to guests.

After the wedding, Rotem and Elad took a trip to the Canadian Rockies; this was Rotem's first visit to Canada, and she wanted to make the most of it. Elad insisted that Andrew stay home to take care of their dog, and he reluctantly agreed. But their excursion made him laugh, thinking that she (and not he) had accompanied his husband on a "honeymoon."

By October of 2011 Elad had still not acquired permanent residency, but he did have a work visa. This allowed him to take a job recruiting Canadian students for study at Tel Aviv University, where he met Kari Zalik, who did the same for the rival school, Hebrew University. Elad and Kari became close friends over the course of meetings and conference travel.[22] In a curious replay of Elad's "honeymoon" with Rotem, Elad, Andrew, and Kari visited Canada's Atlantic areas—Prince Edward Island, New Brunswick, and Nova Scotia. They stayed close to home, since Elad's citizenship status meant that he might have difficulty reentering Canada if he should leave. Andrew called this vacation their "mini-moon."

WEDDING BELL BLUES

In fact, the magical "fairy-tale" wedding did not start out that way. The joining together of "the fabulous couple" on a glorious Sunday afternoon had no hint of the bitter back-and-forth that had preceded it. Andrew was committed to having a traditional Jewish wedding in which he and Elad would sign a ketubah (marriage contract), be escorted to the chuppah (canopy) by their parents, have a rabbi perform the ceremony under the chuppah, provide a kippah (brimless prayer cap) for male guests, crush a glass wrapped in cloth when the ceremony was completed, and listen to guests shout, "*Mazel tov!*" (Good luck!).[23] But Elad had objected strongly to having a wedding of this kind, insisting on a ceremony that was completely devoid of Jewish rituals.[24]

According to Andrew, "He [Elad] wouldn't allow anyone to wear a kippah at our wedding. He did not even want a rabbi to marry us. You know, I wouldn't say he was antireligion, but Israelis come from a very different perspective. You know, in Israel, there's no such thing as

Reform Judaism—you're either Orthodox or you're secular, and he was secular. And so, for him it was that way when we moved to Toronto in 2010, and then he [Elad] started to plan this wedding many months later. I'm like, 'We need the kippot, and we need the rabbi.' And he's like, 'Whoa, whoa, whoa, whoa.' In his mind, it's like I'm trying to make this an Orthodox thing."

Elad admits that they argued vehemently over how their wedding would be conducted. "I refused to have any shred of religiousness on my wedding day. I regret it now, but back then I was so antireligion [that] I did not want a rabbi, so we got a justice of the peace who happened to be Jewish. He did sign a ketubah [marriage contract], but it's a secular, humanistic document. We did break the glass because it's a fun tradition." This act, typically performed by the groom, recalls the destruction of the Jewish temple in Jerusalem. In a departure from tradition, Andrew and Elad did it together with their arms wrapped around each other.

The couple also stood under a chuppah, the justice recited the kiddush (blessing over the wine), and everyone danced the hora. But there was no lighting of candles, no blessing over the meal, and no wearing of kippot. According to Andrew, "In hindsight, he [Elad] looks back and says, we should have had a rabbi and we should have had kippot—some people improvised by placing napkins on their heads. This was a Jewish event, and we should have been more Jewish about it. But he's evolved and changed. Our level of religiosity has increased since Elad started working [at IKAR]." The fragments from the broken glass frame the ketubah that hangs in their home.

Pictures show off Andrew and Elad's wedding attire but not the conflict that surrounded it. Andrew wanted to wear a black tuxedo and urged Elad to wear a white one, since his dark skin would set it off well. But Elad's traditional bent led him to choose a dark ensemble; in fact, he wanted both men to wear black tuxedos. Andrew was annoyed. "I chose white just to spite him!" he admitted. But memory of that altercation is fading. "He [Elad] pulled off an incredibly beautiful wedding."

Andrew and Elad's commendable compromise, played out on August 14, was a memorable moment for them and for every guest present. No one would imagine that a series of bitter disagreements and reluctant concessions had preceded that glorious day. And while Andrew had wanted a rabbi to marry them, he and Elad were delighted by their choice of Jeremy Citron as justice of the peace. Originally from Wales,

Elad (L) and Andrew breaking the glass, a tradition in Jewish weddings done to acknowledge the destruction of the Temple of Jerusalem by Nebuchadnezzar II of Babylonia in 587/586 BCE. This event has several interpretations but is generally thought to be a reminder that in moments of great joy there is sadness. *Photo credit*: (Left) Paul Cheney, 360 Photography in Toronto. (Right) Andrew and Elad's ketubah or wedding contract, framed by the shards of glass they created together from the glass-breaking ritual at the end of the ceremony. *Source*: Photo courtesy of Andrew and Elad Dvash-Banks.

Citron is a licensed wedding officiant in Toronto. He is well-versed in many religions, as stated on his "All You Need Is Love" website.[25] "He was ready to do for us whatever we wanted, you know, different than how I envisioned it," Andrew recalled. Given Citron's background and performance, it is likely that many guests mistook him for the usual leader of a Jewish congregation. I noted earlier that Andrew's mother praised the "rabbi" who married her son; she was stunned when I revealed to her that Jeremy Citron was not a rabbi at all.

A LIFE TOGETHER

Andrew and Elad continued their life in Canada as a happily married couple. They moved to a beautiful condo, purchased a car, and held jobs they enjoyed. They had a wide circle of friends and enjoyed visits from Andrew's relatives in Toronto and from family members in the United States and Israel. But by 2013, Elad had tired of the cold Toronto winters, and both partners were eager for international travel. They booked an eight-day trip to Jamaica, replete with endless perks thanks to Andrew's new management position at Gogo Vacations—five-star hotels, complimentary cocktails, and other luxuries. It was a risky decision because Elad was still not a permanent resident; however, one week prior to their departure his residency papers were approved, letting the couple fully enjoy their time away. It was a real honeymoon this time. They took lots of trips after this as a way of "making up for lost time."[26]

As a Canadian resident and in accordance with his earlier plan, Elad enrolled in a master's degree program in global affairs at the University of Toronto. As part of his program, he worked part-time for the Egmont Group of financial intelligence units (FIUs) that monitors money laundering and tax evasion.[27] Andrew continued his work at Gogo Vacations. By this time the travel cravings they had experienced earlier were satisfied. The thought of moving to America was on hold for a while, but the idea of having a family was not.

• 4 •

Altruistic Surrogacy: Aiden and Ethan

"Aiden looks just like Andrew, and Ethan is a 'mini-me.'"

—Elad Dvash-Banks, 2022

Aiden and Ethan look like an ordinary pair of fraternal twin brothers. Aiden is fair-haired as Andrew had been as a child, while Ethan's hair is dark, like Elad's still is. Fraternal twin differences in hair color and texture are not unusual between non-identical twins; depending on the whims and fancies of genetic transmission, each twin can inherit different genes, making them resemble one parent more than the other. These five-year-old boys are close in height, and their facial structures are somewhat similar although not identical, also consistent with fraternal twinning. But unlike most fraternal twins (and non-twin siblings) who share 50 percent of their genes, on average, Aiden and Ethan share only 25 percent, on average.[1] As such, they are an exceptional twin pair—genetically equivalent to half-siblings. This reproductive quirk occurred because *the boys have the same egg donor but not the same father.*

Aiden and Ethan are not the only twins who have this unusual parental arrangement. The first medically documented case was reported in 1810, in which one twin girl was white and the other twin girl was half white, half Black.[2] This pair was impossible to miss, but some pairs are hard to detect, especially when the two fathers share physical features like hair color and eye color. For this reason, a Japanese twin pair with different fathers might have been missed if not for the big difference in the twins' crown-to-rump length seen on their sonogram at the thirteenth gestational week.[3]

The pregnancy that produced Andrew and Elad's sons came from a conception that was orchestrated by their fathers, in concert with a fertility specialist, an anonymous egg donor, and a surrogate who carried the twins as close to term as possible. What they did replays a naturally occurring reproductive process called *superfecundation* that sometimes yields *heteropaternal twins*, i.e., twins with different fathers.[4] This can happen if a woman releases two eggs simultaneously and each egg is fertilized by a different partner. Once ovulation occurs, there is a twelve- to forty-eight-hour window during which time a sperm can penetrate an egg. Sperm can survive in the uterine tract for as long as seven to ten days. Of course, *superfecundated twins* can occur if a woman releases more than one egg and engages in intercourse with the same partner on separate, but closely timed, occasions, but these twins would be an ordinary fraternal pair, sharing about half their genes.[5] In contrast, heteropaternal twins are a unique subset of superfecundated twins due to their nonshared paternity.

HETEROPATERNAL TWINS: RARE OR UNDETECTED?

Heteropaternal twinning is presumed to be rare, largely because only twenty-four such cases have been reported worldwide.[6] Its presumed rarity is also based on the low frequency (2.4 percent) of lawsuits (out of all legally disputed paternity cases) brought against mothers by fathers upon discovering that one twin is not biologically theirs.[7] However, no one really knows how often such twinning occurs; the 2.4 percent figure was reported in 1992 and needs updating.

I suspect that many naturally occurring cases of heteropaternal twins are not described in medical journals because not all cases enter statistical studies, not all cases come to a courtroom, and, as indicated, some cases may never be detected.[8] In further support of the possibility that heteropaternity is more common than believed, 29 percent of women between twenty-five and forty-nine years of age have two to four lifetime sexual partners, and 62 percent have between five and over fifteen.[9] Of course, these relationships would have to occur close in time for heteropaternal twinning to occur. There is also suggestive, but mixed, evidence of a link between fraternal twinning and frequency of sexual intercourse, based on an increased frequency of fraternal twins conceived outside of wedlock.[10] Also consistent with a fraternal twinning–sexual frequency relationship are the higher rates of HIV infection observed among twins than singletons during the 1990s.[11]

It is likely that heteropaternal pairs will be revealed in greater numbers in the near future due to DNA tests offered by 23andMe, Ancestry.com, and other gene analysis companies. In fact, I know several sets of twins who underwent genetic testing to learn about their ethnic origins and were stunned to discover that they did not share both parents. But unless these twins bring their cases to medical and/or legal attention, they will not be included in statistical studies.

I believe we are on the brink of a new source of twins with common mothers and different fathers. Unlike the first documented case in 1810 that happened naturally, these new cases would reflect changes in medical intervention, federal legislation, and societal values. Methods for assisting reproduction are steadily improving, rates of same-sex marriage are on the rise, and societal acceptance of such marriages has increased.[12] More and more same-sex male couples are likely to consider having families via Andrew and Elad's plan. Some already have. Simon and Graeme Berney-Edwards from the UK conceived opposite-sex twins, Calder and Alexandra, with the help of a Canadian surrogate.[13] Simon fathered Alexandra, while Graeme fathered Calder. New York City couple Al DiGiulio and Chris Soucey are fathers to twin boys, Tommy and Luca; and Vernon Leftwich and Ricardo Cooper, also of New York City, are fathers to twin girls, Harper and Knox.[14] The biological relationship of these fathers to their twins was not disclosed; understandably, some parents prefer to keep that knowledge confidential. In 2021, Pete Buttigieg (formerly "Mayor Pete"), the 2022 US secretary of transportation, and his husband Chasten (Glezman) Buttigieg, brought home opposite-sex twins, Penelope Rose and Joseph August (Gus). Whether one or both partners are the twins' biological fathers, or if the twins were adopted, has not been disclosed.[15]

A FEMALE-FEMALE COUNTERPART?

There is no naturally occurring heteropaternal twinning parallel for same-sex female couples. In other words, *a naturally occurring case of twins sharing their father's genes, but not their mother's genes, is not a biological reality.*

However, it is possible to create hypothetical (but achievable) reproductive scenarios that would mimic this outcome. For example, suppose the same male impregnated two biologically unrelated women close in time. The two developing fetuses would share half their father's genes and none of their mother's genes; however, they would not share the same womb, as would heteropaternal pairs. In fact, I would not classify such children as twins because they violate one of the important criteria I have developed for defining twinship: *gestation by the same woman at the same time*.

My full set of criteria, with the exceptions noted below, are 1) simultaneous conception, 2) shared parentage, 3) common intrauterine environment, and 4) shared familial/cultural events. Exceptions to these conditions are twins resulting from heteropaternal conception, whether natural or replayed, as in the case of Aiden and Ethan; twins resulting from conception during different cycles, known as superfetation (see endnote 4); twins delivered days apart; and twins reared in different homes, and possibly different countries.[16] I believe these exceptional cases clearly qualify as twins.

There is another achievable scenario I can imagine that more closely approximates heteropaternal twinning: Two embryos could be created using eggs from two unrelated females and sperm from the same male. The embryos could be implanted in the womb of one of the women or a surrogate. The pregnancy outcome would be two children who share their father's—but not their mother's—genes *and* shared a womb. I *would* classify such children as twins.

I do not know if such a procedure has been intentionally conducted, but it happened by chance in 1993, at a fertility clinic in the Netherlands. Two embryos created by a white couple, Wilma and William Stuart, were implanted into Wilma's uterus. In December of that year, Wilma delivered twin sons—Teun, who resembled her and her husband, and Koen, who hardly resembled either parent due to his dark skin color. It was eventually revealed that a Black couple had visited the clinic on the same day, also hoping for children, and the gentleman's sperm was accidentally combined with Wilma's egg. Wilma and William love both boys, and they nicknamed them *duo penotti* (a Dutch treat of chocolate and vanilla cream, slathered on bread).[17]

As I thought more about this issue, I realized that *there is an allegedly rare, but real and naturally occurring, female-female version of heteropaternity*. It would involve a woman diagnosed as a chimera, a condition in which a person inherits two distinct sets of DNA.[18] Only a handful of such cases have been identified. In 2002, Karen Keegan of Washington State was utterly shocked and completely baffled to learn that two of her three sons (whom she had physically delivered) were unrelated to her but were related to her husband. The situation was serious because Keegan risked losing her bid for public assistance, as well as custody of her children. The dilemma was unresolved until doctors used DNA evidence to show that Keegan was a chimera— apparently, two of her sons had inherited different cell lines found throughout Keegan's body. *Had she conceived her related son and one of her "unrelated" sons at the same time, the children would have shared their father's genes but possibly not their mother's genes, replaying the processes giving rise to heteropaternal twins.*

Andrew and Elad had never heard of superfecundation or hetero-paternal twinning until I described it to them. They knew only that they wanted a family and that the medical technology allowing them to become fathers was available.

BABY STEPS

"Canadian surrogacy is illegal unless it's a surrogacy of compassion."

—Andrew Dvash-Banks, 2022

Since their wedding in the summer of 2011, the newlyweds had been enjoying life—dining out, taking trips, watching movies, and going dancing. These diversions were made possible by the couple's grow-ing financial security. Andrew had been promoted to manager at Gogo Vacations, and Elad had finished his master's degree at the University of Toronto and was made senior officer at the Egmont Group. By 2015, Elad and Andrew wanted to have children, although Elad was more highly motivated.

"I remember Elad was pushing harder to move forward with the process of starting a family, and I was the one kind of dragging my heels. I still had a bit of the Peter Pan syndrome," Andrew explained. This syndrome, named after the fictitious boy who wouldn't grow up, is not a clinically recognized condition,[19] but unfortunately the term has become part of everyday speech. Andrew, feeling somewhat hesitant over forfeiting his carefree life for one of serious responsibility, invoked it loosely. In the end, he and Elad compromised, as they usually did when they disagreed. "Compromise has been a theme in my life with Elad. We're always compromising," Andrew reflected, then laughed. "Elad ends up getting everything anyway!"

Their compromise was a series of baby steps. They would complete phase 1, which involved hiring an attorney (to create a client–donor contract), choosing an egg donor, creating the embryos, and freezing them. They would wait to begin phase 2, which included finding a gestational surrogate (the woman who would carry the pregnancy), finalizing the surrogate contract, and implanting the embryos into her uterus.

All phases of assisted reproduction are expensive—phase 1 alone can cost tens of thousands of dollars[20]—so waiting would allow them to replenish their savings in anticipation of phase 2. It is worth noting that Canada's reproductive policy is that of "altruistic surrogacy"—donors and surrogates are not paid for their services but are reimbursed only for personal expenses.[21] This feature of the process appealed to Andrew and Elad, because the individuals involved act largely out of generosity, not self-interest. The reduced expense of Canadian surrogacy relative to that in the United States may explain why some American couples go to Canada to create their families via assisted reproduction; still, the accumulated costs for all services are high.[22] Andrew and Elad's decision to have their children in Canada was determined not by the reduced cost but by their inability to marry in California and consequent Canadian residence.

In addition to researching the various reproduction-related topics, Andrew and Elad benefited from the guidance of their friends, Trevor and Zal, who had conceived twin boys using donated eggs and sperm. Two years earlier, their friends had directed them to Little Miracles, Canada's only consultation program that unites egg donors with prospective parents,[23] and to ReproMed (Toronto Institute for Reproductive Medicine).[24] Once their donor had been chosen, they worked with ReproMed's medical director, Dr. Alfonso P. Del Valle, known for his high rate of successful pregnancies.

But before any of this happened, they had to arrange legal representation.

In April 2015, Andrew and Elad contacted Michelle Flowerday, of Flowerday Fertility Law, a firm she founded in 2010.[25] After experiencing the joy of having her own three children, Flowerday realized that "family building was her calling." Her practice is "very niche"—she drafts agreements for individuals involved in third-party reproduction, e.g., infertile couples, same-sex partners, egg donors, sperm donors, and surrogates. Flowerday represented Andrew and Elad, whom she described as "such a personable, loving couple"; one of her colleagues represented the donor and the surrogate. "You could see how united they were and what their families meant to them," she noted. "They were very much family-oriented people, and they loved each other's families."[26]

I asked Flowerday what motivates some Canadian women to donate their eggs, since they cannot hope to benefit financially by doing so. Based on her conversations with countless donors, she explained that "they just want to give a gift." Many women do not intend to have children of their own but want to help others who do. When a baby is delivered, the donor knows the joy it has brought to an otherwise childless couple. Some donors have returned seven times to offer their eggs. Flowerday also noted that same-sex couples deal with infertility the same way the infertile community does. There are some same-sex couples and some opposite-sex couples who cannot have a child together but seek a genetic connection to a child they can create through a third party.

By early 2016, Andrew and Elad had completed the first leg of their journey toward fatherhood. The donor agency membership fee of 1,500 Canadian dollars grants online access to the life stories, medical histories, and color photographs of registered donors.[27] However, preserving the anonymity of clients and donors is paramount; names and identifying personal information are not provided to either party.[28]

Andrew and Elad had several important requirements in mind: Their donor had to be tall and slim (to avoid weight problems), young and healthy (to increase the chance of multiple egg production), and dark-haired (for reasons I explain below).

NOT YOURS, NOT MINE—OURS

Andrew and Elad narrowed their choice of a donor to two young women, one blond and one brunette. They ultimately chose the twenty-year-old brunette, who had twice donated eggs that had resulted in successful pregnancies. While the donor was also "beautiful," her dark hair was the deciding factor; that is because Andrew and Elad hoped to avoid comments such as "He must be your child" and "He must be his child," or questions such as, "You fathered this twin, correct?"

They reasoned as follows: Children inherit genes from both parents. Dark hair is a dominant trait, meaning that a child will be dark-haired even if he or she inherits some genes for light-colored hair. In contrast, blond hair is a recessive trait, meaning that a child will be blond only if he or she inherits genes for light hair. Blond donors can only pass on genes coding for blond hair.[29] Andrew, who now has chestnut-colored hair, could carry some genes linked to being blond (he was fair-haired as a child). Thus, Andrew and Elad believed that if they used a blond donor, they might conceive a blond child, and people would assume that Andrew was the father. They also believed that Elad could transmit only genes linked to dark hair, since he and most of his family members have dark hair.

However, their reasoning breaks down somewhat, because Elad *could* carry some genes coding for light hair, since his paternal grandmother was blond. If present, they would have been overridden by the genes coding for dark hair and never expressed across generations of his family. Were Elad to transmit those "hidden blond genes" to a child, using a blond donor, the child would also be blond—but would likely be linked to Andrew in the minds of many. A dark-haired donor could also carry "hidden genes," but for Andrew and Elad, it seemed a safer bet. Their egg donor was also half-Indian, of Punjabi descent, making each twin one-quarter Indian.[30]

The ideal situation for Andrew and Elad was for each to biologically contribute to one twin.[31] This was an experience they had hoped to share as a couple, but having a family was more important than whose sperm fertilized one—or both—eggs. Assisted reproduction offers no guarantees; depending upon the quality of the sperm, receptivity of the endometrium (inner lining of the uterus), and other factors, either Andrew *or* Elad might potentially father both twins.[32] Or perhaps just one fetus would make it to term and either Andrew *or* Elad could be the father. Both prospective parents knew that any one of these different scenarios was possible. Above all, they were adamant that, regardless of outcome, *the identity of the father(s) would remain hidden from their family members and friends—loving and treating each child equally would not be compromised.* Of course, subsequent events surrounding their move from Canada to California forced Andrew and Elad to disclose the twins' paternity, information that would eventually become public.

Eggs vary in quality, so ten to fifteen mature eggs are typically retrieved for IVF procedures.[33] However, forty eggs were extracted from the couple's anonymous egg donor, classifying her as a "high responder." Their fertility specialist, Dr. Del Valle, was delighted that they had heeded his advice and chosen a youthful donor. Healthy young women can produce twenty or more eggs per treatment cycle, although over fifty eggs have been retrieved in some cases.[34]

In vitro fertilization (IVF) is the process by which eggs are combined with sperm to create embryos.[35] It is best to have egg retrieval and fertilization performed on the same day to enhance embryo quality. Elad recalled, "She [the anonymous donor] was in one room and we were in two separate rooms to deposit our sperm. Del Valle proposed creating thirty embryos in total—fifteen eggs to be combined with sperm from me, and fifteen eggs to be combined with sperm from Andrew. Then the doctor did his magic and we got updates [on the embryos] for several days after that." Ten remaining unfertilized eggs would be frozen. According to their contract with the donor, Andrew and Elad owned these eggs and could use them at a future date.

Embryos are allowed to mature in the laboratory for about five days prior to implantation. They vary in quality, with only 50 to 60 percent developing into a five-day-old blastocyst (hollow cell mass) that is either implanted immediately or frozen and then thawed for later implantation.[36] Not all embryos survive; over the course of the five-day waiting period, some will be viable and some will not.

Reproductive math can be dizzying. Because two sperm donors were involved in Andrew and Elad's case, the elimination process reminded me of a dance-off, in which the less competitive couples are asked to leave the floor, and only the best ones remain. Eventually, there is just one winning pair. The thirty embryos that were created dwindled to sixteen—eight fertilized by Elad and eight fertilized by Andrew. Then, based on microscopic inspection, the eight that received the highest ratings were chosen for preimplantation genetic screening (PGS) tests.[37] (PGS testing identifies embryos free from chromosomal defects, providing a high chance for a successful outcome. However, as I explained earlier, PGS does not test for specific diseases.)

Testing was performed on four embryos created by Elad and four created by Andrew. It eventually turned out that each prospective father had fertilized exactly one top-quality embryo. Elad reflected, "It's almost [like] fate wanted one high-quality embryo from my sperm and one from Andrew's." These two top-quality embryos would be frozen until Andrew and Elad found their gestational surrogate.

The process of finding a surrogate can take months, even years. The extreme intimacy of what will take place—carrying another family's child to term—requires confidence and trust on everyone's part. Women planning on becoming surrogates review the files of couples who are searching, and some will be overlooked for various reasons. Andrew and Elad knew couples who had waited as long as eighteen months. Arrangements that seem promising on paper may fall short of expectations once in-person meetings take place.

Andrew and Elad were lucky in this respect because they did not have to look for very long. In fact, the right surrogate found them almost immediately once their embryos had been created.

THE SURROGATE-PARENT PARTY: "THEY WERE MY DREAM COUPLE"

In August 2015, Andrew and Elad and other prospective parents attended a gathering of surrogates who had recently given birth. This informational session was organized by Canadian Surrogacy Options. The event was intended not to match couples with clients but to provide information about surrogacy in an informal social setting. Andrew explained that these particular surrogates were chosen *because* they had recently delivered and were unlikely to do so in the near future, keeping the mixer "from becoming a meat market."

Andrew and Elad arrived at the get-together wearing casual clothes and feeling relaxed. It was an opportunity to ask questions rather than to focus on making the best impression. They were fully prepared to wait a long time to find the best person. According to Elad, "We went, and she [Amanda Adams, one of the surrogates—who agreed to the use of her real name and the names of her family members] was there, and we met her." The conversation moved swiftly and easily, perhaps because there was no pressure on either side. Then everything changed suddenly and unexpectedly. "A week or two later the manager of the agency called us, [saying] 'Amanda can't stop thinking about you. She just gave birth a month ago, but she wants to [take this] journey with you,' " Elad recollected. Andrew hardly exaggerated Amanda's response when he said, "She just fell in love with us right away."

Amanda's perspective as a "once and future surrogate" reveals more about what actually transpired at her fortuitous meeting with Andrew and Elad. The sponsoring agency had asked each surrogate to describe their ideal couple—what the two people would be like if they could be hand-picked. According to Amanda, "I actually fantasized about a gay couple. I wanted to help a really down-to-earth, super happy, full-of-love couple. They could be interracial. And I wanted two people who were just so madly in love. . . . I found at the beginning, when I was looking into surrogacy, there were a lot of surrogates who were not choosing same-sex couples. And I thought that was such a shame, because my best friends in high school were gay, and I absolutely loved them; it didn't make a difference. I love the concept of you love who you love, and that's pretty much it. So, when I thought about my ideal couple, they would be a gay couple. Super fun-loving and just full of life. . . . The fact that both of them happened to have a penis is irrelevant."

In the previous chapter I suggested that where we go and what we do reflects fundamental aspects of who we are. This could largely explain why people with similar interests, desires, and outlooks tend to congregate. Amanda's selfless intentions aligned seamlessly with the reproductive desires of Andrew and Elad. Of course, chance also played a role—Amanda had been asked to think about her ideal couple, Andrew and Elad were not matched with a surrogate, and all three had attended this particular meeting.

Amanda recalled, "They were my dream couple exactly. I met them and I absolutely fell in love with them at the time. . . . I wanted to be their best friend, help them through their journey, and answer any questions they had. Finally, it dawned on me that they were *actually looking* for a surrogate [that is, it seemed they were not there just for informational purposes]. And I was like, 'Oh, my goodness!' I told the agency, 'Don't give them out to anyone. I want them!' I was maybe a month postpartum, and I was like, 'I absolutely want them!' I did my screening and the doctor said that everything was clear. We [Elad, Andrew, and I] decided to match, and we transferred in February." Amanda had delivered a baby as a first-time surrogate just six months earlier, so she needed to be certain it was safe to do so again on such short notice.

Two months into the pregnancy, Andrew's father Jim was the only family member who had been told that twins had been conceived. By then Andrew and Elad had obtained ultrasounds and knew that two boys were on the way.[38] Despite promising to keep this news confidential, Jim posted the images on his refrigerator and told all of his clients; after all, it was tax season, and his accounting business was booming. Perhaps the

Andrew and Elad's surrogate, Amanda Adams (center), who carried the twins until their birth. This was the couple's first public announcement that "we are expecting," June 2016. Amanda's T-shirt reads, "Their Peas—My Pod"; Elad (L) and Andrew's T-shirts read, "I Can't Keep Calm, I'm Going to Be a Daddy—TWICE." They were attending Toronto's Gay Pride parade, June 2016. *Source*: Photo courtesy of Andrew and Elad Dvash-Banks.

familiar thrill of becoming a grandfather and the close relationship he and Andrew had developed in later years overpowered his vows of secrecy. Despite his battle with cancer, he planned to be present when the twins were born. Sadly, that was not to be. As I explained earlier, Jim passed away three months before Aiden and Ethan were born. It may be that Andrew and Elad confided in Jim to bring him joy and to strengthen his will to live.

AMANDA: COMPASSIONATE SURROGACY PERSONIFIED

Before writing this book, I had never heard of compassionate surrogacy. I am, however, familiar with the compassion and self-sacrifice expressed between most identical twins.

When former Olympic skier Phil Mahre believed he had completed a gold medal performance at the 1984 games, he turned to his brother Steve, who was about to compete in the same event, and said, "Here's what you have to do to beat me." When Tracy Winterhalder was advised that a pregnancy would imperil her health, her identical twin sister Marcy carried a fetus for her—twice—forfeiting opportunities to add additional children to her own family. And when Anna Cortez required a kidney transplant, her identical twin sister, Petra Martinez, donated an organ of her own, in the first transplant operation performed on identical twin patients by identical twin surgeons.[39]

Perhaps these generous acts make sense because they help close family members, even at some cost to the self.[40] Surrogacy also involves acting altruistically, but usually for the benefit of a stranger. Surrogates in the United States and elsewhere are paid for their services, but Canadian surrogates are not. I wanted to understand Amanda's enthusiasm and drive to become a surrogate under these circumstances.

I spoke with Amanda in March of 2022. She was thirty-four years old at the time and in a committed relationship. She is also the stepmother to twelve-year-old Jordan, the biological mother of nine-year-old Ellenia and two-year-old Darius, and, until recently, the foster mother of a one-year-old baby boy whom she was hoping to adopt.[41] When we spoke, Amanda was pregnant as a surrogate for the third time, with an anticipated delivery date in September 2022. She and her fiancé, Akeem, plan to marry next year, "in a kind of weird and different [ceremony], just because we're weird and different." The couple will have their own family and continue as foster parents, with "adoption never off the table."

Amanda is from the Scarborough district of Toronto, in Canada, but lives in Mississauga, just outside the city. Although she is a registered veterinarian technician, she is now a full-time mother. Shortly after her son Darius was born, COVID-19 was rampant, and she was afraid to place her infant in day care. She decided to train as a law clerk, because the unpredictable hours of caring for animals interfered with her mothering. But being a law clerk brought Amanda no pleasure. "I don't do the desk life well," Amanda said. "I love large-animal medicine—I'd rather be shoulder-deep in a cow's behind. It's a job that has my heart."

The story of Amanda's surrogacy began in 2013 when she was twenty-six years old and pregnant for the first time. When she experienced "gushes of blood" early on, her doctor ordered a pap smear to identify the underlying cause and discovered precancerous cells in her cervix. She was advised to have an abortion, with the promise of another pregnancy at a later date.

"I didn't like the idea," Amanda told me. "I prayed to everyone out there that if I could just have this one healthy baby, I would help another couple have one, as well. My daughter Ellenia was born, and she was a happy, healthy, and amazing child. As soon as I got the all-clear, I signed up immediately, in September, as a surrogate. I was matched right away and was pregnant by November."

The following year, in August 2015, Amanda delivered a baby girl for a childless couple but experienced uterine prolapse—weakening of the pelvic muscles and ligaments that support the uterus.[42] She completed the recommended exercises and other treatments to overcome the condition and showed up at the surrogacy get-together. Six months later she would be pregnant with Andrew and Elad's twins.

PREGNANCY

"It wasn't like, 'Oh, which embryo do we use?' " (Andrew)
"We only had two." (Elad)

Today, high rates of successful pregnancies are generally achievable following implantation of a single good-quality embryo.[43] However, this was not always the case, prompting doctors in the past to implant several embryos in the hope that one would produce a healthy child. The downside to this earlier practice was that it sometimes led to high-risk multiple pregnancies. Twins, triplets, and higher-order multiples are more likely to experience premature deliveries, lower birth weights, and increased rates of prenatal and developmental complications, relative to non-twins.[44]

Knowing this, Andrew and Elad were at a crossroads. Elad explained, "Part of us wanted twins because you do it once and you get it over with. But it's expensive and emotionally taxing, and it's a high-risk pregnancy. So, we said, 'Look, we're going to implant two embryos if there is a chance that *none* of them will take.' And what the doctor told us—[he actually said] there is a high chance that *one* of them will take. But there is also a chance that *both* will take, and that's what happened." Based on prior testing, Dr. Del Valle was confident that both embryos would implant successfully. Andrew and Elad weren't fully persuaded, but they ultimately decided to implant both embryos and were prepared for all outcomes. Dr. Del Valle's predictions were correct, but that would not be known for some time.

Amanda had delivered just one baby as a first-time surrogate, but two embryos had been implanted. Therefore, she assumed that two embryos were always used for reproductive procedures. Still, she sensed that her surrogacy with Andrew and Elad was "different" because the embryos were conceived by different partners. She called the journey "insane" but "phenomenal."

Few surrogates have delivered children for both heterosexual and homosexual couples. Amanda observed that when you're working with heterosexual couples, as much as you want to bond with them, it's a little bit different. She had a close, "almost best-friend-type relationship" with the wife during her first surrogacy, but once the baby was delivered, that relationship ended. She believes it is because most young girls think about becoming mothers, yet one day their dream dies. When Amanda was pregnant, she hesitated to complain to the woman about her morning sickness. "I would have felt terrible saying that to someone who wants so badly to feel what I feel." In contrast, she explained that "gay men don't sit there as children and dream of carrying a baby for their husband." That is another reason why Amanda chose to work with a same-sex couple like Andrew and Elad—"They wouldn't know what they were missing."

But they might have missed not having a baby shower had one of their friends not hosted one for them. One of the party guests described the event as "jam-packed with people and presents and so much fun."[45]

PREGNANCY AND DELIVERY

Amanda's pregnancy lasted for thirty-two weeks and six days, and it wasn't easy. In the beginning, she felt sick to her stomach "seventeen times" each day, requiring steady doses of Diclectin. Once her morning sickness eased, the medication was stopped, and things proceeded smoothly—until doctors discovered that she had a competent, but short, cervix, a risk factor for premature birth. This new finding required Amanda to remain on modified bed rest until week twenty-eight. During this time, Andrew and Elad made frequent visits to her home, helping with housework, bringing snacks, and taking her young daughter to the African Lion Safari park in southern Ontario. "They missed nothing—they came to my lactation appointments, and I swear they would have come into the bathroom with me!"

A more worrisome development presented itself at week twenty-nine—Baby B (Ethan) wasn't growing. This condition, known as intrauterine growth restriction (IUGR), is a situation in which the fetus is too small for its gestational age. [46] It was time to visit a different hospital that offered the best maternal fetal care possible. Amanda recalled, "We went there to see the doctor every other day for the rest of *our* [emphasis added] pregnancy."

When IUGR is detected, it is likely that the delivery will occur before the expected due date. Amanda was told she would probably deliver in a week to ten days. It was a delicate balance because she had to stay pregnant long enough to give Baby A the best possible outcome without further impairing Baby B, whose best chance of good health and survival required an early delivery. Baby B was expected to be only two pounds at birth, so Amanda was referred to a high-level (level 3) neonatal intensive care unit (NICU).[47] However, there was no room for her at that facility, so she, Andrew, and Elad returned to their original hospital. It was then that they learned that Baby B was showing signs of brain sparing, a condition associated with IUGR. (Brain sparing involves the restriction of oxygen and nutrients, preventing access to substances the fetus needs for proper brain functioning. In response to this condition, the arteries dilate to increase blood supply.[48]) At this juncture, Baby B was safer *outside* the womb than inside the womb.

A large-scale study of Australian mothers found that twins born at thirty-two weeks or later fare best when the delivery is vaginal and uncomplicated for both twins, or is done by elective cesarean section.[49] For pregnancies in which one twin shows growth restriction, the risks of stillbirth and newborn death are higher. Balancing these two risks alone does not determine the best time for delivery; increased monitoring is required, as was done in Amanda's case.[50] When her pregnancy had lasted a few days past thirty-two weeks, the moment seemed right for delivering the Dvash-Banks babies.

Amanda sent Andrew and Elad home to rest, but almost immediately her doctor informed her that the only level 3 hospital with available space was in Detroit—a distance of about 250 miles. Amanda could be airlifted, but that was prevented from happening since she didn't have a passport and she didn't want to travel alone. However, plans suddenly changed in her favor when a nurse discharged several babies from the closer level 3 NICU, making space for the twins.

Elad drove Amanda to the level 3 hospital, picking up Andrew on the street along the way. They made it in time. Andrew and Elad were in the delivery room for the entire birth. Labor was easy, and once Baby A's water was broken, he arrived quickly—his crying was immediate, and at five pounds, two ounces, he was big and healthy—"a chunky, beefy little man."[51]

Then, according to Amanda, "the world stopped." Doctors lost track of Baby B, unable to follow his heart rate until a nurse held the monitor directly over Amanda's uterus. Then a doctor reached into Amanda's uterus and pulled the baby down and out by his feet. He didn't cry right away. He opened and closed his hand, urinated on himself—and finally cried. Looking back, Amanda proclaimed that interval "the longest four minutes of my life." Fortunately, Baby B was heavier than anticipated, weighing exactly three pounds, but he was still tiny. Andrew and Elad could not immediately engage the babies in kangaroo care (skin-to-skin contact) as planned, and Amanda couldn't lactate at first. It was not a perfect birth experience, but "it was the per-fect birth experience [for us]," Amanda recalled.[52]

POSTPARTUM

Baby A remained in the NICU for three weeks, and Baby B remained there for nearly one month. During this time Amanda's close relation-ship with Andrew and Elad continued. Her milk arrived several days later, and she traveled to the hospital in the evenings to hold the babies, bottle-feed them, and bring milk in special bottles for their daytime feedings; she also delivered bottles to Andrew and Elad for ten weeks af-ter the babies went home.[53] Familiar with parenting challenges, Amanda occasionally babysat the twins to allow Andrew and Elad opportunities for "date nights." Amanda's daughter, Ellenia, sometimes went with her. During her mother's pregnancy, Ellenia would sing the song "Twinkle, Twinkle, Little Star" as she sat beside her. On one occasion, mother and daughter arrived when Andrew was bathing one of the twins, who wouldn't stop crying. Ellenia started singing the familiar song, and the crying stopped. She was so proud.

Despite Amanda's continued involvement with the twins, I won-dered if she sensed a kind of emptiness or longing to mother the children she had just delivered. Women who are pregnant are hormonally primed to be exquisitely sensitive to the needs of their newborns.[54] Amanda admitted that when you deliver a baby, "it's a real high, an overwhelm-ing feeling of love." She did feel "weird" leaving the hospital empty-handed, but she also explained that, as a surrogate, the relationship is with the parents, not with the baby.

NAMING THE TWINS: FAVORITE AND FIGHTER

Andrew went to middle school with socialite and influencer Paris Hilton. He didn't know her well, but as the granddaughter of Conrad Hilton, founder of the Hilton Hotel chain, Paris Hilton enjoyed a cer-tain celebrity. Because of her, Andrew decided it would be "cool" to name his children after cities; if he had a son, the child would be named London, "for sure."

He presented this idea to Elad when they were living in Tel Aviv and still dating, but Elad thought it was "the most ridiculous thing he had ever heard." Perhaps in an effort to deflect a future conflict—and because he was "super smart"—Elad settled the situation almost immediately, using strategic foresight.[55] When he and Andrew first set eyes on their new dog—the pug-terrier mix they acquired in 2009—Elad announced, "That's our London!," thereby preventing a future child of theirs from having that name. Andrew recalled, "I was so overcome with emotion, I was like, 'Yes, this is London!' "

There are other stories behind the actual naming of the twins.

I was aware that each child's name had the same first letter as the father who had conceived him—Andrew–Aiden and Elad–Ethan. This observation was puzzling because the genetic link was information they wished to keep private—each twin was to be "ours," not "yours" or "mine"—but matching the biological father–son initials was just partly intentional.

It happened that both fathers liked the name "Aiden," a biblical name that derives from the Hebrew word "adan," meaning "ardent" or "fiery." He was the firstborn ("Twin A"), and at the delivery they learned that he had received Andrew's genetic material. They chose James for his middle name in deference to Andrew's father Jim, also named James. Naming their second son was trickier because they wanted a name that "worked" in both English and Hebrew; the discussion even got contentious at times. They finally decided that since "Twin B" had received Elad's genetic material, an "E" name would be appropriate. (However, if Twin B had been born first, he would have been named Aiden.) "Ethan," in Hebrew, means "strong" and "resilient," and as Elad explained, Ethan's birth captured those words fully. Ethan was in distress, not just in the uterus, but also during the early days and weeks of his life in the NICU. At the time I was writing this chapter, he was only five years old but already a clever little boy. "My mother says he will be president someday because he defied all odds."[56] Ethan's middle name is Jacob, also to honor Andrew's father, whose Hebrew name was Yakov.

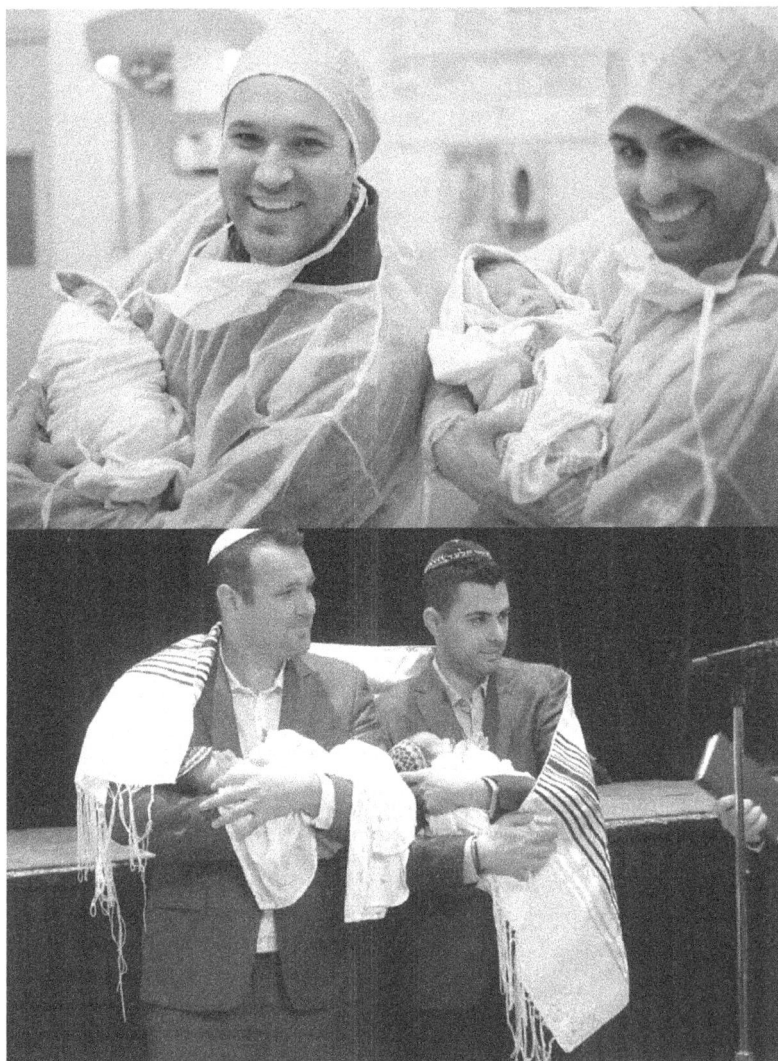

(Above): Andrew (L) and Elad with their newborn twin sons, shortly after their delivery on September 16, 2016, at the Credit Valley Hospital in Mississauga, Ontario. Andrew is holding Ethan, and Elad is holding Aiden. *Photo credit*: Meaghan Milne Photography. (Below): The twins' bris at Temple Sinai in Toronto. This ceremony is usually held when male infants are eight days old but is postponed when there are health concerns; the twins were a little over one month old at the time. Andrew (L) is holding Ethan, and Elad is holding Aiden. *Photo credit*: Ann Banks, Andrew's mother.

THE BRIS

It is a Jewish tradition to hold a *brit milah* (bris)—the rite of circumcision marking entry into the covenant of Abraham—for a male infant on his eighth day of life. It is a celebratory event, attended by family and friends, and followed by a joyful reception. The bris is performed by a *mohel*, an individual trained in Jewish tradition and surgical hygiene. The baby is carried into the room by the *sandak*, the individual chosen to hold the infant on his knees or on his thighs during the procedure. This role is traditionally given to the baby's grandfather.[57] A drop of wine is placed in the infant's mouth upon conclusion of the prayer.[58]

In accordance with Jewish law, the twins' bris was postponed until they were a little over one month old and healthy enough to withstand the procedure. It was a glorious day, marred only by the absence of Andrew's father, who would have served as the *sandak* for one of the twins; in his place, it was decided that Elad's father, Moti, would hold Aiden.

The two fathers with their two-month-old twin sons in their Canadian condo. Andrew is holding Aiden (L), and Elad is holding Ethan. *Photo credit*: Images of Life by Ashli.

Elad's eighty-year-old paternal grandfather, Chaim, felt extremely honored to assume that role for Ethan, his first great-grandson.

Friends and family members met the twins before, during, and after the bris. Ann's first glimpse of her grandsons actually occurred *before* they were born, in an ultrasound video that she keeps on her phone.[59] "It was incredible to watch the interaction between the twins. One of them, I don't know which twin it was, hit the other one with his foot and the one who was hit did this [Ann demonstrated the gesture by slapping her hand on her forehead]. It was like a little old man going 'Oy!' " When Ann finally saw Aiden and Ethan, she wanted to "grab the babies and run with them—grandmother them with love and protection. They were so tiny, I didn't want them to be injured."

Elad's friend Kari called the newborns "teeny weeny, little, delicious babies—I remember giving them a bottle. It was a joyous, happy, happy time." Andrew's younger brother James described his new nephews as "precious little bundles of love." Andrew's half-sister Ashli, a mother of twins herself, simply said, "I love those little boys like you wouldn't believe." And Andrew's sister, Jen, a mother of two sets of

Two-month-old Ethan (L) and Aiden pose for a picture at naptime. *Photo credit:* Images of Life by Ashli.

twins, helped with bottle feedings. Thrilled at their birth, she was "just too happy" to give the twins back to their parents!

Elad's sister, Yarden, first saw her nephews at the bris in Canada. "Becoming a first-time aunt was very emotional. And it was special and beautiful seeing a gay couple with twins." The boys' Israeli grandparents, Tovi and Moti, regret only that Andrew and Elad did not choose Israel as their home. Aiden and Ethan were the celebrated firstborn sons of their firstborn son. They would know Andrew as "Dad" and Elad as "Abba," the Hebrew word for father.

LIFE HAPPENS

Upon returning to Canada from Florida, Andrew and Elad focused on their planned move to California. It was January 24, 2017, the twins were four months old, and they had tickets to fly to California three weeks later. They expected that their visit to the US consulate in Toronto to obtain passports for the children would be "boring and uneventful." They had completed the immigration application, taken the required photographs, obtained the cashiers' checks, and printed the

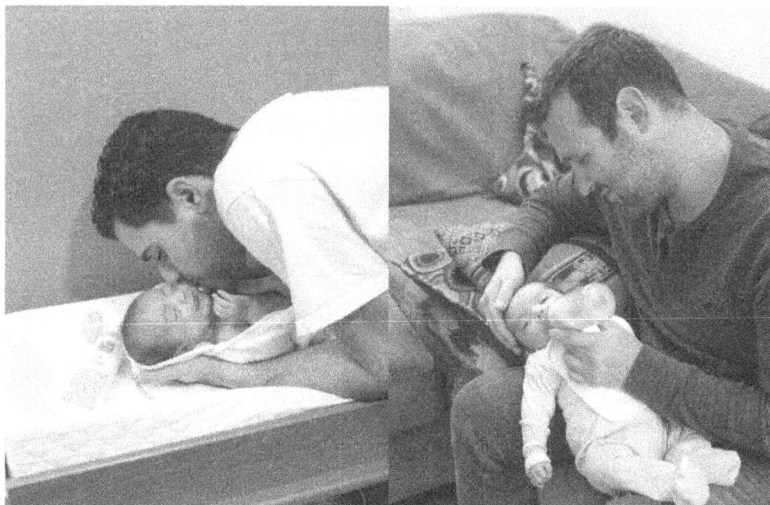

Elad (L) is drying Ethan after his bath; Andrew (R) is giving a bottle to Aiden. *Photo credit*: Images of Life by Ashli.

marriage and birth certificates. Still glowing with gratitude toward the doctors who had successfully delivered their twins, it never occurred to Andrew or Elad that their fate would turn on Ethan's lack of a biological American connection. And looking back, Amanda's lack of a passport for entering the United States, to deliver at the level 3 facility, was far more significant than anyone had realized at the time. Had the babies been born in the city of Detroit, granting Ethan US citizenship would not have been challenged. In that case, both boys would have received their passports as United States citizens.

What followed from the meeting at the consulate would catapult Andrew, Elad, and their twin boys into world news.

TWINS X TWO?

Amanda is ready to become a surrogate just one more time to provide Aiden and Ethan with a little sister. But if Andrew and Elad wanted a second set of twins, she would do that, too. "We had such good luck last time and they were super supportive. There is no other couple I would do that for," she insisted. Unlike her desk job, this is a job that has her heart.

• 5 •

Crossing the Border: Cruel Questioning

"We were going to take the right road [regarding Ethan's
US citizenship]. Like, I pay taxes to my government, but it
has fucked me over multiple times in my life because I was
born the way I am [a gay man], and I accepted it. A part of
me feels so stupid for doing that. Why did I do that? And
then this [denial of citizenship] happened to my child, and
that's where we drew the line."

—Andrew, 2022

THE ONE THING WE DID NOT EXPECT

Armed with the required documents and an ample supply of diapers
for their four-month-old twins, Andrew and Elad headed to the US
consulate in Toronto. The couple's plans for relocating their family to
Los Angeles were nearly complete: Elad had a Green Card, allowing him
to work in the United States, and they had found tenants (a same-sex
couple expecting twins) to rent their condo. Airline tickets had been
purchased, and they were scheduled to leave Canada in three weeks.
The only remaining task was to obtain passports for their twin boys.

Andrew and Elad expected the visit to the consulate to be quick
and easy because they were well prepared. They had assembled their
marriage document, the twins' birth certificates, the egg donation contract, the surrogacy contract, the twins' photographs, and a cashier's
check together in a single file. But perhaps conditions on the ground
foretold a different story. It was a freezing cold January day and snowing

heavily. People applying for passports or conducting other official business had to stand outside the building before going through security, with an estimated wait time of forty minutes. Nevertheless, Andrew and Elad felt secure and undeterred. Soon they would be basking in the Southern California sun surrounded by family members and old friends.

It was not so simple. Facing the couple from across the Plexiglas window, Vice Consul Terri N. F. Day asked, "Who's the father?"[1]

Once again: "Life is what happens to you while you're busy making other plans."

An unexpected chain of events stalked Andrew and Elad's consulate visit, their journey from Toronto to Los Angeles, and the four years that followed. The fact they didn't anticipate what would eventually take place exemplifies John Lennon's honest, blunt, and jarring line from his hit song "Beautiful Boy (Darling Boy)," which became famous because of Lennon's celebrity—and because the words are true.[2]

The couple waited outside in the cold with their infants for thirty minutes before proceeding through security. They received a number and were asked to remain in the waiting room until it was their turn, a period of about two hours. When they were finally called to the window, they presented their documents to Vice Consul Day, who looked them over, declared their file "complete," and directed them back to the waiting area. She called them back shortly after that to take an oath testifying to the accuracy of the information they would provide. By then their payment for these services had been accepted.

During their time in the waiting room, Andrew and Elad watched television, fed the twins, and changed the babies' diapers. But as time passed, something didn't seem quite right. It felt different from the boring, uneventful procedure they had expected. It was taking too long—over an hour—and the two fathers were running out of diapers. "It was, like, if my kid shits one more time, I don't know what I'm going to do," Andrew recalled.[3]

Still, they weren't seriously worried; they even felt reassured by a photograph tacked on the wall, showing Canada's prime minister Justin Trudeau and then US president Barack Obama in a warm embrace.[4] Andrew felt they were in "friendly territory"; according to immigration attorney Aaron C. Morris, the Obama administration had enacted some policy changes that favored equality for same-sex couples.[5]

After administering the oath, Terri Day began posing a series of shocking and humiliating questions. She wanted to know: How did you have the kids? How did it happen? How did you create the embryos? Are the children genetically connected? Are your children both genetically related to you [Andrew]? Day brought her manager, Maggie Ramsey, into the case at one point, but ultimately, the decision to grant or deny Ethan's citizenship was hers.[6]

Andrew and Elad were clearly confused by Day's line of questioning. "Where was she going with this?" they wondered.

Elad filled in some details. "We went through the process of how we deposited our sperm. And I'm, like, a US official is asking, 'How did you have your kids?' It shook me to the core." Other officers and the people seated close to "window C" took notice of the back-and-forth between Day and the couple, because everything said was within earshot.

Andrew later claimed that Terri Day and her manager (whom Day had consulted when she disappeared) were getting "kind of aggressive" with them. (According to Andrew and Elad, the manager was the "bad one.") "The situation escalated and was very unpleasant, to say the least," Andrew recalled. But they answered Day's questions as well as they could, because they needed passports for their children.

Then they were told that they would have to provide a DNA test to the consulate to prove they were the children's parents—even though each child's birth certificate named Andrew Dvash-Banks and Elad Dvash-Banks as such.[7] This was the first time anyone had made a distinction between their children or questioned their parentage—their greatest fear as a same-sex couple.

In fact, Andrew and Elad already had DNA test results. Andrew started to tell Day he had this information but suddenly panicked and changed his story. He admitted to me that he was "scared" because he knew that Ethan lacked a biological connection to a US citizen parent. So he said they wouldn't do the test. Then he "pivoted," telling her they already knew the results because a test had been performed by Maxxam Analytics.[8] In 2016, Canadian surrogacy policy required immediate DNA testing of surrogates and babies to rule out a biological connection between them.[9] (A genetic link is unlikely, but it's possible if the surrogate engaged in sexual activity with a partner around the time of implantation. In such cases, infants' paternal DNA would come from the

partner, not the sperm donor.) The test revealed that Aiden was genetically related to Andrew, Ethan was genetically related to Elad, Aiden
and Ethan were related to each other, and neither infant was related to
the surrogate, Amanda.

Andrew was adamant. "That [information] was going to stay between the three of us [Elad, Amanda, and me]. No one else knew, and
no one was going to know . . . not even my mother." They saw the
confidentiality of their biological ties as critical for fostering family fair-
ness and avoiding thoughtless remarks from others. As Andrew insisted,
his mother Ann did not know the biological origins of her grandsons
when they were born, but it didn't matter to her. Elad's parents, Tovi
and Moti, also had no idea, which was something the two fathers had to
struggle with. People are curious. They want to know details but often
lack understanding.[10]

BIOLOGICAL RELATEDNESS AND LEGAL COMPLEXITIES

There is a legal presumption that when a person gives birth, that person becomes the legal parent. In order to have the birth registered in
someone else's name, that presumption must be rebutted. In 2016, when
Aiden and Ethan were born, a court application was launched by their
attorney, Michelle Flowerday, requesting a declaration of parentage for
the parents and a declaration of non-parentage for the surrogate and her
spouse (if she had one; Amanda was unmarried at the time). The signed
court order was then presented to the government by the lawyer, who
explained that the parents did not give birth and that the baby needed
to be registered in a different name, or names. The birth was registered,
and birth certificates were produced. "They were equally the parents of
the two children [Aiden and Ethan], regardless of any genetic connection," Flowerday said.

But I wondered—if the donor had been an American citizen living
in Canada, might that have made a difference in Terri Day's assessment
of the situation? Speaking only for Canadian reproductive law, Flowerday said, "No—the donor is not a factor. No legal rights flow through
the donor. Genetic relatedness [of the donor to any child] is irrelevant."
According to the contract, as soon as the eggs leave her body, the donor
no longer claims ownership.[11]

University of Michigan law professor, lawyer, and legal historian Kristin Collins agrees that the nationality of the donor would not have played a role in this case. Collins also notes that how much discretion consular officers may exercise is a "really interesting question"—statutes (laws passed by legislative bodies) may be understood literally, but there are also "ambiguities and uncertainties."[12] Yale University law professor Cristina Rodríguez believes consular officers have considerable sway in their decision-making because most decisions go unchallenged. And it takes greater effort and resources than most people have to overturn a decision.[13] To the extent that consular officers exercise discretion in their decisions, I still wonder what the outcome would have been in this case if the donor had been an American citizen.

When I spoke to Elad, he posed a simple rhetorical question directed at the government: "Why was it a big deal for [Ethan] to become a US citizen?" He reasoned that Ethan's other father is a US citizen, and they had a birth certificate, which is a legal document produced by Canada, "not some place in the middle of the ocean." In addition, the birth certificate for Aiden *and* for Ethan names Andrew as one of the parents. "So why were they [US consulate officers] doubting that you [Andrew] were one of Ethan's parents? They were not doubting that Andrew was the parent of Ethan; they were doubting that there was a biological connection. Why did they need a biological connection; where was it [that requirement] coming from, and why? And both children were born abroad—if they were born abroad, why is Aiden a citizen at all? Because there is the law that if you are the child of a US citizen, and you're born abroad, you get your US citizenship at birth, immediately."

Elad was also bothered by the fact that it is very hard for people to understand how you have twins from two different fathers, created with two separate eggs from the same woman and placed together in utero. But at the end of the day, what he and Andrew really wanted was for people to know that they are a family like any other family; they love their kids like any other parents love their kids. Unfortunately, this message is sometimes overshadowed by the technical side of how the twins came to be. But according to Elad, "The thing we feared most was that our twins were being treated differently by the government." He recalled the discrimination he experienced as a dark-skinned Sephardic Jew living in an upscale area of the mostly light-skinned Ashkenazim. "I didn't want our kids to deal with what we dealt with. But those fears existed within us before they even happened—and then they happened."

Andrew and Elad now speak openly about their relatedness to their children, but this change in perspective was not by choice. As I explain later, once their lawsuit was under way, their various media appearances made it necessary for them to do so. This may have desensitized them to their situation to some degree. Nevertheless, Elad recalled that when he and Andrew first came forward publicly with this information, it was "extremely difficult—it was important to us that no one knew." Andrew echoed Elad's thoughts as he often did during their conversations. "It was really private in the sense that, when we chose our embryos, we took the two highest-quality embryos, and one was from my genetic material, and one was from Elad's." The reproductive process proved challenging to consular officials, whose decisions rely on information included in the *Foreign Affairs Manual* (*FAM*).

The *FAM* and its associated handbooks specify the policies and procedures used by the US State Department, US Foreign Service, and other agencies in matters such as diplomatic security, political affairs—and births abroad. Volume 8 references Form FS-240, a "consular declaration of the fact of acquisition of U.S. citizenship at birth."[14] Such declarations rest upon the following:

- Local certification of the birth
- Evidence regarding the physical presence of the US citizen/national parent(s)
- Evidence of the physical relationship between the US citizen and child
- Evidence of the legal relationship between the US citizen and child
- Evidence of citizenship/nationality of the US citizen/national parent(s)
- Consular adjudication of the child's claim to US citizenship

In cases of artificial insemination, surrogacy, and related situations, officers have the right to ask a couple to provide a DNA test to prove that the child in question is biologically connected to a US citizen. Elad further explained that officers may use discretion in applying these requirements in individual cases. However, Elad also said that the State

Department was interpreting the US Citizenship and Immigration Act as requiring a biological connection between a US parent (citizen) and a child. In fact, the act states that "a person born abroad in wedlock to a U.S. citizen and an alien acquires U.S. citizenship at birth if the U.S. citizen parent has been physically present in the United States or one of its outlying possessions prior to the person's birth for the period required by the statute in effect when the person was born."[15] It also states that "in all cases, either the U.S. citizen parent(s) or their alien spouse must be a genetic or gestational parent of the child to transmit U.S. citizenship to the child."[16]

By way of illustration, Elad presented two hypothetical scenarios, the first one paralleling his own to some extent: A married Israeli man and American woman conceive a child in Canada, using a Canadian donor and Canadian surrogate. The egg was fertilized by the husband's sperm, meaning the child is biologically connected to an Israeli father and a Canadian donor. The couple decides to move to the United States. They furnish their child's birth certificate that names the husband and wife as the baby's parents. In this case, the child would lack biological connectedness to an American citizen, as did Ethan. However, it is highly unlikely that any such couple would be asked to provide a DNA test, given the assumption of parentage.

As Elad noted, every individual or couple that exits Canada for residence in another country is not asked about the biological origins of their child (or children). Suppose an Israeli woman holding an infant wished to cross the Canadian border to live in the United States. Without documentation, the consular officer would be unable to tell if she was genetically related to the child. Would she be asked to take a DNA test? When asked about this, Elad claimed that Day referenced her right to exercise discretion in such cases. "That's when I got upset. Andrew was [visibly] emotional—he was crying hysterically." Day appeared uncomfortable and swallowed. This all occurred against the backdrop of the picture showing Trudeau and Obama in a warm embrace. And, as Andrew observed, "They [the consular officers] were literally in the process of getting a new boss [Secretary of State Rex Tillerson, appointed in the Trump administration], who, I'm sure, none of them were happy about—this former CEO of ExxonMobil."[17]

Andrew expanded upon Elad's vignettes with a real-life story. One of his female friends is an American citizen who relocated to

the United Kingdom, where she met and married her British husband. She was unable to conceive a child, so she sought the assistance of a British donor, whose egg was fertilized by her husband's
sperm. As such, the infant was biologically connected to a British male and a British female (who had no claim to parentage)—
and the embryo was implanted into Andrew's friend's womb. No questions were asked at the US consulate when the couple applied for US
citizenship for their new child. The lack of questioning is most likely
explained by the fact that the couple was heterosexual. In contrast, same-
sex couples (especially males) "invite" questioning because conception
cannot occur without reproductive assistance. As Elad said, "That was
our argument with the US consulate—if we were a heterosexual couple,
a man and a woman, no one would have asked us, 'How did you conceive your kids?'"[18]

Andrew and Elad were unaware of the *FAM*'s stipulation regarding a physical relationship between the parent and child. (As it turned
out, the provision was improperly applied in their case, which I will
describe in a later chapter.) They did not bring the hospital's DNA
report with them to the consulate visit, assuming that their children's
birth certificates were sufficient proof of their relationship to the twins.
I believe their reasoning on this issue was sound, and not bringing the
DNA report was not an oversight on their part; recall that Terri Day
had reviewed the contents of their file and declared it "complete." Now
Day insisted that without DNA evidence, neither twin would receive a
US passport.[19]

Day would not have accepted the hospital's report even if it had
been available because the consulate worked with only one laboratory,
in Toronto. The fee for DNA analysis was $1,000. When Andrew ob-
jected to this inordinately high expense, Day was unmoved. She insisted
that the consulate had to know how the babies were "obtained."

"*Obtained?*" Andrew and Elad asked in disbelief.

Seeing how distraught Andrew had become, the supervisor asked
them to leave. The application fees they had paid totaled about $700 US
dollars but would not be returned.

They left the building feeling a mix of emotions. They contacted
lawyer Michelle Flowerday to see if she had any answers. She recalls the
"surprise and horror" they felt at the treatment of their children. She
shared their feelings, knowing that both parents' names were on both

children's birth certificates, which should have been sufficient for grant-ing Ethan US citizenship.

SHORT-TERM SOLUTION

Andrew and Elad had little choice but to complete the second DNA test. They reasoned that at least one of their twins would have a US passport and that they would eventually find a solution for their other twin. But they knew all along that "something was not right, that a mistake had been made."

The second set of DNA findings was sent directly to the consulate; Andrew and Elad never saw a copy. As it happened, both twins traveled to the United States on their Canadian passports, since the final docu-ments had not yet been received.

Despite their being twins, having shared a womb for seven months, and being delivered just four minutes apart, their futures appeared quite different. Aiden was a US citizen at birth and could live freely and in-definitely in California, while Ethan would stay a Canadian citizen and come to California only as a tourist. He would be allowed to remain in Los Angeles for no more than six months.[20] The twins' official ac-ceptance and rejection letters, and Aiden's passport, reached the family a month or two later, after they had left Canada.

It is tempting to ask what might have happened if Andrew and Elad had applied for Israeli citizenship for their family. In that case, Ethan would have been a citizen, given his biological connection to Elad, who is Israeli by birth, but Andrew and Aiden would have been required to make *aliyah*. (This Hebrew term for "ascent" or the "act of going up" has become synonymous with "immigration to Israel."[21]) Israel's 1950 Law of Return allows citizenship to all Jewish people if they emigrate to Israel. Applications can be submitted online, but processing takes time.

In any case, Andrew and Elad wanted to live in California, and Andrew did not want his twins to perform mandatory army service. "I have just two boys," he explained. It seemed likely, but not certain, that Andrew and Elad would have additional children from the frozen em-bryos stored in Canada. Given the arduous process of having their twins, Andrew did not wish to risk their lives at any time.

LANDING IN LA—TWICE

Andrew and Elad and their three-month-old twins left Toronto for Florida in December 2016 (a month before their trip to the consulate) to visit Andrew's mother and brother James. They returned to Toronto for several weeks then headed to Los Angeles for about two months. This relatively short stay in Los Angeles was intended to convince them that the decision to relocate was right, and also to find jobs. Ann Banks was surprised when she first heard that Andrew and Elad were leaving their home in Toronto. They would be exchanging their beautiful, modern condo for a studio apartment in Los Angeles that had no parking space and no washing machine and dryer. The apartment was actually a converted garage.

As I explained, both twins traveled to Los Angeles on their Canadian passports, since their parents had not yet received any documents from the consulate. It turned out that the papers had been forwarded to the tenants renting their condo in Toronto. Andrew and Elad urged the renters to examine them and report back. A thick packet contained Aiden's passport and certificate of birth abroad; a thin envelope delivered Ethan's rejection letter, dated March 2, 2017. The letter, signed by Terri Day, restated what she had told them in Toronto, but seeing it in writing gave it a gravity that her spoken words did not quite capture. "I regret to inform you that after careful review of the evidence you submitted with your child's application, it has been determined that his claim to U.S. citizenship has not been satisfactorily established, as you are not his biological father. . . . The Immigration and Nationality Act (INA) of 1952, as amended, requires, among other things, a blood relationship between a child and the U.S. citizen parent."[22]

Meanwhile, Andrew and Elad began looking for work. Both fathers were still on a one-year parental leave from their jobs in Canada.[23] In April 2017, after several months of searching the Internet for job postings, Elad noticed a position at IKAR. It was the week before they were flying to Tel Aviv from Los Angeles to spend Passover with his family, after which they planned to stop in Toronto to formally end their jobs.

After a preliminary discussion, Elad was invited to visit IKAR in person to complete a second interview and to meet board members. However, given the family's travel plans, his interview was conducted over Zoom. He was offered a job. This was fortunate, because after returning to Canada after six weeks in Israel, the family would be relocating to the United States. They would be renting an apartment in the Brentwood neighborhood of Los Angeles, and they needed to shore up their finances.

Taking Ethan out of the United States wasn't risky at this juncture, as he was only about halfway through the first six-month stay allowed for tourists. When they returned to Los Angeles for the second time in June 2017, after stopping in Toronto to formally end their jobs and relinquish their condo, Ethan's six-month tourist visa began again. Andrew and Elad had just a few months to resolve their son's citizenship status.

Meeting them at the Los Angeles airport in June 2017, Andrew's mother immediately sensed something was wrong. Knowing nothing of what had happened at the consulate office, she assumed that Andrew and Elad had had a fight. Or perhaps the stress of moving with two newborns and the fact that only one father was employed was wearing them down. She had to find out.[24]

Andrew explained the situation and asked his mother to "please not talk about it." She told me later that her son felt ashamed and blamed himself for what had happened. I was surprised to hear this; Andrew had expressed anger and disappointment at the rejection of Ethan's US citizenship, as well as dread and uncertainty over how he and Elad would right this wrong, but he'd never voiced feelings of shame or self-blame.

Calling herself a "mama bear," Ann reminded him that all his life he had stood up to adversity—the bullying at school, the unkind remarks about his sexual identity. Now Andrew and his family were being tormented by the US government. "Get the boxing gloves on," she insisted, assuring him they would fight this together, drawing upon all of the contacts and resources they had accumulated over the years. "I've never asked for favors, but I absolutely put it out there. This is wrong. Really wrong," she said.

Meanwhile, Ann would be sleeping on the floor on an air mattress when she went to help them settle in, which didn't matter to her; being close to family remained her top priority. I will say more about their apartment later.

LANDING AT SPACEX

Elad's new work schedule left Andrew alone at home with nine-month-old Aiden and Ethan. The couple couldn't afford to hire a nanny, and the children required constant care. Andrew began to wonder if he had the patience to parent. The hours after midnight when the twins were asleep were set aside for job hunting over the Internet.

After weeks of discouragement, he saw a notice for a job as travel manager at SpaceX. Despite his experience at the travel agency in Canada, he hesitated to apply because he had been turned down so many times. But Elad "pushed him to do it."

He did, and SpaceX contacted him. "It was the call of my life," he told me.[25] It came from Suzanne, the woman who would later become his boss at SpaceX. Andrew completed the initial screening on his cell phone, then scheduled the next interview to take place during the twins' nap time. The session lasted for thirty minutes, about half the time the twins usually stayed asleep. Andrew was invited for an in-person interview, received an offer, and has been with the company ever since.

WORRIES OLD AND NEW

On the surface, life for Andrew and Elad and their children was favorable. They finally had steady jobs, and plenty of friends and family members lived close by. They hired a nanny named Gaby and began making plans to move to a house of their own.

But the question of Ethan's citizenship status hung in the balance. When Elad and Andrew left for work each day, they worried that someone from US Immigration and Customs Enforcement (ICE) would come to their home and snatch their young son once his visa expired—which it eventually did.

Their concerns were not without substance. Andrew and Elad explained that what happened to them was particularly frightening because of the zeitgeist of 2017. This was during the early days of Donald Trump's presidency (he had been sworn into office just two days before the couple's visit to the consulate). His administration began massive deportations of undocumented immigrants and issued a ban on travelers from seven predominantly Muslim countries to the United States.[26] In 2018, it was reported that the children of migrants from Mexico and Central America entering the United States were separated from their parents and housed in wire-mesh cages in the state of Texas.[27]

The couple's nanny was from Guatemala, not a native English speaker, so how she might respond to an intrusion by immigration officers was uncertain. Elad asked, "Would she [our nanny] have called me? What if she said, 'There are police here and they're taking Ethan'? I would immediately have dropped everything, gotten into my car, and started driving one hundred miles an hour. But I wouldn't make it, because I work far from home. Would I ever see my son? Realistically, my brain would tell me it would be okay, since social services would contact me—but my parental instinct to protect my child would take over."

Elad continued, "I just don't have words to explain the fear and the physical impact it had on us. I didn't sleep, I cried, I was shaken. I wasn't able to focus on work because of a fear that something would happen. Literally, I would have my phone next to me, like I have it right now, and every five minutes, I would check to see if there was a message or an unanswered call. Every day when we came back home, we would hug Ethan so tight—it was, like, another day passed without anything happening to him. And sometimes I remember asking Andrew when we were going to sleep, 'Why are we doing this to him? Can't we just take the easy route? Let's just give up. Let's just get him a Green Card like I did and wait a few years to get him citizenship. I just can't handle this.' This was such a terrible, awful time in our life. We lived like this for over a year."

Neither Andrew nor Elad were in the United States illegally, but Ethan soon would be. Ethan's tourist visa was due to expire toward the end of 2017. That was when Andrew's mother became worried about a knock on the door from immigration officials. "In my mind, I was readying myself to come and grab that baby and go to Canada," Ann Banks recalled, "because I've got a Canadian passport, too. They were not going to get him."

As I explain later in this chapter, the media attention that the family eventually arranged successfully attracted public support as well as legal assistance, as intended. However, it also publicly identified Andrew and Elad and their twins, making them visible to officials who might be seeking children who were in the country illegally.

Ethan did not have US citizenship as their case moved forward. The possibility that one of his parents would have to leave the United States with him was real. The fabric of this family—a married couple with twins, made up of four parent-child pairs (each father with each son)—would unravel beyond repair.

BABY STEPS AND A GIANT LEAP

There was more than one way to solve the dilemma of Ethan's citizenship. The easy solution was what Elad called "the Green Card route." Elad had a Green Card, allowing him to live and work in the United States and to qualify for citizenship in three to five years.[28] As such, he could have sponsored Ethan for a Green Card and then waited for his son's citizenship to be approved. However, according to the Child Citizenship Act of 2000, certain requirements must be satisfied before children under eighteen years of age can become US citizens:[29]

- They must have at least one US citizen parent by birth or naturalization.
- They must be admitted to the United States as an immigrant for lawful permanent residence.
- After admission to the United States, they must reside in the country in the legal and physical custody of a US citizen parent.
- If the child is adopted, his or her adoption must be full and final so that the adoption process is legally complete and fully recognized by the US state where the child is residing.

It was a tempting choice, because Elad values his privacy—even more than Andrew does. The Green Card route would have preserved the confidentiality of the biological relationships of the two fathers to their two sons. However, as I indicated, becoming a citizen by this process can take several years. The minimal age at which a child can be granted US citizenship in this way is unclear. The two fathers were adamant that their twins be treated the same and that Ethan be able to fulfill his full potential. "What if Ethan wanted to become the president of the United States?" they asked. (Recall that Tovi, the twins' grandmother, suggested that he might!) That is a right reserved for US-born citizens.

Andrew and Elad were running out of time.

They decided to seek the assistance of an immigration attorney, but finding the right one—or finding one at all—was not easy. Initial consultation is usually free, but subsequent legal fees run high, and their existing legal expenses were already depleting the couple's finances. Elad summed it up: "We weren't asking to stand out or asking for a fight with the State Department. We were just asking for our children to be treated equally, and they weren't being treated equally." They experienced anger, frustration, and near-desperation after these meetings.

"I GET BY WITH A LITTLE HELP FROM MY FRIENDS"[30]

Andrew's older half-brother Jon once owned Pitch, an advertising agency whose clients included Burger King, Netflix, and Pepsi. Jon retired in 2014, continued as chair for several years, then left the business entirely. When we first met on Zoom in April 2022, I explained my interest in his brother's case and named the main themes I had identified at that time: same-sex marriage, citizenship policy, intercultural families, egg donation, surrogacy, and twinship.

Jon, who followed the different phases of Andrew and Elad's Toronto to Los Angeles journey, said he "smiled internally" upon hearing the "confluence of hot button issues" that had attracted me to this story. He was also amazed that not one lawyer had agreed to take the case. "You can never count on people doing the right thing and doing the smart thing—but it boggles the mind that young, enterprising, hungry lawyers couldn't see what you articulated in one sentence at the beginning of our conversation."[31]

Jon does not have a legal background, but over the course of his career, he dealt with different issues involving attorneys. And he knows a lot about advertising. He gave Andrew and Elad some simple, straightforward advice: "You need a strategy—get the case out and people will come to you. And the way that they're going to chase you is by you framing up the narrative." Jon worried that they would end up with "some Joe Schmo who has a one-person office," rather than the "real heavy hitters" they deserved. He assured his brother and brother-in-law that once their unique and important story went public, "the lawyers would be beating a path to your door." And that is just how it happened.

Jon didn't have media contacts at the time, but Andrew's sisters did. Ashli, Andrew's older half-sister, saw the wisdom of bringing the story to a television audience. "As soon as somebody sees it on TV, it's real, you know what I mean?" Ashli reached out to her friends at some of the television networks, as did her husband, who has media contacts in cosmetic dentistry. None of their leads were coming up with pro bono lawyers; however, Ashli had a friend who worked for CBS News and found her on Facebook. "I asked if she could cover the story. It wasn't her area, but she agreed to pass it on to the appropriate person."[32]

Andrew's other half-sister, Jennifer, also played a significant role in the media coverage. According to Andrew, she "spearheaded" the whole process. Jennifer was a kind of public figure in her own right, an expert in navigating social platforms and getting the message out. "She put us in the right place for getting public attention, and to get ourselves the lawyers that set this whole thing in motion." Jennifer told me she wrote a blog at the time with a very large following. She also had a lot of media contacts, as well as friends at CBS News, who did a story about Andrew, Elad, and the twins. "Obviously, it was all over the news," Jennifer said. Her efforts made a difference, but it would be their eventual connection with Immigration Equality in New York that gave them the legal support they needed—and the media appearances that drew attention to the case. "My job as a sister was to be supportive," Jennifer said, "and to spread the word about the injustice that was occurring to help make others aware."[33] In fact, the situation would become known worldwide. Attorney Flowerday's Canadian clients often mentioned it during their legal consultations, and Elad's family and friends read about it in Israeli newspapers.

In the end, Jon said the family's public relations campaign "worked beautifully." More than one attorney came forward, willing to take the case, so "we could afford to be picky—the heavy hitters called, and it was all pro bono. They [Andrew and Elad] were a perfect case study or test case for what was needed to challenge the policy. And they [the lawyers] delivered in ways that were incredible."

IMMIGRATION EQUALITY

I will say a lot more later about the mission of Immigration Equality (IE) and the work they did on Andrew and Elad's behalf. When I spoke to the lead attorney and executive director of IE, I learned that Jon was right—the timing of this case could not have been better. For now, it is important to understand the perspectives of the two fathers as they considered this opportunity and chose to accept it.

Elad remembered his utter devastation when his parents removed him from the private school he loved and placed him in the public school he loathed. They took the "easier route," the one Elad refused to follow as a parent. Getting a Green Card for Ethan would have avoided public attention, lawyers, and lawsuits, but this plan came with serious drawbacks. Elad replayed his reasoning for me. "We could have bowed down and said, 'Okay, this is the law. But we [had] made a decision. What [would] eventually be harder now, with the media exposure and the challenges to our privacy, time, and resources, [would] be better for the kids, and for Ethan specifically in the future, to be considered a born American citizen—and equal to his twin brother."[34]

Elad continued. "I think what convinced me was that one day, Andrew said, 'Just think about what this will mean to our kids. Not the fact that Ethan got the citizenship, because he would have gotten that in some way. Think about what it would mean to them if they knew—they will know—that we fought for them, and we did what was right. It was Ethan's right—he was a US citizen from birth. And the fact that the State Department took it away from him was a wrong we had to make right. When he grows up, what we're going to tell him is that we not only took care of him, but we probably started something that would take care of many other people in the future.' And that's what made me do it [cooperate with Immigration Equality]—because I didn't want to put my life out there. It's not who I am."

In the chapter that follows, I will examine the couple's associations with the lawyers and staff at Immigration Equality and their attorneys at Sullivan & Cromwell. I will also trace the timeline of legal events that brought them temporary relief and those that presaged unthinkable pain. Most importantly, perhaps, I will consider why Immigration Equality chose to act on the Dvash-Banks case from among the hundreds of applications they receive. I will also assess the legacy of the court's final decision for same-sex transnational families who just want to have children.

The coming together of an intercultural couple, a Canadian donor, a Canadian surrogate, and a United States consular officer laid the basis for a seemingly insurmountable predicament. An agile and committed legal team gave them the chance they needed—but could not promise the outcome they craved.

Immigration Equality: Policies, Practices, and the Twinship Angle

"The life experiences of individuals who find themselves in the spotlight, by choice or by chance, shape their country's written history."

—Fiona Hill (2021)[1]

*T*he roots and resolution of Ethan's citizenship problem were "bigger than both of us," according to Andrew and Elad. They knew that the final decision and what lay behind it would affect not just their own family but all same-sex transnational couples who delivered their children abroad. Chance brought them to that moment, but choice kept them there. Their efforts and those of their attorneys were to shape a significant portion of our nation's citizenship and immigration history.

LOOKING FOR LAWYERS

In the previous chapter I alluded to Andrew and Elad's frustration in their search for an attorney to represent them. Later, I learned the full extent of their difficulties, as well as how their association with Immigration Equality evolved.

One of several complicating factors in finding the right attorney was President Trump's January 2017 ban on citizens from seven predominantly Muslim countries, an act that prevented these individuals from entering the United States. This meant that most immigration attorneys could be found at Los Angeles International Airport (LAX), where their services were badly needed. Moreover, as noted in the previous chapter, the entry of families from Mexico and Central America to the United States at the US-Mexico border was perilous in 2017 and 2018—parents and children were separated, and children were housed in compartments reminiscent of wire cages.[2] These developments directed the efforts of immigration attorneys away from private clients seeking legal consultation.

Andrew and Elad finally met with a lawyer who charged them a $300 consultation fee, then suggested that Andrew adopt Ethan. However, when they informed him that Andrew's name was already on Ethan's birth certificate, the lawyer dismissed that possibility. The next option the lawyer proposed was for Andrew to become Ethan's stepparent, an arrangement that would let him adopt his son at a later time. But this idea did not feel right to Andrew and Elad; it seemed absurd, because Andrew was already Ethan's legal parent. They also believed their problem was significant and far-reaching, needing more than a fast and superficial fix. As Andrew recalled, the lawyer rested his foot on the table and chewed gum when they entered his office. "He was really unprofessional, but we were so desperate. He told us, 'You're pretty much screwed. There's nothing you can do.'" They left the law office feeling more defeated than before, because he was "literally the only lawyer that would talk to us."

As I described in chapter 5, a media campaign succeeded in calling attention to their case, and once it became more visible, several attorneys expressed interest. They explored other options. A September 22, 2017, letter regarding Ethan's citizenship was sent by California congressman Ted W. Lieu to Carlos Hernandez, country officer at the Office of American Citizens Services and Crises. Hernandez's reply expressed his concern while noting that "it is common for our Embassies and Consulates to ask persons [who] engage in surrogacy overseas—regardless of sexual orientation—to go through DNA testing. . . . Please be assured that recommending DNA testing is not a form of discrimination but a means of discouraging fraud and ensuring that U.S. citizenship transmission requirements are met. . . . Also, we suggest that, in addition to finding an immigration lawyer who can help explain the avenues through which his son can acquire citizenship through naturalization, he may also wish to consider applying for a certificate of citizenship directly from USCIS [United States Citizenship and Immigration Services]."[3]

Andrew and Elad wanted Ethan to have what was rightfully his. They also wanted a meaningful fit between themselves and those working with them—a relationship that would achieve a significant goal that they and their prospective attorneys would share. Ultimately, it did not take a village to find the right representation; it took a community—it took IKAR.

As Elad explained, IKAR is not just a synagogue; it is a place for learning and a community of individuals committed to solving social justice issues. Many of its members hold prominent positions in the arts, sciences, and entertainment industries. Thirty-five-year-old Yoni Fife, a lawyer and chair of IKAR's board of directors at the time, had seen Andrew and Elad's first CBS interview in the summer of 2017. He told Elad that his law firm had done pro bono work with Immigration Equality, an organization of which neither Elad nor Andrew were aware. Fife also explained Immigration Equality's missions and goals to Elad: advocating for immigrants and families discriminated against due to their sexual orientation, gender identity, or HIV status. Their efforts included applying direct legal services, policy advocacy, and impact litigation.[4] Yoni advised Elad and Andrew to present their story to the organization, which they did.

BREATH OF FRESH AIR

Elad led me through the different phases of the couple's application process. First, he and Andrew filled out an online inquiry form available on Immigration Equality's website.[5] Next, they completed a telephone interview, during which a Board of Immigration Appeals (BIA)[6]–accredited representative recorded their answers to dozens of background questions: Who are you? Where are you from? What is your relationship to one another? What problem are you hoping to solve? This experience, while demanding, was exactly what they had hoped for in their search for someone to take their case. "We were talking to the intake person [BIA representative], and he was *listening* to us. It was, like, [for] the first time, someone was *listening*," Andrew declared. "And then, around the same time, I was starting to tell my family about the undisclosed details. We were being very private at first because I was trying to respect the law [requests that we not speak publicly so as not to compromise our chance for success]."

One week later, Immigration Equality invited Andrew and Elad to a Zoom interview during which they discussed their case with key personnel. They were introduced to Jackie Yodashkin, director of public affairs, and Aaron C. Morris, Immigration Equality's executive director. During this session Andrew and Elad answered more questions about what they wanted to achieve and why. When the conversation ended, they were told that someone from Immigration Equality would get back to them. They expected to wait at least a couple of weeks.

That's not what happened.

An e-mail from Immigration Equality with the subject line "Your Case" arrived about one week after the conversation ended. Elad recalled, "I guess they did their work. . . . It's kind of like we knew what we were going to hear, what we were supposed to hear from them." He said it reminded him of applying for admission to a university—you wait for the letter, you open it, and you feel so excited. "So, when we got the e-mail, we opened it immediately and started reading, reading, reading, and it says, 'We would love to extend an invitation to represent you pro bono in this case against the State Department.' And we were just so excited because we had no idea how we were chosen or who made the decision."

It was a breath of fresh air.

Looking back, Andrew described the deep gratitude he felt—and still feels—toward Yoni Fife for approaching Elad. He is also indebted to Elad, who spoke honestly and openly with his IKAR colleague. "Thank God he said something. If it was me, I would have been telling everyone, but Elad is more private, as you know."

Andrew and Elad had one more decision to make—but there was little to decide because of the goal they had in mind. Akin Gump Strauss Hauer & Feld LLP, a renowned law firm in Los Angeles, had met with them several times and was interested in taking their case. Akin Gump offers a wide range of pro bono immigration services to their clients, such as "permanent resident ('green') cards, waivers of inadmissibility, and family-based immigration."[7] Their list does not include discrimination due to sexual orientation or gender identity, the niche for which Immigration Equality is famous and which was so well-suited to Andrew and Elad's situation.

"We ended up choosing Immigration Equality because it was not just a law firm that would represent us," Elad explained. "They [Immigration Equality's lawyers] were also going to make this a matter of public education—educating the public about this subject and drawing media attention. All the other lawyers just wanted the facts of the case to litigate. That's how we chose Immigration Equality."

The first press release describing their case—along with a case involving the children of a same-sex female couple—and the injustices done to both families was issued on January 22, 2018.[8]

AARON C. MORRIS: EXECUTIVE DIRECTOR, IMMIGRATION EQUALITY

Immigration Equality is selective and rigorous when it comes to choosing the individuals and families they represent. According to communications director Kristen Thompson, in 2021 the staff received over 5,000 calls on their legal helpline and served 791 individuals, although not all cases were requests for legal representation.[9]

I wanted to know why the organization saw special significance in Andrew and Elad's story, distinguishing them from the large pool of prospective clients. That opportunity arose in 2022 during a trip to New York City, my first trip anywhere since the COVID-19 pandemic rearranged our lives in March 2020. I was in New York to celebrate the publication of my 2021 book, *Deliberately Divided: Inside the Controversial Study of Twins and Triplets Reared Apart*. A reception with family, friends, colleagues, and contributors was scheduled for June 12, 2022, at the Museum of Jewish Heritage in Lower Manhattan.

Before leaving California, I had asked Andrew and Elad to send an e-mail introducing me to Immigration Equality's executive director, Aaron C. Morris. I assumed he and I would eventually arrange a Zoom session to discuss the case, but just as I arrived in New York, Andrew wrote, "He [Aaron] said he would be happy to chat with you. . . . He is located in NYC, so perhaps if your schedule permits you could meet in person."

I immediately sent an e-mail to Morris suggesting some dates and times.

Aaron C. Morris, executive director of Immigration Equality. In 2017, he received the Peter M. Cicchinio Award for Outstanding Advocacy in the Public Interest. Morris also serves on the board of directors of the Khalid Jabara Foundation, an organization dedicated to improving relationships within communities through social justice programs. *Photo credit*: Tony Gale.

He wrote back:

Hi, Professor,
   The guys [Andrew and Elad] did tell me that you would be in contact. I'm going on vacation to Yellowstone on Tuesday and trying desperately to get everything accomplished before I sign off. But I am also having dinner at a friend's Monday night [June 13] at 7 PM on the UWS [Upper West Side]. Could we meet near his apartment at Vin Sur Vingt wine bar at like 5:30?[10]

"Yes, I can do that," I replied. I had planned a celebratory dinner with my boyfriend, Dr. Craig Ihara, for that night, but I could not give up this opportunity. Craig and I agreed to meet at the wine bar at 7:00 p.m. after my meeting and enjoy our special dinner another time.

I arrived at the wine bar early to find a table that was outside (for COVID safety reasons) and as far from the noisy New York City traffic as possible. I was reasonably certain I would recognize Morris from a photograph posted on Immigration Equality's website, showing a mustached man in his early forties wearing a pink button-down shirt, beige vest, and patterned tie.[11]

Instead, a thinner version of the man appeared, wearing a white V-neck T-shirt and shorts and carrying a bag that contained slacks he would later change into for the dinner at his friend's home.

"Professor Segal!" he declared when he found me.

I motioned for him to sit in the seat across from me and asked him to call me Nancy. Knowing we had limited time, I presented him with my publisher's standard consent forms, one for the interview and one for a photograph. He signed the first one, explaining that if he agreed to an interview, there would be nothing to prevent me from writing what I wanted. He didn't sign the second one, because the use of a photograph was a question for his communications department/public relations staff; I would revisit that possibility later if needed.

Then I handed him a signed copy of my book, *Deliberately Divided*, in appreciation for his time. He seemed surprised but pleased to accept this gift. He was unaware of the 1960s study of intentionally separated twin pairs I had investigated and written about.

I began our meeting by explaining the kind of book I wanted to write about Andrew and Elad, whom Morris immediately described as "effusive and kind." After he provided some context for the case, he told me why Immigration Equality had decided to support them.

Morris and his colleagues had seen a pattern of abuse/discrimination by the US State Department regarding the citizenship of children born to same-sex transnational couples, which they felt could be solved only by litigation. After the Supreme Court declared the Defense of Marriage Act (DOMA) unconstitutional in 2013 (and in *Obergefell v. Hodges,* 2015), the Obama administration did a good job of incorporating reforms and accepted recommendations from Immigration Equality.[12] However, an issue that immigration attorneys and other professionals struggled with was *administrative advocacy*—positions concerned with influencing the "formation, application, or change of rules that government agencies put in place to implement statutory law."[13,14]

The key issue in Andrew and Elad's case was parenting [i.e., the citizenship of one of their twin sons, despite his same-sex parents' legal marriage]. To find a solution, Immigration Equality needed several such couples. Prior to accepting Andrew and Elad as clients, they had already agreed to work with Allison Blixt and Stefania Zaccari from New York City, whose story parallels that of Andrew and Elad in many ways.

INDIVISIBLE BY FOUR

Allison Blixt and Stefania Zaccari met in New York City, fell in love, and moved to London, where same-sex marriage became legal in 2014.[15] Stefania, a citizen of Italy, delivered a son, Lucas, in 2015, and Blixt, a citizen of the United States, delivered a son, Massi, in 2017. The UK government recognized both women as the parents of both children. However, the US State Department would not recognize Allison as Lucas's mother, thereby denying Lucas US citizenship when they tried to return. Immigration Equality held that the policy as applied by the State Department was for unwed mothers only, and, by doing so, the government failed to recognize the marriage between the two women.[16]

Morris explained that once Immigration Equality accepted Andrew and Elad as their clients, they were able to build a strategy to bring litigation. Not only did Andrew and Elad present a compelling case, but they had come to the attention of Immigration Equality at the perfect time.

Two more cases were added to their effort. Jonathan Gregg and Derek Mize married in New York City in 2015. Both men were US citizens—Mize was born in the United States, and Gregg was born in England to an American mother and British father. The couple had a daughter, Simone, conceived through surrogacy and delivered in England, then moved to Georgia. The State Department viewed Simone as a child born out of wedlock, simply because Gregg did not meet the five-year residency requirement for granting US citizenship to a child. Simone was given a tourist visa valid for just three months.[17]

A fourth case involved a same-sex male couple, Roee and Adiel Kiviti, whose daughter Kessem's citizenship was in question. Roee was born in Israel and raised in Southern California, and he became a US citizen in 1993. Adiel was born in Israel and became a US citizen in 2019. The men married in California in 2013 and lived abroad until 2015, when they returned to the United States.

Their first child, Lev, was born in Canada by surrogacy and was recognized as a United States citizen at birth; his application was processed in Los Angeles. In 2019, the couple welcomed Kessem into their family. Kessem had also been born in Canada. When Roee and Adiel applied for her US passport, the term "surrogacy" was entered on the form by a staff member, and the required fee was paid. But the next day, Adiel was informed that his residency was being examined and that Kessem's citizenship would be determined by a provision in the Immigration and Nationality Act that applies to children born out of wedlock. This provision states that the child must be biologically related to a US parent who has lived in the United States for five years.[18] The decision by the State Department was denial of US citizenship to their daughter.[19]

Lawsuits on behalf of the four families—Dvash-Banks, Zaccari-Blixt, Mize-Gregg, and Kiviti—were filed by Immigration Equality, in conjunction with various co-counsels that differed across cases. The Dvash-Banks and Zaccari-Blixt filings were done in January 2018; the Mize-Gregg and Kiviti filings were done in July 2019 and June 2020, respectively. These couples are listed under "Impact Litigation Family Stories" on Immigration Equality's website. Impact litigation is brought or defended when a case typically involves more than one individual.[20]

Each case was unique, but they shared significant themes: the US government's failure to acknowledge their marriages, the rejection of US citizenship to children born abroad (some of whom lacked a biological

American parent), and discrimination based on the sexual orientation of the parents. Most importantly, there was one overriding consideration that defined them all: They were indivisible as families, and they intended to stay that way.

THE DVASH-BANKS CASE: TWINSHIP ANGLE

Immigration Equality is a nonprofit organization that works in concert with law firms willing to serve clients pro bono. Lawyers at Immigration Equality identify the problem, find potential clients, and set the strategy. At the time of the Dvash-Banks case, Aaron C. Morris was the lead attorney for Immigration Equality, with lawyers from New York and Los Angeles's Sullivan & Cromwell firms agreeing to participate.[21] Co-counsel included Jessica M. Klein, Alexa M. Lawson-Remer, Theodore Edelman, Scott E. Blair, Alexandra Moss, Andrew K. Jennings, Rebekah Tillander Raybuck, and Lauren Goldsmith.[22]

When I first learned of the Dvash-Banks case in January 2018, several points of contention were evident: failure to grant US citizenship to the child of a US citizen born abroad, discrimination against a same-sex couple, and the possible breakup of a family.[23] However, as a psychologist specializing in twin studies, I noted that the potential dissolution of a *twinship* was a neglected angle. Having worked closely with reared-apart twins, I could attest to the sadness, anger, and bitterness that twins experience at the loss of a uniquely celebrated relationship.[24]

Twins arouse universal interest, no doubt explaining their powerful presence in drama, literature, and film. When twins share careers, marry other twins, or deliver babies on the same day, these events become headline news. Understandably, separating twins who enter the world as a pair is seen as cruel and unfair by virtually everyone. Twins have, however, grown up apart for reasons such as maternal death, family poverty, parental divorce, and accidental switching of newborns. In the 1960s, several New York City twin and triplet sets were intentionally adopted apart and tested secretly in a controversial study.[25] Regardless of the reason, the twins suffer when they learn of their lost relationship, and the public mourns the loss along with them.

The Dvash-Banks case reminded me of another event that threatened to separate twins. Early in my career I was asked to write a letter on behalf of thirty-six-year-old Russian twins whose assigned immigration status prevented the two women from relocating to the United States together. The letter, addressed to the Washington Processing Center and to Congress, reviewed research on the significance of the twin relationship and the personal devastation following its loss. Ultimately, the twins were allowed to stay together, a decision that their uncle attributed largely to my effort.[26]

I was convinced that a similar approach would strengthen the Dvash-Banks case because their twin sons were closely connected. Aiden and Ethan were just sixteen months old when Immigration Equality filed their lawsuit in January 2018—but twins as young as four months of age can react by becoming motionless when their co-twin vocalizes, or appearing disoriented when their twin is temporarily out of sight. Given the series of filings and appeals, the case did not settle until October 2020, when Aiden and Ethan were four years old and each other's best friend.

I had sent an e-mail to one of Sullivan & Cromwell's attorneys, Alexa Lawson-Remer, on January 24, 2018, with the subject line "Twin Toddler Case," cc'ing her colleague, Theodore Edelman. In the message, I offered my assistance, highlighting the importance of twinship. Lawson-Remer thanked me and said I would be contacted if and when my expertise was needed. There was no follow-up or response to my subsequent messages from either attorney, even months after the case had settled. (After my meeting with Morris in June 2022, in August I was motivated to request brief comments from attorneys Scott Blair and Alexandra Moss but received no reply.)

I did not understand why the twinship angle was not addressed until I met with Aaron Morris in June 2022 (and finally spoke with Lawson-Remer in September of that year, as I will describe in chapter 8).

Morris ordered his first of two glasses of rosé wine just after I raised the topic. He explained that the Dvash-Banks case was not just about twins but about separating a family—a "legal whole." Even if he were to concede that twin separation was "worse" than sibling separation, it wouldn't matter, because the law favors families, regardless of whether the children are twins or singletons. Morris asserted that "the interesting angle was that Aiden and Ethan were literally born in the same way and at the same time—they had the same surrogate—but one twin was a US citizen, and the other twin was not."[27] Thus, he placed less importance on psychological damage to the boys from their possible *separation as twins* than on how the *circumstances of their birth* bore upon the case.

I found his explanation perplexing, because *the birth events he described uniquely defined Aiden and Ethan as twins!* Morris admitted that the Dvash-Banks case was "more stark" than the other three cases involved in the suit, because of the similarity of the boys' birth. Of course, the fact of twinship and the similarity of events that define multiple births are completely confounded.

I confessed to Morris that if twins had not been part of this case, my interest in the situation and its outcome would have been reduced. "That is not unique to you," he replied. "They got more publicity than the other couples. A lot." I maintained that the twinship angle was responsible for this, and he replied, "Probably."

Communications director Kristen Thompson, who joined Immigration Equality in April 2019, felt that the media frequency matched across the four families, each of which posed unique legal challenges. She believed that the visual images of loving parents and young children who were so mistreated (regardless of twinship) conveyed their anguish to the public in a powerful way. Still, Thompson acknowledged that there is a universal fascination with twins—and observed that Aiden and Ethan were adorable.[28]

Jackie Yodashkin, who headed communications prior to Thompson, concurred, although neither she nor Thompson had the data to confirm or refute their impressions. Yodashkin called the scenes and situation of the four families "heart-wrenching." She also noted that people really connected to the stories, "especially when there are twins—they're born minutes apart, but they're being treated differently and risk separation. It's remarkable. . . . It's easier to see the injustice with twins—it's an easy story to tell in that it sort of tells itself."

Yodashkin remembered the time a camera crew recorded the twins at a playground—"Just watching twin brothers play, it was so cool." She noted that journalists from places that had never previously requested information from Immigration Equality's communications department were interested in Andrew and Elad.[29] Elad's friend, Rotem, first learned of the case on the local news in Israel, but she heard more later when she was stranded on Cebu Island in the Philippines, in 2020, due to the COVID-19 pandemic; she contacted Elad immediately after that. Immigration Equality also received inquiries from a British couple whose surrogate was from Cyprus and from a Brazilian couple based in Rio de Janeiro.[30]

Law professor Kristin Collins sided with Morris and me when it came to the effects of twinship on thinking about the Dvash-Banks case. While Collins hadn't thought much about this aspect of the case, she asserted that twinship "really called the lie on the policy and the absurdity. It set it in such stark relief." Note that Collins and Morris used similar language ("stark relief"; "more stark") to describe the twinship effects.[31]

Twinship was at the core of Andrew and Elad's media strategy. "When you say 'twins' to the average American, [it's like] you are talking about the same person," Elad recalled. "They're in utero together, they're born together, they're the same age, and they go through everything together in life. . . . It's the exaggeration of how ridiculous this thing is. . . . I think it helped us media-wise—it made the whole concept of separation between the two of them impossible in people's minds. We repeated that in every single interview."[32]

Knowing the popularity of twins in the media and in the public consciousness, I suspect that the Dvash-Banks case may have attracted somewhat greater attention than the other three—if not in the number of articles and appearances, at least in public sympathy. (I do not have the data to support this view, but these reflections from the staff are telling.) Morris also pointed out that, with respect to the other families, he didn't wish to overemphasize the twinship. That is understandable, and it is likely that the staff assigned to these cases shared his view. That being said, the Zaccari-Blixt and Dvash-Banks lawsuits were filed at the same time, yet the Dvash-Banks case moved ahead more swiftly than the others.

LEGAL INTERPRETATION/MISINTERPRETATION

According to Morris, the government executed a form of "legal gymnastics" to come up with their interpretation of the law, even though the law was so plain. The Supreme Court "could not have been clearer on the validity and extension of equality for marriage, but it felt like double-speak—we acknowledge that you are married and are the parents of these children, but we treat your children as though they were born out of wedlock."[33]

Prior to August 2020, the State Department's policy was that a child delivered by a surrogate outside the United States is considered born out of wedlock, even if the genetic parent is a United States citizen. That policy was, however, based on the Immigration and Nationality Act of 1952—twenty-nine years before in vitro fertilization was performed in the United States (1981) and sixty-three years before same-sex marriage was legalized (2015). The policy was developed in the 1990s to conform to existing law, but the Trump administration was criticized by many for its continued implementation.[34] In June 2019, nearly twenty Democratic senators and eighty congressional representatives sent a letter to Secretary of State Mike Pompeo, urging him to reverse the policy that denied citizenship to children delivered abroad who were conceived by American parents by assisted reproductive methods. The Dvash-Banks family situation was highlighted in that letter.[35]

Nine months later, in May 2021, the State Department announced it would no longer deny citizenship rights to children conceived by same-sex couples via in vitro fertilization and surrogacy. This change in policy was conveyed to all United States overseas posts and to Congress. It resulted from the lawsuits filed against the department by same-sex couples (Zaccari-Blixt, Dvash-Banks, Mize-Gregg, and Kiviti), which produced decisions that favored the families. Morris noted that the State Department has yet to issue a public correction of regulation or formal policy, although they are granting citizenship cases to children for the most part.

Three months later, the US Citizenship and Immigration Services (USCIS) also made a change. It announced that it would grant citizenship to a child who, at birth, was genetically or gestationally related to at least one parent who was a US citizen or to their non–US-citizen spouse and updated its policy manual to reflect this change.[36] Attorney Ellen Trachman, while applauding this progress, questioned the additional genetic or gestational requirement; the original code simply specified "parents." She argued that the expanded use of assisted reproductive technology could eliminate a genetic and/or gestational aspect of a given case. Trachman favors basing citizenship on the legal parent–child relationship, without the added requirements. "The broader interpretation would be consistent with the law, and inclusive of all children of U.S. citizen parents," she wrote.[37]

MORRIS ON MEDIA

A central tenet of Immigration Equality is to educate as well as litigate. Morris can never judge the extent to which media attention affects judges' decisions. He did say that when Americans care about a problem, it pushes the government to modify policy. "Andrew and Elad were game for almost anything—fighting for family and eager to do what they could [on behalf of other parents]. I understand and appreciate that. They were justifiably angry."[38] But it's a delicate balancing act. The Dvash-Banks case was a collaboration between the couple and the members of Immigration Equality's communications department. The public message had to be carefully controlled until the legal portion of the case was over, out of concern that someone might say something publicly that could later be used against them in court or might contradict prepared testimony. This explains why I and others interested in writing books or producing documentaries were not allowed to speak with family members. It also explains why staff members wouldn't talk to me until the case settled.

Morris continued. "We had a press plan—a coordinated, all-hands-on-deck strategy for, not just how to talk to the press, but for how to articulate what we were doing. To avoid wonky thinking and getting lost in the weeds of the law (details that no one understands or wants to know about), we asked: What is the simplest way to articulate the issue at hand, and how does it affect the people? The communications department, Andrew, Elad, and I thought a lot about it, and we stuck to the plan." Both Jackie Yodashkin and Kristen Thompson worked directly with Andrew and Elad, preparing them for the kinds of questions they might receive and the best answers they could provide. Media attention escalated dramatically following what Thompson called the "big moments," such as circuit court decisions, State Department appeals, and changes in immigration provisions.

Morris knows that speaking to the media isn't easy for everyone. "What they [Andrew and Elad] did was admirable but rough—you have to be so open and have your privacy invaded regularly, and often."

Elad, especially, had difficulty with the media in the beginning. "I had a problem that when Immigration Equality took us on, they said people will know your story, people will know who you are," Elad recalled. "We're going to come into your home. We're going to take pictures. People will ask questions. There will be nasty comments on social media. So just prepare yourself for this and know what you're going into."

Public response was generally positive, but Andrew and Elad received some very disturbing and stressful comments and postings, as I will describe in the next chapter.

Of course, despite going public and gaining widespread support, the outcome was uncertain. Elad reminded me, "Our legal team never promised us that we were going to win. No good lawyer will do that. And they said, 'You might lose after going through all of this. We're very confident, but you never know what judges you'll get and what the government will do.' So, it was a very big decision to [move forward] after all [that]."[39]

Elad was right.

On May 6, 2019, the government appealed (contested) a decision that was favorable to the Dvash-Banks family, brought by the federal district court to the Ninth Circuit Court of Appeals. There was no explanation for their action. It happened that the appeal coincided with the family's invitation to a dinner hosted by Immigration Equality. I reviewed both a videotape and a transcript of their speech, addressed to the many supporters who had followed their story. They described their meeting, their marriage, and the birth of their twin sons. They also expressed deep gratitude to the attorneys and staff at Immigration Equality and the Sullivan & Cromwell law firm for their commitment to their case.

Taking turns throughout, Andrew showed how his government had failed him on three separate occasions but underlined the couple's determination to fight for what they knew was right. He said he was "shocked" by the appeal as he tried to determine their next steps in the process toward gaining US citizenship for their son Ethan. Elad acknowledged that while this setback left them "heartbroken," the family remained an "unbreakable unit of four." He concluded the speech by saying, "The arc of the moral universe is long, but it always bends toward justice." Nearly three-year-old Aiden and Ethan were with their parents on the podium—Elad was holding Aiden, and Andrew was holding Ethan. When Aiden grabbed the microphone and Ethan yawned unashamedly, the audience was utterly charmed. It was hard not to be.

Journalists also sought comments from the couple's attorneys, especially during key moments, such as judgments and appeals. Morris admits to feeling frustrated when some news outlets want to sensationalize a story, but as someone who talks to the press, he feels it's reassuring to know you have autonomy in an interview. And he welcomes the coverage. "It's never about me," Morris notes. "It's about how the press can help us fix the problem."

It is possible to catch the attention of a policy maker previously unaware of the issue, or to build public support that can then pressure the government. In the middle of litigation, Andrew and Elad appeared on NBC's *Andrea Mitchell Reports* from Los Angeles, while Morris was interviewed by a reporter in New York. "It felt really good and positive," Morris recalled. He could not name any negative media experiences with Andrew and Elad's case, but he recalled unfavorable moments with some others.

Morris noted that most reporters who covered the Dvash-Banks case seemed "confused and irritated" by the government's position of denying Ethan US citizenship. Then he suggested that "exasperated" was a better word—"Like, how can that be?"

Unlike Morris, not all attorneys speak publicly about their cases, although it's hard to know if their law firm's policy or their personal preferences are responsible. Prior to coming to New York, I had e-mailed Jessica Klein, another Sullivan & Cromwell attorney, who also failed to reply. I mentioned this to Morris, who had been told of my request. I learned that Klein was "totally not interested in talking to me."[40] I wondered if it was because I had contacted her without an introduction from Andrew and Elad, but Morris believed it was law firm policy.

I was not discouraged. As I said earlier, I had sent e-mails to the other co-counsel members involved in the case and to all of them in 2022. By then, Blair and Moss were no longer associated with Sullivan & Cromwell, so I felt optimistic about hearing from them. I didn't.

ALMOST TIME FOR DINNER

It was close to 6:30 p.m., leaving just thirty minutes before Morris needed to leave for his dinner event, which was actually a small fundraiser for Immigration Equality. I asked him what he would ask me if he were writing a book about the case. He thought a moment, then posed a question for which he said he had no answer: "Why does the government fight so hard to keep this policy [of denying lawful citizenship to children] when they keep losing?"[41] He noted that Immigration Equality had successfully litigated all four family cases, and while the government did not appeal the Mize-Gregg case in Georgia, it had appealed the Dvash-Banks case in Los Angeles, more than once. Morris could only speculate that issues related to resource allocation or organizational payoff must explain why the Mize-Gregg case wasn't challenged. It was also unclear why the government had withdrawn its appeal of the Kiviti case.

According to Andrew, Trump was aware of their lawsuit, based on information from a friend of Andrew's mother, Ann.[42] "What would have happened if Trump had been reelected US president in 2020?" I asked. Morris said it was hard to know. "The Trump administration did remarkable things to appeal the decision that we won, such as asking the Ninth Circuit Court for an *en banc* review [the hearing of a case by all judges of a particular court, not just a select few], and completely giving up on the Georgia case when we won. So, it was hard to read the tea leaves about what their strategy was."[43] In June 2019, Immigration Equality filed its fourth suit on behalf of the Kiviti family and won the case in June 2020. The State Department withdrew its appeal in October 2020.[44]

MEETING FINALE

I am interested in how people choose the careers that they do. With a second glass of wine in hand, Morris traced his early professional development from undergraduate classics major to Harvard-Smithsonian administrator to law school student. After interning at several LGBTQ (lesbian, gay, bisexual, transgender, queer or questioning) organizations, including the newly formed Immigration Equality, he joined a group focused on law, policy, and human and civil rights for two years. (Immigration Equality wasn't hiring at the time.) He then joined a law firm created by the people who had created Immigration Equality but left after six months when IE began hiring. He worked his way up at Immigration Equality from staff attorney to senior staff attorney to legal director in 2014 and executive director in 2016.

The wine bill came as we were still talking. I wondered if I should have paid, because the interview was at my invitation. However, I did give him a copy of my recent book.

As Morris prepared to leave, I thanked him for his time. "I think of all the time Andrew and Elad gave to us—for a bigger moment—which is why we are having this conversation," he said.

"Is it your payback to them?" I asked.

"Just an acknowledgment of their effort, how open they were," Morris said. "From the inception they were clear that they wanted it to be about more than just their family. Because they knew other families through social media and through word of mouth that had the same problem but weren't positioned to go forward publicly."

Morris also mentioned a law review article I might read, although he couldn't name the author or the source. He had discovered it while searching for something else and thought, "Wow, someone wrote about all the things I did."

I wasn't surprised, since I had discovered six or seven such articles while looking for Elad's master's thesis, and I have found several more articles since then. The case encompassed timely topics of universal interest I have emphasized throughout this book, especially same-sex marriage, citizenship policy, twinship, and family.

Soon after the case settled in 2020, Morris was in Los Angeles and met with Andrew and Elad, this time for a social visit. They insisted on taking him to dinner and chose In-N-Out Burger, a popular California fast-food chain since 1948 that now operates in seven Western states.[45] They told him, "You don't have this [In-N-Out Burger] where you are, and it's our favorite place." For some reason, Morris had kept that dinner detail to himself, but he agreed to let me include it in the book.

TOGETHER AS ONE

Family life continued for Andrew, Elad, Aiden, and Ethan despite their pressing problems as the lawsuit against the State Department moved forward. The couple had professional responsibilities to fulfill and two young children to raise. They had to think about their twins' education, religious training, physical health, and overall well-being. Daily routines were established as parent–child relations and twin–twin interactions were taking shape—even as Ethan's uncertain citizenship status continued to darken their days.

· 7 ·

Family Ties: Parents and Plaintiffs

> "They [Andrew and Elad] were definitely a joint client re-
> lationship in terms of advising and making decisions. They
> were great parents, and they were co-parenting through-
> out this whole thing."
>
> —Alexa M. Lawson-Remer,
> former attorney at Sullivan & Cromwell

*A*s of January 22, 2018, Andrew and Elad were leading dual lives. They were plaintiffs in a lawsuit filed against a set of defendants, namely the US State Department and Secretary of State Rex W. Tillerson. The document was filed jointly by Immigration Equality and the Sullivan & Cromwell law firm.[1] Favorable outcomes are never guaranteed in any legal proceeding. Whether or not Ethan would be granted US citizenship was unclear—but only a favorable decision would calm the fears of his parents and those of families in similar circumstances. Adding to this uncertainty was the length of time required to resolve the situation, impossible to judge in any judicial undertaking.

While the legal process was moving forward, Andrew and Elad were committed to fulfilling parental responsibilities to their twins. The two new fathers were intrigued by their twins' early behaviors and the evolving relationships between each twin and each parent, and they shared some wonderful moments and exciting observations with me.

Like all parents, they had to consider the children's social development, physical health, and day-care needs, and when the children were a little older, their educational activities and religious instruction had to be arranged. Unlike most parents, however, they had less time for the fun part of parenting, because these typical decisions had to be made against

133

Elad and Ethan (L) with Andrew and Aiden, walking in a park near their home in North Hollywood, California, 2017. Ethan appears to be reaching out to "explore" his twin brother, Aiden, as their parents look on. *Photo credit*: **Images of Life by Ashli.**

the menacing backdrop of the case. Events linked to the lawsuit were regular intruders in their daily lives, often disrupting caretaking activities and family plans.

Then, in March of 2020, the COVID-19 pandemic led to a national shutdown, shifting workplaces to homes and day-care responsibilities to parents, further complicating the lives of the Dvash-Banks family. Travel was severely limited, causing Andrew constant worry over losing his dream job as SpaceX's travel manager. He wondered if he should start taking classes in case he had to change professions.

Andrew admitted that Elad carried most of the burden during this tense time—working for IKAR, caring for the family, making meals, and giving him the emotional support he needed. To save time in the morning, every night Elad chose the children's clothes for the next day and placed them on the kitchen island, where they would be visible. "[Elad] is very task-oriented when he's on a mission," Andrew noted.

"He is not only the love of my life, but the most incredible human being in the world." Elad struggled, too, and could be hard on himself—like the day he forgot to pack the twins' water bottles. Elad accepts his partner's strengths and weaknesses—"Andrew can barely make scrambled eggs!" Elad confessed.[2]

In this chapter I will look at how the two fathers and two children were becoming a close, loving, and *ordinary* family despite their extraordinary circumstances and the restrictions imposed upon them by the pandemic. Even though Andrew and Elad were immersed in a network of close friends and relatives, everyone had responsibilities of their own.

EARLIEST DAYS

Andrew's brother Jon flew to Toronto in September 2016, becoming the first family member to see his newborn nephews. The funniest part of his experience happened when he arrived. Talking to Jon in the hospital lobby before he saw the twins, Andrew insisted that it was very important to treat the boys as though he and Elad were both equally their parents, regardless of where their DNA came from. "And, just so you know, we're not telling anybody, *including you*, which boy is whose in terms of our DNA." But once Jon saw the babies, he remarked, "You don't have to be Sherlock Holmes to crack this case!" As I indicated earlier, it was obvious to everyone that Andrew had conceived Aiden and Elad had conceived Ethan. Over the course of my interviews, someone jokingly asked, "Where's the donor?" as if to imply that the children were clones of each parent and a donor was not part of the process.

Recall that Andrew and Elad and their twins spent February and March of 2017 in Los Angeles before visiting Israel in May. During their first brief stay in California, they decided to "sleep-train" the twins in between looking for jobs. They hired a Toronto consultant who assisted them remotely. An important part of the process was that each boy had to sleep in his own dark space apart from his parents with a white-noise machine turned on. The only possible solution in their tiny studio apartment was to place each boy in a separate travel bassinet in their walk-in closet. Once this was decided, they followed the prescribed routine, and "it worked like magic"—the boys slept twelve hours each night and continue to do so.

Elad laughed thinking about that time. Because the closet led to the bathroom, he and Andrew had to relieve themselves in the backyard to avoid disturbing the twins. But what seems funny now was stressful then.

Once the family moved to Los Angeles permanently in June 2017, Jon insisted that they get together as often as possible, which was not always easy. Although Andrew and Elad's first apartment in Brentwood was just a few miles from Jon's house in the Pacific Palisades, Jon and Andrew's other siblings, Ashli, Jennifer, and Brian, had children and teenagers of their own to attend to. Andrew's brother James lived across the country in Florida, as did his mother, Ann—and Elad's parents and siblings lived thousands of miles away in Israel.

Andrew and Elad also had very limited financial resources in those days, so they chose a "really shitty run-down apartment that had the thinnest walls." They lived on the first floor of a two-story building, below three male foreign students from UCLA. "You could hear every single footstep above your head," Andrew recalled. One night, Andrew knocked on his neighbors' door to complain about the noise and discovered "mountains of diapers"—apparently, the father of one of the students had a diaper business and was hoping to break into the market. Had the three students been more considerate, they would have found some eager buyers just downstairs.

As their new life began, Andrew felt the pangs of parenting doubts. In June 2017, when Elad began working at IKAR, Andrew was still unemployed and remained at home alone with their nine-month-old twins. The infants were teething and screaming in pain. Andrew was so overwhelmed, he never asked Elad how things had gone on his first day at work. "I need to get out of here," he said to Elad. "They [the twins] are crazy. I cannot do this. I'm not built for this." The situation stayed this way for several weeks. "Every day was crazy, crazy, crazy. . . . I needed a job so we could hire a nanny." As I indicated earlier, Andrew's job at SpaceX finally came through, allowing the couple to hire a nanny when the twins were a year old. But their family life was plagued by worries. Chief among them was an issue I raised earlier: Would immigration officers try to steal Ethan from his home while his parents were at work?

I posed this question to legal professionals.

University of Virginia law professor Amanda Frost, special assistant defender Ashley Craythorne, and immigration rights attorney

Meredith Luneack described the couple's concern as "possible, but unlikely."[3] Yale University law professor Cristina Rodríguez felt it was "unfathomable" that US Immigration and Customs Enforcement (ICE) agents would deport a young child without a parent. But as a mother of two daughters, as well as a daughter of immigrants, she conceded that Andrew and Elad's constant worry was understandable. "It was not an impossibility. One never knows where there is legal authority."[4]

Thus, a slim element of possibility that Ethan would be removed from his family was real. Worrying over whether your child will be home at the end of the workday is a fear most parents do not face, and it consumed Andrew and Elad—and at least one of the other three families represented by Immigration Equality, referenced in the previous chapter.[5] I thought about Elián González, the six-year-old Cuban boy who was found clinging to an inner tube in the Florida Straits, in November 1999. His mother and nine other people had drowned trying to reach the United States. Elián stayed with relatives in Florida while a custody battle ensued between his family members in the United States and his biological father in Cuba. US immigration officials decided to put him in the custody of his father, who came to the United States in April of 2000, but when his relatives refused to release him, Immigration and Naturalization Service (INS) agents raided the home and took the child.[6]

As Andrew and Elad said many times, their love for their son Ethan is what drove them to persevere through these trying times. Their words reminded me of a line I heard during a performance highlighting the plight of Ukrainian families affected by the 2022 Russian invasion. A mother with limited eyesight insisted, "When your child is in danger, your vision returns."[7] Andrew and Elad knew they had six months—until December 2017, when Ethan's tourist visa would expire—to solve their son's citizenship problem. Meanwhile, they had twin boys to raise, and their first birthday was approaching.

BIRTHDAY PARTIES AND A FAMILY VACATION

When the twins turned one on September 16, 2017, the family invited relatives and friends to a party at a nearby park. A "smash cake" had been specially ordered for the celebration. I had never heard of such a thing, but I learned that it's a small treat made specifically for a baby's first birthday. Andrew said they bought the cheapest one they could find at the local supermarket—a wise decision, since it does not last long. When presented with the cake, the infant usually does a lot of "pounding, smooshing and eating."[8] The occasion offers great photo opportunities, and Andrew and Elad made the most of them before hosing the boys down. The twins' second birthday party in 2018 was held at Los Angeles's Griffith Park, with a ride on the train that circles the Travel Town Museum. In between these two festive occasions, Ethan's tourist visa had expired. He was now in the United States illegally.

However, in 2018 the couple's attorney, Aaron C. Morris, contacted US Citizenship and Immigration Services, stating that their case was pending and requesting that the family be allowed to travel outside the country and return. (When tourist visas expire, reentry into the United States is prohibited if the individual should exit.) The request was approved, allowing Andrew and Elad and their children, joined by Elad's parents and sisters, to vacation together in Puerto Vallarta, Mexico. This trip helped to ease the tensions brought on by the legal proceedings, albeit temporarily.[9]

The first two years of a child's life span the period of infancy and toddlerhood, after which early childhood emerges, lasting until about age six.[10] It was time for Andrew and Elad to think about sending their children to preschool.

Aiden (L) and Ethan celebrating their first birthday, September 16, 2017, with their own smash cake. This milestone provided some moments of happiness and joy to their fathers, who were desperately searching for a path to Ethan's citizenship. In early 2018, Andrew and Ethan would add "plaintiff" to their respective family identities as parent and toddler. *Photo credit*: Images of Life by Ashli.

Aiden (L) and Ethan enjoying their second Halloween, October 2017. The boys are dressed in penguin costumes. *Photo credit*: Images of Life by Ashli.

IT TOOK A COMMUNITY—AGAIN

When news of their story first appeared on CBS, IKAR honored the couple with an *aliyah*, an honor typically reserved for individuals who become engaged, get married, publish a book, or achieve another noteworthy goal. Prior to the Torah reading during Shabbat, Elad and Andrew were invited to read the blessing that precedes this part of the service. "When we did that before the entire community of about three hundred people, we felt their warmth and love. It was very special," Elad recalled.

IKAR operates a preschool program for children who are two years of age and older. Children are admitted either on the first of September or the first of January; because Aiden and Ethan would not turn two until September 16, 2018, they were nearly two and a half years old when they enrolled at the preschool in January of 2019. Even though they were cared for by Gaby—their Guatemalan nanny who was wonderful with the children—having them at home for an extra half-year compounded the stressful conditions.

The family was fortunate: Because Elad worked at IKAR, the twins' tuition was reduced, a benefit enjoyed by all of IKAR's employees. They could not have afforded this expense otherwise. At this time, the family also ended their association with their nanny but found her a job caring for the children of Andrew's high school friend.

During the fourteen months that followed, Elad escorted the children to and from preschool, which lasted from 8:30 a.m. to 5:30 p.m.

Aiden and Elad (L) with Andrew and Ethan. The twins, now about one year, one month old, are standing and walking alone but need some support from their parents. Children vary in their physical development, but the average ages at which these skills appear are 11 months for standing alone and 11 months, 3 weeks for walking alone. *Photo credit*: Images of Life by Ashli.

Aiden and Ethan were always the last children waiting at the end of the day. "Don't the other kids' parents have jobs?" Andrew wondered. They would race home, have dinner, put the twins to bed at 7:30 p.m., and then work on their laptop computers until 1:00 a.m. The late-night hours were necessary, as the days between January 2019 and March 2020 were often interrupted by lawsuit-related tasks, such as copying documents, forwarding messages, finding photographs, and meeting attorneys at their Century City offices. Judicial decisions were announced without warning, some encouraging, others alarming. In spring 2019, the couple won their case in the federal district court, but the State Department appealed. And while this was all taking place, there were media obligations to fulfill as part of their agreement with Immigration Equality.

GOING LIVE

Many mornings and afternoons were filled with interviews, podcasts, and live television appearances, often involving their children. Elad had an easier time taking days off from work than Andrew, since IKAR is a relatively small, person-oriented institution. Andrew's tighter schedule meant that Elad took part in some interviews alone—not easy for him, given his penchant for privacy.

Elad remembers the time the family appeared on a Los Angeles morning television program. "We had to be there at 6:00 a.m., all dressed up," he recalls.

Jackie Yodashkin, Immigration Equality's former public affairs director and mother of a young child, remarked on the "immense thing" Andrew and Elad were doing. "They were trying to ensure the rights of their children and other children like them, but also trying to do the day-to-day parenting of twin toddlers, which I'm sure is much harder than the daily parenting of just one child—and that is extremely hard. . . . The twins were just happy toddlers, never knowing the peril they faced."[11]

Elad described the couple's mood on the day of the live morning show. "We were like, 'Is this all going to be worth it?' We were asked questions like, 'Who's the mother and who's the father in your relationship? Why did you each conceive one twin? If you knew this would be a problem, why didn't you just use sperm from Andrew, the US citizen? Why didn't you do the surrogacy in the United States if you wanted to live here—why choose Canada?' Each of these questions has answers that are not simple, and sometimes you're exhausted, repeating everything that everyone asks, but you have to repeat it. We were literally telling the same story hundreds of times [especially during the days after CBS first aired our story]. I felt like there was nothing private in our life."

Looking at the videos and newspaper photographs from those days reveals two adorable, endearing, and obedient twin toddlers. But these sunny scenes reflect skillful editing, because the boys were rambunctious from the start. After one of their shows, the family returned to the green room (the waiting room or lounge of a television studio or theater) to produce a segment for Facebook Live. Aiden and Ethan began throwing magazines stacked on the tables and became intrigued by the tacks pushed into the corkboard. "They were tired, hungry, and falling apart," Elad recalled. "And it was all recorded by Facebook." But Elad also remembers moments when the boys' behavior was extremely appealing. "Seeing them with their little button-down shirts and saying little words during the interviews was just so cute. They [the boys] will always remember those moments." These visuals proved quite powerful, as the idea of separating twins gave the story the commanding edge it would not have had if the boys had been non-twin siblings. Recall that twinship is a large part of what attracted me—and others—to this story.

The media opportunities orchestrated by Immigration Equality were instrumental in bringing public attention to the case. Many people posted opinions on social media platforms, most of them supportive. But some comments were nasty, homophobic, and/or anti-Semitic. Some people hoped the family would burn in hell. Jackie Yodashkin[12] advised Elad and Andrew to stop reading those remarks, written by bored people who were not their intended audience. Although they agreed, it was hard knowing they were out there.

"I had to keep reminding myself that we were doing this for Ethan," Elad explained. "We were fighting for Ethan to be equal to his brother and to any other US citizen. What we were fighting for was ours by right—no one was doing us a favor. We were fighting for him and for all other families that will never, ever—hopefully—have to go through this. If we were successful, it would be bigger than us." Despite this core belief, there were still times when Elad complained to Andrew that "enough is enough—I don't want to do any more media."[13]

Andrew and Elad argued a lot during that time, but as Elad observed, it was a test of their relationship as a couple and their role as parents. And he reminded himself that the situation "was bigger than us." Meanwhile, they had twin boys to raise.

RAISING TWINS

Raising twins is profoundly different from raising non-twins. Twins are part of a unique pregnancy in which two fetuses compete for prenatal space and nutrition, and they are more likely than non-twins to be born prematurely and with congenital difficulties.[14] In addition, twin infants, toddlers, and children experience many developmental milestones together, such as birthday parties, date of school entry, and first visit to a museum. Like non-twin siblings (who also share half their genes, on average), fraternal twins tend to differ in their abilities, tastes, and temperaments. But because they are matched in age, they are more closely compared by others and sometimes subjected to unkind remarks, especially as they enter kindergarten and beyond. Which twin is more attractive, more athletic, or more intelligent may be thoughtlessly pointed out by those around them. These situations pose challenging moments for parents who try hard to be fair and just.

Fortunately, local, national, and international multiple birth organizations offer educational resources and support services tailored to families with twins, triplets, and beyond. These organizations are located worldwide, and many nations set aside days—even weeks—to heighten multiple birth awareness.[15] Close association between researchers and families is encouraged to facilitate dissemination of information to parents and to identify problems needing further study. I have addressed gatherings of parents of multiple birth children in the United States, England, Canada, New Zealand, Australia, Israel, Japan, and Hong Kong. However, twin organizations cannot prepare parents for everything; sometimes it takes a grandmother.

In July 2019 the family flew to Israel to spend summer vacation with Elad's parents. The twins were two and a half years old and not yet toilet-trained—the ongoing lawsuit, the children's medical appointments, and other family matters conspired to delay this significant developmental achievement. "We didn't have the emotional capacity to invest in it," Elad confessed. When they arrived in Tel Aviv, the twins' grandmother, Tovi, was shocked to learn this was the case—Israeli youngsters are entitled to free prekindergarten classes, contingent upon being able to use the toilet. Tovi removed their diapers, and little toilets were placed in the backyard. "The boys would pee, then go over and explore," Elad recalled. This effort was only partly successful. When the family returned to Los Angeles in September, Ethan had mastered the technique, although he had occasional accidents for the next six months. Aiden had a harder time, transitioning from training diapers to night diapers before being trained by age four. "There were a lot of clothing changes," Elad remarked.

In September 2019 Andrew and Elad hosted two birthday parties—not for each boy separately, but for the different sets of Andrew's siblings that didn't always get along. These celebrations were held in the backyard of their home with pizza, cake, and other party foods. In retrospect, it was fitting to hold two parties that year, because in September 2020 (when the twins turned four), such gatherings were highly restricted or even prohibited due to the COVID-19 pandemic. Vaccines were not available for adults until December 2020 and not administered to children under age five until June 2022.[16]

UPROOTED (AGAIN), PLUS WORRIES OLD AND NEW

The worldwide spread of COVID-19 disrupted family and work routines everywhere. In March 2020, IKAR's preschool closed, and Andrew and Elad began working from home. Without their nanny, the two fathers became full-time caretakers as well as breadwinners, remaining within the confines of their home with their twins for the first few months of the lockdown. They also had their lawsuit to contend with, since Zoom sessions between lawyers and clients became efficient ways of moving events ahead. Andrew described this time as the "toughest period of his life," bumping down the aftermath of the consulate visit to second place.

With parks and playgrounds closed due to the pandemic, there was no place to take the children, who often got "out of control." One day, out of desperation, Andrew and Elad ripped away the yellow warning tape around the swings and seesaws at the local playground to give their children some fun. And on a hot May afternoon they relaxed on a closed beach.

It was about this time that they first noticed Aiden's unusual behaviors, possibly because they were with him on a more constant basis. Unlike Ethan, Aiden couldn't sit still in front of the television. He had trouble making eye contact and easing into conversations, developmentally atypical behaviors that were worsening with time. Observation and testing by his pediatrician in the spring of 2020 resulted in a diagnosis all parents fear—three-and-a-half-year-old Aiden had some form of developmental delay and attention-deficit/hyperactivity disorder (ADHD).[17] Fortunately, the diagnosis came with the assurance that with this early detection, followed by effective interventions, Aiden would soon be indistinguishable from any other child.

Medication to lessen his ADHD symptoms would be administered. They were also told that treating Aiden would need some work. Given the lingering stress from the lawsuit and the new stress imposed by the pandemic, Andrew's response was not unexpected. "I was like, literally, the only thing I needed you [the physician] to say was that it's not going to require work. But I had no choice; it was the most important thing." Andrew and Elad made certain that Aiden received all the help he needed.

Solutions to one situation can trigger trials of a different sort when twins are involved. Andrew and Elad not only had to care for their son with special needs but also had to be careful not to overlook the unaffected (or typical) twin, who can suffer, too.[18] As Andrew observed, "If we just had one child with special needs and that's what we knew, that would be like normal to us. But we're constantly comparing the twins, which isn't necessarily fair."

Andrew and Elad were initially reluctant to speak openly about Aiden's special needs for fear of attaching an indelible stigma to their son. And, as I indicated earlier, the couple disagreed somewhat over who in their family should be told, if at all. Ultimately, Andrew and Elad agreed to go on record, knowing their experience would help other parents with special-needs twins.

Andrew and Elad's new focus on Aiden meant forfeiting attention to Ethan. There were consequences; for example, Ethan wondered why the behavioral therapists who came to work with Aiden didn't work with him. And when his preschool reopened in August 2021, Aiden sometimes left the classroom early for therapy sessions, leaving Ethan perplexed over why he couldn't leave, too. His jealousy and resentment escalated—understandable, since despite his cleverness and competence, Ethan was still a little boy. And despite their brotherly bond, Ethan recognized a kind of competitive edge between them—what one has, the other must have, too. To get attention, Ethan sometimes mimicked Aiden's atypical behaviors, such as throwing tantrums, having figured out that these actions brought attention. "Is today the day you are coming to pick me up early?" Ethan asked constantly.

One of the twins' preschool teachers at IKAR was Maria Garcia. The twins were in her class from February to June 2019 at age two, and again in January 2020, when they were age three. But the pandemic two months later caused classes to be held virtually for the next three months, until the school ended those, as well. Some parents, including Andrew and Elad, opted for pod learning, in which a five-student group met with Ms. Garcia in a home offered by one of the families.

School did not reopen until August 2021. The children stayed in school from 8:00 a.m. until 3:00 p.m., followed by aftercare until 5:45 p.m. It was during 2020, before the pandemic shutdown, that Ms. Garcia had first noticed Ethan's difficulties. She believed his unusual behaviors—throwing toys, shouting out loud, telling his teachers to *sheket* ("be quiet" in Hebrew)—were linked to the extra attention his twin brother, Aiden, was receiving from his parents and therapists. In contrast, Ms. Garcia described Aiden as easygoing, content to play in the sandbox, digging for treasure.

The solution to Ethan's troubles was giving him opportunities to feel empowered. Ms. Garcia had him come inside to do "heavy work," such as helping her wipe the table, stacking the chairs, arranging the children's clothing. She also mentioned a plan to separate the twins one summer, explaining that Ethan "likes things to be a certain way" and would intervene if Aiden was doing things differently. However, Elad's upset at the idea of separating the twins prevented it from happening. Perhaps Elad, who now favors kindergarten separation, felt the twins were too young at the time and very closely bonded.

According to Ms. Garcia, Aiden verbally expressed his affection for his brother ("I love you, Ethan"), whereas Ethan acted in ways that showed protection and concern for his brother's whereabouts. It was not unusual for the twins to hug each other. Their teacher was also impressed with their behavioral differences, characteristic of fraternal twins. Aiden had excellent hand–eye coordination. He was adept at jumping, hopping, and climbing, and he was the first child in his group to scale the small dome stationed in his classroom.

Ethan preferred riding a bike. He was a leader, but one who walked away from situations that did not progress according to certain rules. He did not share Aiden's joy in collecting gems and sequins (Aiden loved the sparkling decorations on T-shirts worn by the girls in his class).

In fact, Aiden's passion for small treasures drew other children to him, curious to see what he had found. He didn't respond to their questions. Instead, he played by running when the other children started chasing after him, thinking it was a game.

Ethan did engage in conversations, but he could become verbally disruptive during "circle time," when the children gathered around their teacher for stories or other discussions. Again, Ms. Garcia attributed his defiance to the attention Aiden was getting—he was a little boy who simply didn't understand. Another teacher suggested that the family hire a therapist for Ethan, to even things out, but that didn't happen.[19]

Whenever possible, Elad took Ethan out for special walks during Aiden's therapy sessions. Ethan's negative behaviors began to subside, and Aiden continued to improve; nevertheless, familiar challenges and chronic concerns continued to surface.[20]

SAME OR SEPARATE WAYS

One of the most common twin-related questions is this: Are same or separate classrooms better for twins? Every fall I receive numerous inquiries from parents of young multiples, most of whom wish to keep their children together but face unsympathetic administrators who support mandatory school separation policies. These policies are usually based on the (unfounded) belief that twins will not establish their own identities if they remain together.[21]

In September 2020, Aiden and Elad returned to their preschool program at IKAR (albeit for reduced hours), while their parents worked from home. The school had been made aware of Aiden's diagnosis and was fully supportive. However, a decision regarding the twins' attendance was soon made for them that had nothing to do with parental wishes or school practices.

The twins had been back at school for three weeks when Andrew and Elad were informed that Aiden could not stay. His behaviors were disruptive, and he would not wear his mask. "It was such a blow," Andrew recalled. So, for the rest of the school year, a therapist spent four hours a day with Aiden at home, while Ethan continued going to school. Because Elad and Andrew were still working at home, one of them would drive Ethan to class and return later to pick him up. What had promised to be a somewhat normal routine was derailed. "It was a very, very, very difficult year," Andrew reiterated.

There was more.

A favorable ruling by the circuit court was brought on appeal to the Supreme Court by US Secretary of State Mike Pompeo. The death of liberal Supreme Court justice Ruth Bader Ginsburg on September 18, 2020 (two days after the twins turned four), also meant that Andrew and Elad had the rest of 2020 to be nervous. The presidential election was two months away. If then president Donald Trump was reelected, a Trump-appointed justice might not be favorable toward their case were it to be decided by the Supreme Court.

When I spoke to Andrew and Elad in December 2021, Aiden and Ethan were five years old. Their birthday party that year had been held at home because the pandemic still limited the range of available options. In September, the twins had relocated to the public school just down the block from their home and were assigned to the same transitional-kindergarten (TK) class. In the California school system, TK is designed for children who were born in September (like Aiden and Ethan), or later in the year, and miss the cutoff for regular kindergarten. Keeping the twins together worked out well because they enjoyed assurance and support from one another as they entered their new school. According to Elad, some children had a difficult time when they first arrived because they were alone. "We were lucky in that way," Andrew observed.

Earlier, I referenced a digital diary that Andrew and Elad were keeping for their boys to read when they were old enough. They wanted Aiden and Ethan to understand the citizenship struggles their parents had gone through, and to let the twins know what they were like as young children growing up. Here is what Elad wrote on their sons' first day of school:

> My boys—
> Today was such a special day; you started TK in big kids' school. Daddy and I [Abba—Hebrew word for Dad or Daddy] are so proud of you, and know you will learn so many wonderful things and grow to become good and compassionate human beings. Remember that there is nothing you cannot do and that we will always be behind you! The two of you were such cuties with your huge backpacks. We love you!

Aiden was also making great progress, largely due to the wonderful resources his new school provided. However, in April 2022 his therapist resigned, so they were waiting for a replacement. Despite the turnover, another therapist was eventually assigned. And as of 2023, Aiden's reading skills have been exceptional.

Transitional kindergarten lasted from 8:30 a.m. until 12:00 p.m., after which the twins attended an aftercare program until 5:30 p.m., when their parents picked them up. The program accommodates two groups of children, allowing Aiden and Ethan to be apart from time to time. Elad's views on separation had changed—he believes it's "great for them to be split up [occasionally] because they are closely attached to each other. They're together all the time, every day, and this gives them an opportunity to develop their own personality."

Twins' school placement is a complex matter. Despite their favorable TK experience, Andrew and Elad decided to place the twins in separate kindergarten classes in the fall of 2022. They reasoned that Ethan is the "alpha twin," whereas Aiden follows behind and depends on his brother in social situations. They worry that Ethan's frequent attention to Aiden might limit his own developmental freedoms.

There are benefits and downsides to separating twins in school, a topic that parents and researchers take seriously. Benefits include the fact that twins can gain confidence by developing talents, interests, and friendships apart from their brother or sister. Downsides include the possibility that one twin may be less ready to separate, have a less welcoming teacher, and/or miss friendships forged the previous year. And because twins may develop separate friendships, only one is likely to be invited to birthday parties from time to time. Andrew and Elad realized they had not considered this last prospect.

Over the course of our conversation, Elad (but not Andrew) admitted that a part of him would prefer keeping the boys together because of the care they give to one another. He thinks of Ethan as Aiden's "guardian." Teachers have told them that when Aiden plays alone, Ethan takes him by the hand and says, "Come, Aiden, and play with us." When they are separated, Aiden will not have this support except during lunch periods and recess. The preschool teachers at IKAR also told the couple that Ethan eventually thrived during the few months when Aiden was at home and Ethan was at school. It seems Ethan didn't feel the same sense of responsibility toward his brother as he had before and was completely free to do what he pleased; in fact, he was performing better without Aiden present.

As I suspected, Elad's hesitancy regarding school separation—especially for Aiden—dates back to the time when his parents removed him from a school he loved and placed him in one he loathed. "I don't want something like this to happen to the kids," he said. Elad thinks the boys may have a few hard days at first, but overall, both parents are confident that they have made the right choice and that the twins understand and accept the decision. They are optimistic about the outcome, since the students, teachers, and school are familiar to their sons. Teachers have also told them that parents suffer more on the first day of school than their children do; most students adapt quickly to their new environment.

I do not favor mandatory school separation polices for twins because every pair is different. Twin type (identical, fraternal same-sex, fraternal opposite-sex) may factor into the decision, because, in general, identical twins have closer social relationships with one another and are more academically matched than fraternal twins, so they are more likely to want to stay together. The situation is different for opposite-sex twins—young females typically develop physically, socially, and cognitively ahead of young males, possibly justifying the separation of these twins. However, research findings provide approximate guidelines, not inflexible rules. I also believe strongly that school placement decisions should be made jointly by parents and teachers who can agree to monitor each pair's situation and make changes if needed.[22]

I often advise parents and teachers that a successful compromise may involve keeping twins in the same class while assigning them to different tables or play groups. Some twins just need to know where their twin is in order to feel content and secure. Elad observed that when Aiden and Ethan play separately, they sometimes turn around to make sure their brother is in sight, "and then they are at ease." (As he was saying this, Ethan entered the living room and asked Andrew where Aiden was.)

In July and August of 2022, the boys attended summer day camp together. They also took several weeks of intensive swimming instruction, since their parents felt they were not progressing with weekly lessons alone. These arrangements give camp counselors and coaches opportunities to notice the special words and gestures that children express away from home. The affection Aiden and Ethan showed toward one another was observed. Parents may see such behaviors less often because of their crowded work schedules and because children are tired at the end of the day—but there are exceptions.

A MOMENT IN TIME

"There are so many crazy, difficult moments being a parent of twins that it's hard to really find those happy moments when your heart just melts. And this morning I had that."

—Andrew Dvash-Banks, December 4, 2020

The first time I spoke to Andrew at length was in November 2020. Their lawsuit had not completely settled, so our conversation was somewhat guarded, but the government's opportunity to lodge an appeal was closing. Andrew was in his car, a place he seems to associate with peace and quiet. On this day, Andrew had just taken his boys to school and would not see them again for several hours.

We discussed the main themes I wanted to cover in this book. Andrew said, "And while it's not a theme, but an emotion—parents will do whatever they can to protect a child." He and Elad expressed these ideas often and in different ways throughout our interviews. I suspected they were still getting used to the idea that they could finally raise their children without fear. This luxury allowed them a chance to enjoy certain moments in time, including the heart-melting experience Andrew referenced above:

They have separate beds . . . for some reason last night, Aiden just really wanted to cuddle with Ethan in his bed. He's never done that before on his own. And then in the middle of the night, Elad moved Aiden back to his own bed. But when I came in this morning, they were both awake, both in Ethan's bed, cuddling. And Aiden said, "Ethan, you're my best friend. I want to sleep in your bed forever."

"WE ARE SO BORING"

Andrew and Elad believe there is nothing unusual about their family, "a point they would love to get across."[23] Like most parents of young children, they take Aiden and Ethan to Disneyland on some weekend days and often watch Netflix movies with them at night. Since the fall of 2021, the twins have been taking Hebrew classes on Saturdays, swimming lessons on Sundays, and karate lessons during the week. Like other young boys, Aiden and Ethan go on play dates, ride their bikes, walk their dog, and play in the park. Elad packs their lunches, and one or both parents walk them to school each morning, pick them up each afternoon, and bring them to medical appointments when scheduled. Andrew and Elad enjoy an occasional night out on their own, as do all couples, but most of their time is spent with their twins.

At the time of this writing, the two parents and two children were in Israel for a two-week visit with Elad's parents, to be followed by a Mediterranean cruise. And like other parents, Andrew and Elad were thinking about how the twins would celebrate their sixth birthday, on September 16, 2022. Elad suggested that they may have a "Kids' Reptile Party," where the children learn fun facts about dinosaurs and tortoises. As the birthday boys, Aiden and Ethan would be zookeepers for the day.[24]

"The only feature that makes us unique is that we're two gay men. Other than that, we're just like everybody else," they observed.

Their perspective should be taken seriously, because the frequency of same-sex male couples having children is rising. Moreover, while the prevalence of marriage in the general population is declining, it is rising among the LGBTQ community.[25] Such couples still face discrimination, especially in states with fewer legal protections. Same-sex parents have experienced mistreatment in restaurants, religious institutions, neighborhoods—and US consulates. But like other parents, same-sex parents remain actively engaged in raising their children. And despite the stigma that some children of gay parents feel, their well-being is consistent with that of children in representative samples.[26] Children of gay and heterosexual couples do not differ in educational outcomes, such as school grades and school trouble. Other research has shown that the children of gay couples tend to be more resilient, compassionate, and tolerant than children from traditional nuclear families but may experience more social-interactional difficulties.[27]

I expect that the problems facing same-sex couples and their children will lessen with time as people gain greater understanding and acceptance of the many ways of becoming a family. Recall that the advent of in vitro fertilization (IVF) in Great Britain in 1978 and its introduction in the United States in 1981 were met with mixed reactions.[28] Some people feared that IVF meant the demise of what it means to be a mother or a father and that sons and daughters conceived in this way were "illegitimate." However, IVF has delivered millions of babies to childless couples, bringing joy, pride, and satisfaction into their homes.

Today IVF is a routine reproductive procedure performed in clinics worldwide. However, its full potential was unimaginable years ago. Developed to assist conception when heterosexual partners could not conceive naturally, it has segued into a viable option for same-sex couples who cannot conceive collectively. Aiden and Ethan are the delightful outcomes of the choices made by their parents. However, with the lawsuit looming, it was hard for them to fully enjoy parenting their twins as they had wished.

Understanding their emotional discord, interspersed with moments of hope and promise, requires a look at the judicial proceedings—the cycle of court decisions and State Department appeals.

• 8 •

Menacing Landscape and Hopeful Terrain: Lawsuits, Negotiations, Appeals, and Resolution

Andrew and Elad's lives were embedded in fear and uncertainty from January 2017 until May 2020. Their only hope rested on the efforts and dedication of attorneys from Immigration Equality and Sullivan & Cromwell. Their first lawsuit was filed on January 22, 2018—nearly one year after their January 24, 2017, visit to the US consulate in Toronto to obtain passports for their twins. Over the years their case alternated among oral arguments, judgments, negotiations, appeals, and extensions; still, Andrew and Elad clearly recall the key events that shaped the victories and disappointments they experienced along the way. Attorneys who were not directly associated with the case offered analyses and insights on the significance and promise of the case and the final decision. Organizations protecting the rights of same-sex couples and their families issued statements supporting the cause for which Andrew and Elad had been fighting.

ALLEGATIONS AND COMPLAINTS

At the heart of the Dvash-Banks lawsuit was the legality of recognizing Ethan as a US citizen from birth. The documents filed on his behalf state his case in legal terms that are important to understand.[1] They fall under the categories of factual allegations and counts.

Factual Allegations

A factual allegation is a statement of truthful matter. However, it stays as an assertion until proven true.[2] There were several factual allegations in the Dvash-Banks case:

a. The Dvash-Banks family (background)
b. The application of the State Department's policy to the Dvash-Banks family
c. The State Department erroneously deemed E. J. (Ethan Jacob) to have been born "out of wedlock."
d. The State Department's policy unconstitutionally discriminates on the basis of sex and sexual orientation.

Counts

A count is the basis for which someone can be held liable or guilty in court.[3] There were several counts in the Dvash-Banks case:

Count I. The State Department's policy violates the due process guarantee of the Fifth Amendment.
Count II. The State Department's policy violates the constitutional guarantee of equal protection under the law.
Count III. Administrative Procedure Act [stating that the plaintiffs suffered a legal wrong because of agency action, and continue to suffer because of it][4]
Count IV. Declaration that E. J. D.-B. [Ethan Jacob Dvash-Banks] is a US citizen.

LEGAL PROCEEDINGS: TIMELINE

I have provided a timeline, given to me by Andrew and Elad, that reflects the couple's most significant moments during their legal proceedings (see table 1).[5] While hundreds of documents were drafted and many decisions were rendered between 2018 and 2020, it is meaningful to track the progress of the case through the sensibilities of the individuals most directly affected. A complete chronology of what transpired among the plaintiffs, defendants, attorneys, judges, and courts is publicly available.[6]

The plaintiffs in the case were Andrew and Ethan, because the complaints were that 1) Andrew was not recognized as Ethan's father and 2) Ethan was denied US citizenship at birth. However, Elad was appointed as Ethan's spokesperson, given that Ethan was under eighteen years of age and needed his own advocate. Elad never exercised this role, since the case did not go to trial. (The family's attorneys filed a complaint; had discovery, in which interrogatories were issued and depositions were taken; appeared before the judge; and engaged in motion practice. However, witnesses were not called, nor were testimonies taken before the judge.) The defendants were the US State Department and Secretary of State Rex Tillerson, until Tillerson was replaced by Mike Pompeo several months later.

Table 1

---

1. The original lawsuit was filed on January 22, 2018, by Immigration Equality and Sullivan & Cromwell, on behalf of Andrew Mason Dvash-Banks and Ethan Jacob Dvash-Banks (plaintiffs). (Their nine attorneys from Immigration Equality and Sullivan & Cromwell are named in chapter 6.) The complaint was directed against the US Department of State and the Honorable Rex W. Tillerson, Secretary of State (defendants). Counsel for the defendants included Vinita Andrapalliyal, Anthony J. Coppolino, Joseph Hunt (District of Columbia), and Lisa Zeidner Marcus (Pennsylvania).

2. The case was assigned on January 24, 2018, to District Judge John F. Walter and Magistrate Judge Jacqueline Chooljian, from the Central District of California.

3. In spring 2018, the State Department, under Secretary of State Tillerson, entertained the idea of negotiating directly with the family. This was done without the explicit acknowledgment that they had been in the wrong. The attorneys at Sullivan & Cromwell favored this idea; Immigration Equality was concerned about the other families they were representing but agreed to go along with what Andrew and Elad wanted.

4. On April 26, 2018, Mike Pompeo replaced Rex Tillerson as US secretary of state. Direct negotiation with the family was no longer possible, given this transition.

5. Lawyers representing the plaintiffs and defendants requested a series of deadline extensions to accommodate their requirements. These negotiations persisted through July of 2018 and beyond.

6. On August 21, 2018, an attempt at private mediation between the parties was dismissed by Judge Walter.

7. The State Department tried to have the case dismissed in August 2018, but this request was denied on November 27, 2018.

To stay consistent with the unfolding of events, I have placed a break in the timeline for the insertion of deposition excerpts—Andrew's and consular officer Terri Day's responses to questions posed by attorneys from the other side. Both individuals were deposed (questioned by an attorney from the opposing side) in January 2019. The order of questioning has been preserved, although some questions and answers have not been provided or provided in full, partly due to repeated responses. I have not seen the complete transcripts of these depositions, which are unavailable for public review. The timeline is completed following the deposition excerpts.

DEPOSITION EXCERPTS: TERRI DAY

According to one of the Dvash-Banks's lawyers, Alexa Lawson-Remer, Terri Day (TD) was most likely questioned by a junior attorney from Sullivan & Cromwell (ATTY-SC). Day's supervisor, Maggie Ramsay, was not deposed because the information needed by the plaintiffs' lawyers was provided by Terri Day, and the legal documents "spoke for themselves." (The excerpts are reprinted as they appeared in the legal documents, so they may not always be grammatically correct.)[7]

ATTY-SC: And I think before you referred to, there's a checklist you go through. Is that a metaphorical checklist, or is that a physical checklist?

TD: That is a metaphorical checklist. We know, based on the *FAM* [*Foreign Affairs Manual*], what documents are required, what things we need to know about the parent[s] and about the parents' relationship with the child.

ATTY-SC: Did you ever consult any other documents or guidance of any kind during the course of your adjudication of US passport and CRBA [Consular Report of Birth Abroad] applications?

TD: I would say no.

ATTY-SC: Did you ever consult the *FAM*?

TD: Yes.

ATTY-SC: Was there anything else you ever consulted?

TD: I can't—I can't say with 100 percent certainty. I don't remember specifically, but in my experience, the *FAM* is the—is the guideline that is followed. If there are any changes and they are communicated to us through our managers, be it NIV [non-immigrant visa], IV [immigrant visa], or ACS [American Citizenship Services].

ATTY-SC: And when you talk about whether you had a question as to the biological tie, was that a subjective determination that you made during the course of the interview, for example?

TD: I would say no, because the—from my understanding, the biological connection is required to transmit the citizenship. So if—you know, someone—so that's not really—you can't really argue that point to say, well, maybe—you know, kind of make a judgment call. I think it's very clear what this—what the guidelines are. So I would say that if the parent indicated to me that—which is normally, like I said, how that would go about. If the parent indicated to me that they had used assisted reproductive technology, then we would go down that line of questioning, if I thought that—if I saw that this was something that had, you know, had happened.

ATTY-SC: And what was your role?

TD: I was the adjudicating officer. So I took in the—I—after the local staff took in the documents, I reviewed them, and I certified copies. I gave an oath to the parents and had them sign the documents. I interviewed them, and then I was ultimately responsible for approving or denying those applications.

ATTY-SC: *Was anyone else involved in that adjudication? And we'll start with E. J. [Ethan Jacob].* [Note: Italics added throughout for emphasis.]

TD: *Can I just say for both of them—*

ATTY-SC: *Sure.*

TD: *Because they were—they were treated as—I mean, all the information that's true for one—in the initial interview phase, as far as I knew, it would have been true for the other.* So no one was—I mean, I consulted with my manager about the case, and she brought in Maggie Ramsay as well. But during the—and during the interview, at a certain point, Maggie Ramsay did speak to the family. So in that way, people were involved, but the ultimate decision was mine.

ATTY-SC: And then what would happen next? What happened next?

TD: . . . If I have any questions about that, I would ask at that time. And then we—and then that's when we would get into, okay, how they were conceived, who—you know, who's biologically related to whom, and then—and on through.

ATTY-SC: Do you remember anything that Andrew and Elad said to you that made you feel like they thought they were being attacked?

TD: I do remember them—especially Andrew—saying, you know, these are our children . . . I mean, they were feeling that they were, you know, being attacked. And it was directed at me, you know, no doubt, not—not necessarily at the *FAM.*

ATTY-SC: Did you consider this document [Ontario court document] to be adequate proof that Andrew and Elad Dvash-Banks were E. J.'s parents?

MS. MARCUS: Objection. Vague as to the term "parents."

MS. GOLDSMITH: You can answer.

TD: I need clarification on the term "parents."

ATTY-SC: Did you consider this document to be adequate proof that Andrew and Elad Dvash-Banks are E. J.'s legal parents?

TD: I would say yes.

ATTY-SC: And have you seen this document before?

TD: I have, yes.

ATTY-SC: And did you consider this document [marriage certificate from the Ontario government] to be sufficient proof that Andrew and Elad were married at the time of E. J.'s birth?

TD: Yes.

ATTY-SC: What is the basis for your opinion that it would not have made a difference whether you had adjudicated E. J.'s application under Section 301 versus 309? [Sections 301 and 309 of the *Foreign Affairs Manual* refer to the citizenship of children born abroad and to children born out of wedlock.]

TD: Because both require the biological link—both require the biological connection.

ATTY-SC: And is your understanding that the basis for that requirement is a provision in the *FAM*?

TD: Yes.

If I could ask Terri Day a question, I would refer her to the italicized portion of her eighth response to the questioning and ask: How was it possible to consider Ethan and Aiden collectively in the initial interview—TD: *Can I just say for both of them*— ATTY-SC: *Sure.* TD: *Because they were—they were treated as—I mean, all the information that's true for one—in the initial interview phase, as far as I knew, it would have been true for the other*—and not during the later phases?

DEPOSITION EXCERPTS: ANDREW DVASH-BANKS

Andrew Dvash-Banks (AD-B) was deposed by trial attorney Lisa Zeidner Marcus (LZM), who has served in the Department of Justice (Civil Division, Federal Programs Branch) since October 2007. She had served most of her career under President Obama, who was in office from 2009 to 2017. Andrew recalled, "She seemed very emotional during the deposition. Frankly, I wanted to reach out and hug her, but couldn't—my lawyer [Alexa Lawson-Remer] was seated next to me. Alexa stressed that this was serious business; it was a deposition, and we're fighting for your son."

Lawyers prepare their clients for depositions to be certain that what they say will help their case. Both Alexa Lawson-Remer and Theodore Edelman worked with Andrew in this regard. Andrew admitted that his lawyers would have been more at ease if Elad had been the one to be questioned by the State Department's attorneys. "I am very loose with my words. I don't think before I speak, and they knew that." Andrew also commented on Secretary Tillerson's 2018 offer to address the matter somewhat more directly with the family; Andrew called it a "white glove experience."[8] However, as I indicated, Andrew and Elad were concerned about the potential implications for the other three families that Immigration Equality was representing, so they did not seriously consider this possibility; then Pompeo replaced Tillerson, and the offer was no longer possible. Andrew reflected, "I got the impression that the Tillerson State Department was not nearly as homophobic as the Pompeo State Department."

LZM: And you—do you currently live with your husband and your children?

AD-B: I do, yes.

LZM: Do you live with anybody else?

AD-B: No.

LZM: Since the four of you have become a family unit, have you lived with anybody else . . . for a month or longer?

AD-B: For a month or longer? Yes, we have.

LZM: Was it one of your parents?

AD-B: Yes.

LZM: Other than that, was there anybody else that you've lived with as a family?

AD-B: No.

LZM: And what was your understanding [from the fertility clinic] at the time?

AD-B: From the information that was provided to me from the fertility clinic, I understood that one of the embryos had my genetic material.

LZM: And what was your understanding with respect to the other embryo?

AD-B: It did not have my genetic material.

LZM: Did it have your husband's genetic material?

AD-B: Yes.

LZM: Do you have any under—do you know the result of this court order?

AD-B: Yes.

LZM: What was the result?

AD-B: The result was affirming Elad and myself's parentage to our twin boys.

LZM: And what was the next thing to happen during the appointment?

AD-B: You mean after that prolonged period of waiting?

LZM: Yes.

AD-B: We were called up to the window.

LZM: And was it a different window from the first window that you were called up to?

AD-B: Yes.

LZM: And there was an individual on the other side of the window?

AD-B: Yes.

LZM: Do you know the position that that individual held?

AD-B: Do I know now? I know—I know now what that person's position was at the time. . . . From my understanding, the person's position was vice consul.

LZM: What other questions do you remember?

AD-B: There were several. Obviously, one really sticks out to me, just because it was a really emotionally charged question. When she asked, Are your children genetically connected—she asked me, Andrew, are your children both genetically connected to you?

LZM: And can you describe how you would display those emotions to the consular officer, please.

AD-B: It's not every day that you walk into your home country's consulate to be told that you're essentially not the parent of your child even though you've produced a birth certificate showing that, even though you've cut his umbilical cord, even though you have, you know, fed him and stayed up all night for what was that? Like, four months at that point for him, even though that you spent seven months—unfortunately, it was seven months; I wish it was longer—but seven months in utero—at every single appointment to have a representative of your country tell you that you're not his parent or question that parentage. So I guess to answer your question, like, my emotions and my husband's emotions were derived from that.

LZM: From your perspective, generally speaking, what are your claims against the Department of State?

AD-B: From my perspective, my claim against the Department of State is that my son E. J. was refused United States citizenship by the US State Department. And my claim is that—that we were wrong[ed] and treated unfairly, and that's an unfair—how do I say this? And—and that he was refused American citizenship because he's considered a child born out of wedlock. And his twin brother born four minutes before him was granted American citizenship.

I wondered if Andrew and his lawyers were aware of several twin-related cases in which twins were delivered in different countries, and what the implications might be for his own situation. I know of two such cases and some other curious and relevant twin-related events that I will describe later in this chapter.

The timeline (table 1) continues below:

Table 1 *(continued)*

8. On February 21, 2019, Judge John F. Walter released his judgment that an in-person trial was not required. His partial summary judgment favored the Dvash-Banks family: Ethan was declared a US citizen. (A *partial summary judgment* means that a trial court disposes of one or more issues in a case when there is no disagreement over the material facts. A party is entitled to judgment as a matter of law.)[1]
9. On April 19, 2019, Ethan's US passport was issued and forwarded to his parents from the State Department.[2] The State Department was given forty-five days to do this once the judge had ruled in Ethan's favor. They were given sixty days to appeal the judge's decision.
10. On May 6, 2019, the State Department appealed their loss to the Ninth Circuit Court of Appeals.[3] The appeal was filed on the fifty-ninth day.
11. During the summer of 2019, the State Department requested extensions of the required timelines.
12. During the summer of 2020 (after the Dvash-Banks case had been decided in favor of the family by a federal appeals court but was possibly subject to further review; see item 16 below), two of the previously described cases similar to that of *Dvash-Banks* were successfully litigated at the district court level by Immigration Equality and legal associates: the Kiviti family (daughter Kessem was declared a US citizen on June 17—the decision was finalized on October 26, when the US State Department withdrew its appeal) and the Mize-Gregg family (daughter Simone was declared a US citizen on August 20—the decision was finalized on October 26 once the deadline for an appeal by the US State Department had passed).[4]

13. Oral arguments were scheduled for October 7, 2020, but were canceled once a three-judge panel ruled again in favor of the Dvash-Banks family, recognizing that Ethan was a US citizen from birth. The official ruling by the US Court of Appeals for the Ninth Circuit Court, released on October 9, upheld a ruling by the lower court. "Both courts found that the State Department had wrongly interpreted the Immigration and Nationality Act (INA). Further, the Ninth Circuit noted that the State Department's interpretation of the INA was foreclosed by settled Circuit case law, which reiterated that the section of the law applying to married couples, 'does not require a biological relationship between a child and the citizen parent through whom citizenship is claimed.'"[5]

14. In extraordinary circumstances—for unsettled issues of the law, or if the court has concerns about a decision made by a particular panel—either party can petition the whole court to review a case; this is called an *en banc* review.[6] The US State Department petitioned to file for *en banc* review following their loss; however, the Ninth Circuit Court denied this petition on January 15, 2021. The request for an *en banc* review, which would have involved a large number of judges from the Ninth Court, was denied.

15. *Note:* The three judges from the Ninth Court who were randomly chosen to render a decision regarding holding an *en banc* review by the Ninth Circuit Court were Daniel E. Bress (appointed by former president Donald Trump), Andrew D. Hurwitz (appointed by former president Barack Obama), and Andrew J. Kleinfeld (appointed by former president George H. W. Bush). The only judge who voted to approve the request was Judge Kleinfeld.

16. On April 27, 2021, Alexa M. Lawson-Remer filed a Joint Status Report: *Andrew Mason Dvash-Banks et al.* (Plaintiffs) v. *Anthony J. Blinken, Secretary of State* (Defendants). The parties agreed in principle to settle the plaintiffs' requests for expenses if the US State Department decided against further review of the case.

17. June 14, 2021, was the deadline for the Justice Department (based on a request from the State Department) to ask the Supreme Court to review the case, but the Justice Department declined. The Biden administration, which came into office on January 20, 2021, decided not to pursue the matter further. The policy was changed in the *Foreign Affairs Manual*, as indicated above.

Notes

1. "Partial Summary Judgment: Definition." https://www.quimbee.com/keyterms/partial-summary-judgment, 2022. Andrew and Elad's claim that the consular officers had violated the Administrative Procedure Act that governs the process by which federal agencies develop and issue regulations was decided in favor of the US State Department. US Environmental Protection Agency, "Summary of the Administrative Procedure Act," https://www.epa.gov/laws-regulations/summary-administrative-procedure-act; "United States District Court: Civil Minutes—General," *Case 2:18-cv-00523-JFW-JC, Document 123,* February 21, 2019.
2. "US District Court: Civil Minutes—General," February 21, 2019.
3. "Notice of Appeal," *Case 2:18-cv-00523-JFW-JC, Document 133,* May 6, 2019.
4. Immigration Equality, "Kiviti Family," https://immigrationequality.org/adiel-roee-and-kessem-kiviti/, 2022; Immigration Equality, "Mize-Gregg Family," https://immigrationequality.org/derek-jonathan-and-simone-mize-gregg/, 2022. The Zaccari-Blixt case, filed at the same time as the Dvash-Banks case, settled in favor of the family on May 18, 2021. Michael K. Lavers, "US to

(continued)

Table 1 *(continued)*

Recognize Citizenship of Married Couples' Children Born Abroad," *Washington Blade*, https://www.washingtonblade.com/2021/05/18/us-to-recognize-citizenship-of-married-couples-children-born-abroad/, May 18, 2021.

5. Immigration Equality (Press Release), "Appellate Court Upholds Previous Ruling that Twin Son of Gay Married Couple Born Abroad Is U.S. Citizen from Birth," file:///Users/csuftitan/Desktop/Nancy's%20Work/Book%20NEXT/Immigration/Appellate%20Court%20Upholds%20Previous%20Ruling%20That%20Twin%20Son%20of%20Gay%20Married%20Couple%20Born%20Abroad%20is%20U.S.%20Citizen%20from%20Birth%20-%20Immigration%20Equality%20_%20Immigration%20Equality.html, October 9, 2021; "Memorandum." D.C. No. 2:18-cv-00523-JFW-JC (*Case 19-5551*), https://immigrationequality.org/wp-content/uploads/2020/10/DVASH-BANKS-Ethan-ninth-cir-order-10.09.2020.pdf, October 9, 2020.

6. Aaron C. Morris, the lead attorney for Immigration Equality, explained that circuit courts have three-judge panels that review a decision of a lower court below. In extraordinary circumstances—for unsettled issues of law, or if the court has concerns about a decision made by one panel—either party can petition the whole court to review a case; this is an *en banc* review. All judges of the Ninth Circuit Court can review the decision of the three-judge panel—and there are many judges in circuit court. The Justice Department under former president Donald Trump took the extraordinary measure of asking them to do this after they had lost; however, the court declined to do so. Aaron C. Morris, interview with Nancy L. Segal, 2022.

Of course, the happiest day was June 14, 2021—the day that Andrew and Elad received an e-mail message from the Sullivan & Cromwell attorneys with the good news that the case was closed—forever. Congratulations from Immigration Equality followed, with a note that they were hearing from "happy couples" who no longer had to consider suing the State Department.

The welcome outcome does not lessen the challenge and uncertainty of the legal process Andrew and Elad and their family went through. Their case raises many important issues in search of solutions.

CONCEIVED TOGETHER, BORN APART

In 2012, I was a consultant for *Guinness World Records* (*GWR*), given the task of providing new and updated records for a section on twins to be published in the 2016 volume. During my research, I discovered that on July 1, 2012, Donna Keenan of Northumberland (a county in northern England) went into early labor. Her first twin, a boy named Dylan Joseph, was delivered on the living room floor of her home, but her second twin was not ready to be born. Because the birth of her second twin was imminent, Donna was rushed to Borders General Hospital, in Melrose, Scotland, located forty-five miles from her home. Dylan's twin sister, Hannah Rose, arrived about ninety minutes later. This unusual case was announced in *GWR* as the first case of twins born in different countries.[9]

Then a new pair suddenly stepped forward to claim this title.[10] Carol Roberts of Wales, mother of identical twins, Heidi Gannon and Jo Baines, had a similar experience nearly forty years earlier. Unaware that she was carrying twins, Carol delivered Heidi on September 23, 1976, at the Welshpool Hospital in Wales. By the time her multiple pregnancy was recognized, there were possible complications, so Carol was immediately transported to Copthorne Hospital in Shrewsbury, England. She gave birth to her second twin, Jo, two hours later. Heidi teases her sister, calling her the "English twin," but Jo regards her birth in England as a minor detail and considers herself to be Welsh. She indicates her English birth only when biographical information is requested on official forms. According to the twins, Jo, as a resident of Wales, has never had problems with anything official. Both her undergraduate and graduate degrees were completed in Wales without difficulties.[11]

The twins in both "binational" pairs are citizens of the United Kingdom and carry passports identifying them as such. The UK does not make citizenship distinctions among individuals born in England, Scotland, Wales, or Northern Ireland. Consequently, Dylan and Hannah, and Heidi and Jo, received identical passports despite being born in different countries. In contrast, Aiden and Ethan—who were born in the same country (Canada) and had the same legal parents—were denied equal citizenship rights. The situations are not strictly parallel given the structure of the UK, but it is worth noting that the same passport was awarded to people born in different nations.

Moreover, the twins Hannah and Jo, who were both born "abroad," enjoy the same voting privileges as their co-twins. Voting in UK parliamentary elections is based on residency in England, Scotland, Wales, or Northern Ireland. Local elections in these four countries have certain age, residency, and registration requirements which all four twins easily meet. Hannah and Jo could also run for elected office, although Heidi assured me that Jo has no such intention.[12] However, Ethan would have been required to complete an official process to obtain the same citizenship status, voting rights, and electoral eligibility as his twin brother, Aiden. Recall that the twins' Israeli grandmother, Tovi, impressed with Ethan's abilities, thought he might become a US president someday.[13] Any route to Ethan's citizenship except the one pursued by his parents would not have allowed this.

ADOPTED FROM AWAY . . .

Since 1998 I have been tracking the behavioral development of Chinese twins raised apart, due indirectly to China's One-Child Policy (1979–2015).[14] This practice restricted urban families to one child and rural families to two. Because of this policy, and because of China's preference for male children, thousands of baby girls were abandoned. Among the abandoned infants were twins who, for unknown reasons, became separated at birth and adopted by different families, many in the United States.

Writing about the Dvash-Banks case made me wonder if, and how, American children born abroad acquire the citizenship of their adoptive parents. Children must be legally adopted when they are younger than age eighteen (as of February 27, 2001) and in the legal and physical custody of their new parents for at least two years. These children automatically acquire US citizenship if at least one parent is a US citizen who has resided in the United States for at least five years (two years prior to age fourteen), if the children are under age eighteen, and if they have been lawfully admitted to the United States as a permanent resident of their US citizen parent. Children under age eighteen on February 27, 2001 (i.e., born on or after February 28, 1983), may automatically acquire US citizenship from their US citizen parent(s) if they have satisfied the statute's requirement before their eighteenth birthday.[15]

The current process seems simple. However, some families in my study who adopted children from China tell a different story. According to one family in Colorado, "We left China with a final adoption but went ahead and also finalized it here; then, using the adoption certificate, we filed for US citizenship. We went to court in Denver for the final decree. Citizenship has to be applied for and is not automatic." A family that adopted twins from Vietnam wrote, "I was unaware that fourteen years after adopting the girls they did not have full citizenship. I had to complete a significant amount of paperwork and pay a substantial amount of money to complete the process."[16]

If Andrew had agreed to adopt Ethan, his son's pathway to US citizenship would have avoided the emotional tumult that the legal proceedings imposed. In fact, an attorney the family had consulted early on had proposed adoption as a possible option. But recall that *both Andrew and Elad were equally recognized as the legal parents of both twins, as confirmed* *by official Canadian document*s processed by attorney Michelle Flowerday. Most importantly, adopting Ethan would have neglected to correct the US State Department's misapplication of the law in ways that treated the couple unfairly, setting a potentially dangerous precedent for comparable cases in the future. Andrew and Elad's belief and persistence in doing what was right for themselves and for other families would not allow that.

SATURDAY, OCTOBER 10, 2020

March of 2020 was the beginning of mandatory lockdowns of public places due to the COVID-19 pandemic. Consequently, my office at California State University, Fullerton, was unavailable to me for months, although access was later allowed upon approval of a formal request to the dean of my division. I began spending weekends at my boyfriend's home in Yorba Linda, California, where I had the use of a quiet study to work.

On the morning of October 10, 2020, while reading the *Orange County Register* over breakfast, I was immediately overjoyed to see the page 13 headline: "Court: Son Born Abroad to Gay Couple is a U.S. Citizen." The article summarized the decision Andrew and Elad had hoped for: The circuit court had upheld the lower court's ruling, recognizing Ethan as a US citizen (see table 1, timeline, item 13). Aaron C. Morris, the lead Immigration Equality attorney, told the newspaper that "the Justice Department conceded in its appeal that it would lose if the court applied the law in the Dvash-Banks case. 'This seems to be an issue they're not willing to budge on. Every federal court that has heard the government's argument has ruled against them.' The State Department said it was reviewing the case with the Department of Justice."[17]

Positioned above the text was an image of the twin brothers, one dark-haired and one fair-haired. At four years of age, neither boy could possibly have sensed the significance of that day, but they will—because their parents have continued placing articles and documents in a digital file for them to open when they are older. "We want them to know how much we love them and how much we fought for them," Andrew explained.

Saturday, October 10, 2020, was a landmark day on many levels. The Dvash-Banks family could celebrate their personal success after a difficult struggle. A welcome precedent was set for the children of other transnational same-sex couples who were born abroad.

October 10 was also the day I could begin this book project—the story of the Dvash-Banks US citizenship case, with the life histories of the parents and children at its center. Of course, sixty days had to pass without serious challenge from the US State Department in order for the last decision to become final—but as timeline items 14 and 15 reveal, requests for further review were declined (see table 1).

Within an hour of learning the news, at 8:34 a.m., I sent an e-mail message to Andrew and Elad, with a copy to Andrew's sister Ashli (with whom I had "secretly" spoken when the case was ongoing):

> Hello, Elad and Andrew!
> I just saw the great news in the newspaper this morning—that both twins are now US citizens! What a journey you have been through. So wonderful that this is all documented for the twins to read when they are older. You are such lovely and thoughtful parents.
> I have just finished the manuscript for the book I have been working on all year: *Deliberately Divided: Inside the Controversial Study of Twins and Triplets Adopted Apart*, to be published in the spring of 2021 by Rowman & Littlefield. I will submit it early next week. I would love to chat with all of you after that to see if you would still be interested in having me write your incredible story. It would be an honor.
> My best wishes to all—and Happy [Jewish] New Year![18]
>
> Nancy

Andrew replied later that evening, at 8:29 p.m.:

> So nice to hear from you, and thank you so much for the nice note and well wishes! We're so thrilled with the news.
> And congrats on finishing your book! . . . We would love to speak with you about writing our story. Now with this issue behind us, I think we are more free to speak about it than previously. I think after the election [November 3] would be the best time to speak? Let me know your time frame and what works.
> Best regards,
>
> Andrew Dvash-Banks

I waited until Thursday, November 5, to contact the couple again and spoke to Andrew by telephone on Friday, November 6, as described in an earlier chapter. It was the first of many phone calls, Zoom sessions, and personal meetings with Andrew, Elad, their twins, and family members that would take place over the next two years.

THE DVASH-BANKS CASE: INSIDE LOOKING OUT

Alexa M. Lawson-Remer had been special counsel at Sullivan & Cromwell for thirteen and a half years when she represented plaintiffs Andrew and Ethan. When I reached her in September 2022, she was senior vice president at City National Bank in Los Angeles, a position she had held for just four months.

Given Lawson-Remer's prominence in the Dvash-Banks case, I was determined to find her. (I knew she had left the law firm and had twice asked her former assistant to put us in touch, but that never happened.[19]) After months of disappointment, I tried again, inspired by my June meeting with Immigration Equality lawyer Aaron C. Morris. Knowing that success with search engines often relies on particular words and word combinations, I persisted until a promising lead emerged. I composed an e-mail message at 1:53 p.m. on September 6 and received her response at 1:56 p.m. We met on Zoom two days later. Perhaps she felt freer to talk since she was no longer associated with Sullivan & Cromwell.

Lawson-Remer's strong attraction to the case was both professional and personal. She sensed the powerful effect the decision could have on same-sex families struggling to secure citizenship for their children. She is also the mother of five-year-old fraternal twin boys. "I could very much understand the frustration that Andrew and Elad were going through because I have [two] kids and the scenario is the same." She explained that she and her partner had each donated an egg that was fertilized by the same sperm donor and implanted into the same womb. Thus, each child was genetically related to one mother but not the other. "The idea that one kid would be treated as less than the other is just—it hurts you so fundamentally."

When Lawson-Remer first heard about the case in 2017, she was "shocked." She wondered if the State Department had made a mistake, or if their interpretation of the law was "real." Digging deeper into the situation with attorney Morris from Immigration Equality, it appeared that the government's policy *was* real and could potentially impact other couples. "That shock turned into 'We need to do something about this,'" Lawson-Remer recalled.

I wondered how confident she had felt about winning the case.

"We had a pretty strong argument and we won very early on," Lawson-Remer noted. "I felt strongly about the merits of the case—not just on the personal or moral levels, but also the interpretation of the law. We were also thinking ahead, developing strategies, how to change course if the opposing party did something unexpected."

Andrew commented on the defense team's twofold strategy as told to him by his attorneys. The first, which occurred at the time of the first appeal (see table 1, timeline, item 7), was to identify their surrogate as an unmarried woman at the time she gave birth, with the idea of showing that the twins were born out of wedlock. However, recall that the couple's attorney, Michelle Flowerday, made it clear that Andrew and Elad were both equally the parents of both twins—and that the record showing the identity of the surrogate could never be released. The defense team's second strategy was to request an *en banc* review (see table 1, timeline, item 14).

I asked Lawson-Remer why her team didn't take advantage of assistance from a "twin expert" that worked close by. She and Morris explained that since the case never really went to trial, the testimony of expert witnesses wasn't needed. (Earlier, I indicated that Morris did not want to over-emphasize the "twinship angle" out of deference to the other families—and that the law did not distinguish between twins and siblings.) Lawson-Remer's confidence in obtaining a favorable outcome was also reinforced by the defense team's "disorganization."

She considers the Dvash-Banks case outstanding in several ways. "It's an alignment of a policy with how it was intended to be. It was an unfortunate misinterpretation of what marriage meant. New questions will come about because of reproductive technology and surrogacy." Given her experience and expertise, Lawson-Remer focused on the significance of the decision for other families. "There was a need for realignment with the societal norm. It's very logical—both kids belong to both parents, but the application and interpretation [of the law] had not caught up." She explained that the case was about more than Ethan getting citizenship rights, the freedom to travel, and the ability to run for president.

"It's that other families were watching this case and saying, 'That's my son, too. That's my daughter, too,'" Lawson-Remer explained. "And so, the State Department decided to change its policy—and I think it's a direct result of the Dvash-Bankses' bravery, since there was a risk they might not win. Countless couples are benefited, not just same-sex couples, and that's great—that's great."

All four cases litigated by Immigration Equality had a significant impact, but *Andrew Mason Dvash-Banks and E. J. D.-B. v. U.S. Department of State and Michael Pompeo* was the first one to settle.

Judges virtually never comment publicly on cases that were under their jurisdiction, but I was undeterred. In September 2022 I contacted the District Court for the Central District of California, asking for Judge John F. Walter to assess the significance of the Dvash-Banks case. Not surprisingly, I never received a reply.

Later that month, I made two inquiries to the United States Court of Appeals for the Ninth Circuit seeking comments from judges Daniel E. Bress, Andrew J. Kleinfeld, and Andrew D. Hurwitz, who issued a 2:1 decision against the State Department's request for an *en banc* review (see table 1, timeline, item 14). First, I spoke with a receptionist who promised to transmit my request to the appropriate individual. Within hours I received a telephone call from Chief Deputy Clerk Susan Gelmis, who offered to pass along to the three judges my request to speak with them. However, I told her I had another plan in mind. By then, I had received a voice message from a court employee confirming that judges rarely comment on cases unless they know they can do so safely and without controversy, but that he would submit an inquiry to the judges. The following day I was told that "all three have respectfully declined to be quoted or interviewed for the book."[20] My disappointment was slight because my expectations had been quite low.

I contacted the four attorneys representing the State Department and Secretary of State Mike Pompeo. I did not hear back from three of them but was stunned to reach Lisa Zeidner Marcus by telephone on my first try. She promised to contact her public affairs office for permission to discuss the case. I understood but also explained that I could present her comments without reference to her name or gender. I contacted her again by e-mail when I did not hear back, and again, she promised to seek permission. I am still waiting.

THE DVASH-BANKS CASE: OUTSIDE LOOKING IN

The Dvash-Banks case attracted considerable attention from attorneys and legal scholars. It became the focus of law review articles and supportive public statements from organizations.

Mary Bonauto is the civil rights project director for GLAD (GLBTQ Legal Advocates and Defenders), a Boston-based organization that provides information and services to members of the LGBTQ community and to HIV-infected individuals.[21] In 2015, she argued successfully before the Supreme Court in the *Obergefell v. Hodges* case that enabled same-sex couples to marry nationwide. Bonauto also led GLAD's support of the court of appeals victory in *Dvash-Banks v. Pompeo*, which explains why I sought her perspective on this case.[22] GLAD's statement is discussed below.

Bonauto saw the case as going beyond genetic relatedness, with broad implications, as did Lawson-Remer. She asserted that the State Department showed disrespect for same-sex marriage and committed a "category error" by treating Andrew and Elad as though they were unmarried. The brief that she helped prepare (see below) restated the right of same-sex couples to marry, giving them access to the benefits and protections that come with marriage. Bonauto noted that in the Dvash-Banks case, the State Department imposed a biological relatedness criterion that would not have applied to heterosexual couples. She also recognized the "possible compelled separation" of the family if one twin was denied citizenship.

On December 19, 2019, GLAD issued an amicus ("friend of the court") brief, "opposing the government's decision to NOT grant citizenship to a child of the Dvash-Bankses." This brief was filed with the National Center for Lesbian Rights (NCL) and the law firm Wilmer Cutler Pickering Hale and Dorr, LLP. It was filed on behalf of Ethan, Andrew, and Elad; Elad was recognized as *guardian ad litem* (legal advocate for a child). A statement on GLAD's website asserts, "The government's policy is to grant citizenship to the child who is biologically related to an American citizen, but not to the child of a non-citizen who is married to a citizen. . . . This policy is unjust and a violation of the constitution." The NCL posted a similar statement on their website.[23]

A clear description of the State Department's misapplication of policy is stated in this brief. Section 7 FAM 1140, Appendix E, of the 2014 *Foreign Affairs Manual* states that children must be born "during the marriage of the biological parents to each other" to be US citizens at birth. However, under that provision neither Aiden, nor Ethan, would qualify. Instead, Aiden was considered a citizen at birth via a provision that affects the citizenship of children born out of wedlock; his twin brother Ethan was not considered a citizen at all.

It is worth comparing relevant sections of the 2014 and 2022 *Foreign Affairs Manual (FAM)*. The 2014 *FAM* included definitions of "birth in wedlock" under which the State Department was operating when the lawsuits were filed. The updated version of the *FAM* does not include this appendix. The 2022 *FAM* reflects the changed definitions of the term "in wedlock" that are now more inclusive.[24]

According to the 2014 *FAM*:
- The term "in wedlock" has been consistently interpreted to mean birth during the marriage of the biological parents to each other.
- To say a child was born "in wedlock" means that the child's biological parents were married to each other at the time of the birth of the child.
- If a married woman and someone other than her spouse have a biological child together, that child is considered to have been born out of wedlock. The same is true for a child born to a married man and a person other than his spouse.

According to the 2022 *FAM*:
- The term "in wedlock" has been interpreted to mean birth during the legally recognized marriage of the parents to each other.
- This includes a child conceived before the marriage and born during the marriage.
- To say a child was born "in wedlock" means that the child's parents were married to each other at the time of the child's birth.

The 2022 *FAM* also specifies that for a child to be a US citizen at birth, then one parent in the marriage is a US citizen and at least one parent has either a genetic or gestational tie to the child. If the parent has only a gestational tie to the child, that parent must also be the legal parent at birth. Thus, a key difference between the 2014 and 2022 editions of the FAM is that a biological connection (genetic or gestational) between the child and the US citizen parent is not required when the parents are legally married to one another.[25]

Attorney Aaron C. Morris believes the Dvash-Banks case was significant in bringing about this change because it was the first of the four cases to settle and had advanced to the Ninth Court of Appeals. The government appealed one other case, then dropped it. "I don't really know how or why the government made the decisions it did," said Morris. "You'd have to ask them . . . though, I'm sure they won't tell you."[26] Officials do not like to talk, but I did speak to someone inside the State Department who described events and decisions behind the policy change affecting citizenship, as I reveal toward the end of this chapter.

Law professor Kristin Collins advised GLAD and associated attorneys during preparation of the amicus brief (see above). She called the State Department's view of Aiden and Ethan's birth as non-marital "an incredible overreach—an absurd interpretation of the statute to treat children born within a marital relationship as non-marital. . . . The part of the statute that deals with foreign-born children of non-marital fathers has a biological requirement—not the section that deals with the foreign-born children of married parents [or fathers]. It was very insulting to these men to be treated this way. And the State Department should have realized that this was an untenable approach for that reason alone. It's also just wrong as a matter of law."

Why the State Department acted as they did was unclear "and frankly shocking." Perhaps their views were unintentional with respect to discriminating against gay couples. The importance of marital rights for gay couples, with emphasis on the children's well-being, was reinforced by outcomes in *Obergefell v. Hodges* (2015) that were still recent in the minds of many (see chapter 3). "Were they asleep for the last several years?" Collins wondered. "Or since gay couples are less numerous than heterosexual couples, perhaps the State Department's 'heartlessness' reflected their inattention to the problem."[27]

Collins sees the Dvash-Banks case as "one of a cluster of current cases that are important with regard to citizenship and naturalization." And like Lawson-Remer, Collins posed timely questions that lack easy answers. Both lawyers believe that gay and heterosexual couples will benefit from the decision in the Dvash-Banks case.

Law professor Cristina Rodríguez views the case as an important example of a court "willing to intervene and say this is a relationship that should be recognized—that biology is not the sole determinant of parentage. In that sense it is pretty significant." Rodríguez further applauded the willingness of courts to affect the transmission of citizenship in ways that promote family values and inclusiveness. And she underlined the relevance of the case for children born through assisted reproductive technology, which is becoming a more prevalent option for infertile and gay couples wishing to raise families.[28]

Collins wonders if heterosexual couples will benefit most, at least in terms of raw numbers.[29] While 63 percent of LGBTQ couples plan to have families, they are more likely than heterosexual couples to do so by fostering or adopting than by seeking assisted reproductive methods.[30] However, other recent data suggest that this trend may be changing. Since 2003, a twenty-one-fold increase in the number of same-sex male couples and single men using assisted reproductive services was observed in a Canadian clinic, albeit in a very small sample. Interestingly, among the twenty-five deliveries, eight (32 percent) were twins, and the twins in every pair had a different father—just like Aiden and Ethan did.[31]

Collins also wonders if more gay couples—especially males who must resort to assisted reproductive methods to conceive biological children—will continue to be burdened by inquiries surrounding parental background and childbirth circumstances. These are questions worth asking, but their answers and solutions remain uncertain.

SCHOLARS TAKE NOTICE

The nature of same-sex marital rights, the significance of "wedlock," the meaning of "out of wedlock," and other citizenship issues were addressed in law review articles about the Dvash-Banks case. These articles were written by legal scholars and other professionals with interests in these topics and related issues.

Google Scholar is a rich source of articles on virtually any topic. Entering the term "Dvash-Banks" into the search box yielded 19 articles and citations in professional journals that referenced this case. The legal databases Westlaw and HeinOnline identified 23 and 27 law review articles and references, respectively, although several duplicate those listed in Google Scholar.[32] Searches on Westlaw and HeinOnline for the other three families represented by Immigration Equality identified fewer entries, respectively: Zaccari-Blixt (7, 11); Kiviti (11, 5); and Mize-Gregg (4, 3). Some articles reference all four families.

During the course of my research, I discovered an insightful, scholarly paper that focused on the Dvash-Banks case but addressed the citizenship consequences for children of same-sex couples more broadly.

I was stunned to learn that author Sasha Hochman was an undergraduate history major at Barnard College in New York City, as this essay could easily have been written by a more seasoned scholar. Hochman argued that for children born outside the United States, the passing of citizenship from parent to child is needed to ensure that children receive the same rights and recognition from the State. She also underlined the fact that families take many forms. "Biology is not the only bond between a parent and child."[33]

I also reviewed a family law professors' brief, authored jointly by two law professors and three practicing attorneys and endorsed by over sixty law professors from across the United States listed as *amici curiae*.[34] The singular (*amicus curiae*) is a professional person or organization that is not part of the litigation but may advise the court in legal matters directly affecting a case.[35] My discovery of this document was accidental and timely, and also a bit embarrassing. Professor Cristina Rodríguez, whom I cited above, suggested I contact her Yale University colleague, Professor Douglas NeJaime, an expert in family law. I sent NeJaime an e-mail summarizing the purpose of my book and asking him for an interview. I even attached a newspaper clipping about the Dvash-Banks case in case he was unaware of it. He replied that he would be happy to talk—noting that he was one of the co-authors of the family law professors' brief!

The brief asserted that citizenship law has looked to and implemented family law principles; that under these principles, biology has never been the single or key factor for establishing parentage; that the government's argument was wrong historically and legally; that Andrew was Ethan's legal father from birth; and that the District Court "properly deemed E. J. [Ethan Jacob] a U.S. citizen from birth."[36] NeJaime believed the brief was needed because many lawyers who were involved at that point did not specialize in family law.

Looking over the list of *amici curiae* appended to the law professors' brief, I was excited to see my friend and colleague, George Washington University law professor Catherine J. Ross, among them. Catherine and I met as panelists at a March 2019 conference, "The Twinning Reaction: Science and Deception," held at the University of Virginia Law School. We both addressed different aspects of the controversial 1960s New York City study of adopted-away infant twins who were separated at birth and followed until age twelve. The twins' adoptive parents were never told they were raising a "singleton twin." Catherine provided excellent insights, included in the book I authored about that study.[37]

She agreed to do the same for the Dvash-Banks case (included later in this chapter).

I also questioned NeJaime on the role the Dvash-Banks case played regarding the change in government policy on citizenship. He explained that there were some discussions he could not disclose to me. Courtney Joslin, a law professor at the University of California, Davis, and one of NeJaime's co-authors on the professors' brief whom I contacted, saw the significance of this case as reflective of a broader point—the importance of non-biological parent–child relationships to children and, thus, the importance of having the law reflect and protect those relationships.[38]

Sometime later I was fortunate to have someone put me in touch with a State Department official who had served in the early months of the Biden presidency. This individual, who wished to remain anonymous, had worked closely on issues related to the Dvash-Banks case and others—e.g., the meaning of wedlock and the definition of gestational ties. I will refer to this person as SDO (State Department official). Over the course of two hundred virtually held meetings that spanned about five hundred hours, SDO brought about some important policy changes. The process was complicated and delicate—and could have been derailed by people holding beliefs with no basis in fact.

SDO described a case predating Dvash-Banks that involved a married same-sex female couple living in Australia. One woman was American, and the other was Australian. An egg donated by the Australian partner was fertilized and implanted into the womb of her wife. Consequently, because the gestational mother had no biological connection to the child she delivered, the child was denied United States citizenship. "I [SDO] said that was 'ridiculous'—the mother carried the child—so we said we needed to modify the term 'biological' to include 'genetic' or 'gestational.' A bureaucratic fight ensued, but we won a change in the rules governing the case in 2011 [and the child received a US passport]."

While Dvash-Banks and related cases were pending, SDO called a meeting of attorneys to see what further changes could be made to assist transnational couples conceiving children by assisted reproduction. Older lawyers were fearful of fraud, such as the marketing of embryos and the selling of babies. Other confrontations followed; however, the younger attorneys were more amenable to changes in policy. Then SDO "shifted the argument" by noting that state laws were changing in favor of families, so "federal and international law should follow suit, rather than fall behind." The question of the citizenship of a child unrelated to both parents was also raised but not addressed at that time since it was not relevant to Dvash-Banks. "We decided to put that on hold and solve the other issue [to eliminate the 'biological' connection altogether]." They succeeded.

Their success was considered a major victory for transnational couples. Comparing the 2014 and 2022 versions of the *Foreign Affairs Manual* (see above) shows that the term "biological" had been eliminated. Of course, other aspects of this change had to be worked out with the Department of Homeland Security, Citizenship and Immigration Services, and the General Counsel's office. The issues were complex, and not everyone had a full understanding of what was involved. And as this process was going forward, SDO was aware that some of the Justice Department litigants were "hostile" toward the Dvash-Banks legal position. Still, SDO credits the Dvash-Banks case as "an action forcing an event—a change in the real life of a family leading to litigation." It happened because SDO persisted, despite being told to "leave well enough alone" by some of the resistant attorneys. SDO persevered, knowing that had this change not been made, additional cases would accumulate. It turned out that attorneys who were initially against the idea eventually agreed to making the change.

SDO defined several critical issues for the future. The term "gestational" remains problematic. "We understood it to mean a woman carrying a child, but it could mean more when you move away from traditional child-bearing." I agreed and pointed out that Elad, while not carrying his child, had the same connection to Ethan as did the Australian egg donor in the earlier case, i.e., contributing a gamete (sperm). As such, Elad should be considered a gestational parent.

A key point that emerged from SDO's negotiations is that if a couple, regardless of sexual orientation, *intends* to have a family and commissions a surrogate, *this should constitute evidence that they are the child's legal parents from birth.* Showing intended parentage is accepted in some states, such as California and Connecticut, regardless of marital status, but not in all states and not in all nations. The 2022 *Foreign Affairs Manual* indicates that a child may be conceived prior to wedlock but must be born during wedlock. However, what is the status of children born out of wedlock but to intended parents? I also believe the *FAM* is vague regarding the significance of a gestational connection, i.e., can it replace genetic relatedness as it did for the American-Australian couple? Is there a legal framework to support such a decision in the future?

MORE LINGERING QUESTIONS AND WHAT-IFS

Recall that at the close of my interview in New York City with Aaron Morris, I asked him what he would have asked me if he had been writing a book about the case. His question was this: Why did the government fight so hard to keep a policy when it kept on losing? He also wondered why the Justice Department asked for an *en banc* review in the Dvash-Banks case but completely gave up on the Georgia case (Mize-Gregg family) that Immigration Equality had also won. He called the request for an *en banc* review "an extraordinary measure after they [the Justice Department] had lost."

Law professor Catherine Ross, a specialist in family law, underlined the Canadian court's order naming Andrew and Elad as the twins' legal parents *and* the United States' usual practice of recognizing such decrees across states and other nations. "Everyone involved in this case—Andrew, Elad, the egg donor, and the surrogate—was in agreement. So, why was the State Department substituting its own conclusion contrary to the intent of the parents?" she asked.[39] There are no clear answers to these questions.

I was curious about Morris's thoughts on an Italian case that raised some unusual issues relevant to gay fathers and their families. A same-sex male couple in Italy who conceived twins via a surrogate was told by their government that their sons would not be recognized as brothers; however, each parent could register as the father of the child to whom he was genetically related. Famiglie Arcobaleno (Rainbow Families), a nongovernmental organization advocating the rights of same-sex parents and their children, regarded this latest development as genuine progress.[40] Morris said that if this case were to happen in America today, he would inform the Biden administration that this decision is contrary to the agreed-upon change of policy. He added, "If the administration felt it was outside their policy, we would have to do something about it."

I suspect that if the Dvash-Banks case had not settled favorably for Andrew, Elad, and their twins, Morris's response would have been swift and without hesitation—he would have kept on fighting. That is one question that can be answered.

Resolved: Together as One

$\mathcal{T}$he first time I visited the Dvash-Banks home was 1:15 p.m. on Sunday, December 12, 2021. The date of our meeting was determined by the family's weekend schedule, and the time was fixed by the twins' swimming lesson on that day. The lesson lasted from 12:00 to 12:30 p.m. Once home from the pool, the boys would need showers and a snack, so Andrew and Elad suggested I arrive at 1:15 p.m. Later that day, the four of them were expected at Lawry's restaurant in Beverly Hills, at 5:00 p.m., for their annual dinner with Andrew's relatives. Given all this, Andrew believed that "the time frame would work perfectly [for our first in-person interview]."

The allotted time worked well because I guessed that several hours would suffice for gathering additional background information about the couple, the lawsuit, and the two children. But the challenges of arranging a convenient time reminded me of my experiences with so many other families whose lives are highly orchestrated by activities scheduled far in advance.

CHILDREN BRING UP THEIR PARENTS

Many people think parents bring up their children, but the reverse is closer to the truth. I argued this point together with my colleague, Dr. Robert Plomin from Kings College London, in an October 2019 public event. We were debate partners in New York City's *Intelligence Squared* (IQ[2]) series, and the motion we supported was "Parenting Is Overrated."[1] I expected the audience to favor the opposing side—they did—because the common belief is that parental rearing practices significantly affect child outcomes. However, twin and other developmental research tells a more nuanced story.

The way parents treat their children is largely shaped by each child's individual personalities, interests, and inclinations.[2] That is why mothers and fathers often find themselves providing different opportunities, resources, and support for each child. I am fond of saying that one-child parents are "environmentalists," whereas parents with two or more children are "geneticists." Parents expect that what works for their first child will work for their second child, but they quickly learn that this is not so. Of course, mothers and fathers who raise their children in the same home provide each child equal access to reading materials, laptop computers, and sports equipment, but home experiences differ across children. An older child may be immersed in historical novels, while a younger child can spend hours playing video games. Sensitive parents adjust their practices to accommodate these differences, even when it comes to bedtime activities. Both Aiden and Ethan love listening to stories before falling asleep, but before going to bed they take their baths—their parents have realized it is best to bathe Aiden first because Ethan is quicker.

In a sense, children create their own environments, partly filtered through their genetically based predispositions. That would also explain why identical twins raised separately by different families show so many common behaviors. All of us play active roles in creating our environments, influenced partly by our unique genetic backgrounds.[3] Parents face the critical task of nurturing their children's abilities, talents, and tastes and providing them with emotional support when needed. For example, parents can help a shy child feel more at ease, but they will probably be unable to turn the child into an extroverted, gregarious sort.

As Aiden and Ethan transitioned from early toddlerhood to young childhood, Andrew and Elad provided them with a wide variety of matched experiences. Some activities were successful and continued (e.g., swimming), while others failed and ended (e.g., soccer). As I was leaving their home after my first visit, I saw Aiden standing at the kitchen table busily pasting bits of paper onto a larger sheet. Knowing he had had a swimming lesson that day, I asked him if it was "good." He replied, "No, it was not good—it was great!"

"Good/great to know this!" Andrew wrote back when I messaged him later. He and Elad are thinking about installing a pool in their backyard sometime in the future, since both twins love to swim and both had progressed well after several weeks of intensive training in the summer of 2022, when they were five. The two boys also took karate lessons for a while, but they were discontinued, partly due to scheduling issues, and also because Aiden had difficulty focusing on the sport. Neither parent is highly involved in athletics, although Elad likes to run, and Andrew was on his high school's swim team. Both parents offer their sons opportunities, hoping they will participate in sports they enjoy. The Toyota Sports Performance Center in El Segundo, the home of the Los Angeles Kings ice hockey team, has three Olympic-size skating rinks. On Saturday afternoons the center offers free recreational skating to the public, and Aiden and Ethan love it. Involving their twins in Little League baseball is an activity Andrew and Elad will try in the spring.[4]

In the fall of 2022, Andrew and Elad enrolled their children in Spanish classes. Spanish is an excellent choice for a third language, given the large number of Spanish-speaking residents in Southern California. (The twins speak some Hebrew in addition to English.) Many educational, cultural, and recreational programs are offered by the California Hispanic Chamber of Commerce, the Museum of Latin Art, and the city of Los Angeles. The twins resumed their Hebrew instruction, which began on Saturday, September 10. As before, they travel to IKAR with their parents for morning Shabbat services, then join other children for their lesson.

During the fall of 2022, Aiden and Ethan reached two significant milestones in their lives: The twins started kindergarten, *and* they were intentionally assigned to separate classes.

SCHOOL DAYS

Monday, August 29, 2022, was the twins' first day in kindergarten and the first time they were apart in a formal school setting. Parents stayed with their children for the full hour that kindergarten was in session. For the first half-hour Andrew went to Ethan's classroom and Elad went to Aiden's classroom, and then they switched places. Tuesday, August 30, was the official opening school day and would last for the usual four hours. The two boys would be apart for most of that time, but they could enjoy lunch and recess together, which they usually do.

Their transitional-kindergarten (TK) teacher was now a kindergarten (K) teacher, and Aiden was placed in her class. And while Ethan and Aiden are close brothers, siblings find it hard to resist an occasional tease. Ethan goaded Aiden slightly by saying, "Oh, you're still in TK—you're still a baby, because you're with the same teacher." Andrew explained to Ethan that Aiden's teacher was now in charge of a kindergarten class, just like his, "but the problem was that she kept her old classroom. That kind of gave Ethan more ammo to make fun of him, but Aiden didn't seem fazed."[5]

I spoke with the twins' swimming coach, Nick Bishop, who is working toward a master's degree in teaching at California State University, Fullerton.[6] He has taught Aiden and Ethan to swim for about a year and a half, at South Bay Aquatics in Redondo Beach. At first, the twins attended their semi-private lesson together, but about "halfway through my journey [with them]," Nick found that he preferred teaching them one at a time.

Aiden had difficulty focusing, which distracted Ethan. "Aiden would look at Ethan, then look at me, and finally listen." Nick (who had experienced ADHD as a child) restored Aiden's attention by giving him a specific task, but this wouldn't work for Ethan. "I ended up disciplining Ethan more." When the twins were crab-walking—moving along the pool's wall with their hands—Ethan traveled at "mad speed," while Aiden was slow and methodical. "So, I had Aiden go first, to set the pace, but Ethan began moving too fast and I was afraid he'd bump into his brother. I got him to slow down, but when I looked away, he'd start doing it again."

Now Aiden has his lesson first, while Ethan reads in the car outside.

The twins perform slightly above the average for children of their age, but some creative effort by their swim coach was needed. By "shortening the goal and broadening the target," Nick helped Aiden overcome his fear of water. "I got him to put his head underwater for just one second and open his eyes without rubbing them." He also got both boys to swim across the pool; he wanted them to keep their hands on their belly, but when that didn't happen, he relaxed that requirement, and it worked. He also said that both boys made great progress during their intensive swimming lessons, given by a different instructor.

Nick detects energy and excitement in Aiden whenever he is at the pool, independent of his ADHD—"and that makes me happy; he's a smart boy." I told Nick what Aiden said to me when I was at their home—that his swimming lesson that day was not good, but "great." That made Nick happy, too.

I wondered how Andrew and Elad would handle situations in which only one twin was invited to a birthday party by a child in his class. They hadn't thought about this until I mentioned it, but they understood it was a real possibility. Both parents agreed that the invitee should attend, and they would arrange a special activity for the one at home. Although they were confident that this was the right decision, they still seemed slightly uncomfortable knowing that one boy would be disappointed. The twins had always gone to birthday parties together.

PARENTING: WHAT EACH PARTNER DOES BEST

I sensed that the children relied on Elad more than on Andrew when it came to their daily activities and tasks. "That's true," Elad confirmed. "I don't know if it's because that's how I was raised. My mom was the parent we went to for everything. But that's what's happening here. I am more the parent in charge of the kids' education and play dates. Andrew is there to help, but I am definitely the main one. It just happened this way—I'm more into it." Elad also prepares most of the meals and does most of the cooking, while Andrew washes the dishes and takes out the trash.

Andrew's view of the couple's parental division of labor aligned well with Elad's description. "I don't want to use the term 'maternal instinct' because there's no mother here. But he [Elad] has this instinct to do everything for me. . . . He's very much a caretaker, and I could see that, because Aiden has increased needs, whereas Ethan is very independent. The kids call for him; they don't call for me. He's the one that keeps this family together."

Still, Andrew is very much involved with his children, just in other ways. On one of my visits, I saw him sitting in the pantry with both boys on his lap, all three deeply engrossed in conversation and laughter. He appeared to be pointing things out to the boys. Andrew also focuses on teaching their children how to handle challenging situations when he and Elad aren't around. He described a scene from their summer

2022 visit to Israel when the boys were playing on a merry-go-round-like apparatus in a park. "Suddenly, two older boys came and kind of pushed them off and took over. We were with friends, and we were all watching. One friend asked, 'Aren't you going to go and intervene?' And I said 'Absolutely not. They're almost six. And they need to figure that out. They need to either stand up for themselves and get back on or find another place to play—or they need to do something with those emotions other than knowing that their daddy is going to come and save them.' Unfortunately, a lot of kids in high school and college still think that Mommy and Daddy are going to get them out of jams. I just refuse to raise my kids that way."

I wondered how the incident in the park was finally settled. Apparently, Aiden didn't fully comprehend what had happened, so he simply moved to another piece of equipment, but Andrew saw that Ethan was mortified. "He just stood there, kind of holding back tears. I think he was trying to process it and understand and trying to figure it out. It was really interesting to watch him, and we watched him very intently. After a few moments, he looked for his brother and ran after him. It was important for me to see them experience that."[7]

Andrew's college friend, Laurel Mintz, called Andrew "a fantastic father, very hands-on, but realistic—one who doesn't sugarcoat the challenges of parenthood." Then she laughed, recalling how she and Andrew had joked about having children together if she never got married—"but then he went and got married and had his children. So, I lost out!"[8]

ASSORTATIVE PARENTING VERSUS ASSORTATIVE CROSS-PARENTING

Assortative parenting is not a term in psychological literature, but it describes a real phenomenon. Assortative parenting comes from the resemblance between a parent and child in appearance and behavior. Mothers or fathers who perceive aspects of themselves in a particular child may feel a certain affinity or identification with that child over another. For example, mothers indicated emotional closeness to children whom they perceived as similar to them in interests, values, life experiences, and approaches to life.[9] Similarity to a parent was one of several factors listed by individuals questioned about the reasons for favoritism in their family.[10]

However, there is a related concept I discovered when I met Andrew and Elad that I call *assortative cross-parenting*. It was captured in Margaret Mitchell's classic 1936 novel, *Gone with the Wind*, in the words spoken by Rhett Butler to Scarlett O'Hara following the death of their young daughter: "I liked to think that Bonnie was you, a little girl again. . . . She was so like you, and I could pet her, and spoil her, as I wanted to spoil you."

Assortative cross-parenting is the special feeling of a parent toward a child who displays the same traits as his partner, i.e., *the traits that attracted the parent to his partner in the first place*. I began chapter 4 with Elad's observation that "Aiden looks just like Andrew, and Ethan is a 'mini-me.'" But the similarities go beyond appearance to behavior—with intriguing consequences.

Elad explained, "I think I read about this in an article in Hebrew from an Israeli paper. It's so interesting. I read it just after the kids were born. I always had that connection to him [Aiden], imprinted on me when he was born. There's an attachment. I cannot describe it. I love Ethan. I'm obsessed with how he looks like me and acts like me. He's my mirror image. He's my soul mate. But there's something else with Aiden. They [Andrew and Aiden] act similarly. So, I think, subconsciously, the qualities that attracted me to Andrew, I see in Aiden. It's just like this attachment—this special thing—that happened almost naturally since they were babies, really infants, when they were born. But if someone asked me, 'Who do you love more?' which is an awful question to ask a parent, I honestly would say I love them exactly the same. But I have this special thing with Aiden—a kind of attachment— that I can't really explain in words. And I think Andrew feels the same way about Ethan . . . it's definitely genetic, because we're raising them exactly the same way. It's like, oh my God, this is Andrew!"

This same attachment to the other father's child was expressed by Matthew and Ed Moreira Bahnson, a married same-sex couple living in North Carolina.[11] Matthew is a postdoctoral fellow at Pennsylvania State University focused on engineering graduate education research. Ed, originally from Uruguay, is a professor of cell biology at the University of North Carolina. Their two-year-old twin daughters, Isabella (Bella) and Victoria (Tori), were conceived like Aiden and Ethan but with one important difference: a different egg donor was used for each twin. It turned out that only one embryo, created with Ed's sperm, was available, and the least expensive and most practical plan was to use another donor's egg. The two girls are twins, but they have no common genes. It is theoretically possible—but practically impossible—for full siblings to inherit none of the same genes from their parents.

Both Matt and Ed claimed that each girl is a "clone" of themselves. Bella has Matt's dark hair and calm temperament, while Tori has Ed's massive curls and high energy. Both fathers identify with the child they fathered because they see their own traits being expressed in them. For this reason, Matt believes he has unique insights into what Bella is thinking or trying to do, as well as what makes her happy or sad. Ed feels the same way about Tori, admitting he can now empathize with his mother and older sister, who "had to deal with me growing up." However, like Andrew and Elad, each father also has a special affinity for the twin conceived by his partner. According to Matt, "I really like Tori's energy and enthusiasm for life, and her unbridled joy at seeing people she loves. They're the same reasons I fell in love with Ed." Ed observed, "I love being around Bella—it's more peaceful being around her . . . she's so sweet, it's impossible not to love her."

Matt and Ed were aware of the Dvash-Banks lawsuit, which became public in 2018, soon after they had made their plans for having a family. They are very grateful that they decided to have their children born in the United States.

Daniel Head and Darek Sady had a different take on the topic of assortative cross-parenting. Daniel is the founder of HeadGlobal, a company offering customized recruitment and business development services to international clients.[12] Darek is the director of product management at Anthology, formerly Blackboard. The couple is raising four-year-old opposite-sex twins, Darby and Darwin. (Friends call the family members the "4D's.") Neither man expressed a special feeling for the child conceived by his husband.[13] Daniel explained that because Darwin is a girl, "It's not like I look at her and am immediately reminded of him [Darek]." Still, both men found the concept of assortative cross-parenting "fascinating," "cool," and plausible—"I could see that happening," Darek admitted.

As our conversation ended, Daniel revealed something he had never told Darek. "If Darek were to die, I wonder if I would use one of the [frozen] male embryos to have a child and name him Darek—a child who looked and acted like him." But Daniel quickly added that this possibility was too strange to consider seriously. Darek thought the idea was "really sweet. I think it's great. It's just that's not the way I think about our kids." Darek sees each twin as a "force of nature," a unique product of genetic and environmental factors. And he is correct in saying that the appearance and behavior of another child would be unpredictable.

Many photographs have been taken of Andrew and Elad with their two children. It is impossible to say for certain, but a considerable number of them show Andrew positioned closer to Ethan, with Elad standing or sitting closer to Aiden. Before my conversation with Elad took place, I had assumed that this photography arrangement was their conscious effort to avoid favoring the child they had conceived; now, I think assortative cross-parenting is an alternative explanation.

HOUSE PARTIES, BOOK PARTIES, AND BIRTHDAY PARTIES

Andrew's half-brother Jon has a house in the Pacific Palisades, a westside region of Los Angeles, where the families gather occasionally. As a father of two, Jon is a sharp observer of children's behavior, confirming what others have said about the twins' interactions. He agreed that Aiden is Ethan's "faithful follower"—they love doing things together, but they are also happy playing on their own. And like non-twins, one brother can become jealous of what the other brother is doing and try to join him. One of the twins' favorite (and most "important") activities at Jon's house is collecting snails around the backyard. "They do this together, but Aiden is more passionate about snail collecting than Ethan. So, Ethan will go off doing something else, but after a while he'll see Aiden with the snails, and he's like, 'Hey, I want this snails thing again.' " Jon also commented that the boys are "rambunctious and get into lots of things. But, on the whole, they're incredibly sweet and well-behaved."

In May 2022, my boyfriend, Dr. Craig Ihara, and I hosted a party to celebrate the release of my 2021 book, *Deliberately Divided: Inside the Controversial Study of Twins and Triplets Adopted Apart*. Andrew and Elad drove to Orange County for the occasion. Knowing that Aiden and Ethan would be with them, I made sure to have an ample supply of apple juice and cookies, as well as paper, crayons, and colorful markers, available for them. Both parents watched over the children, Elad a bit more than Andrew, before leaving early for a family get-together near Los Angeles. I was sorry they missed the formal program we had planned, but family social calendars fill up fast, as I noted earlier. I still have their gift of a white orchid and the card that came with it: "Congrats on the book. . . . We are so honored to be your next muse (subjects)." The card was signed "Andrew, Elad, Aiden & Ethan," with a heart drawn next to the four names.

The twins turned six years old on Friday, September 16, 2022. A family celebration took place on Saturday, September 17, followed by a children's birthday party on September 18. The invitation sent to the twins' friends announced a two-themed extravaganza—*Alice in Wonderland* (Aiden's obsession) and *Star Wars* (Ethan's fixation). The invitation, shown below, was created by a graphic designer who cleverly combined both boys' wishes. Andrew thought it looked "pretty cool."

Andrew's sister Ashli arrived late to the children's party, which by then was in full swing, with about twenty children and their parents. "It was awesome! As a mum of twins, I love that they did a double theme—they didn't try to make the boys compromise. . . . They had separate birthday cakes, decked out with their names and all the appropriate decorations and special flavors—red velvet for Aiden and chocolate fudge for Ethan. It took me a while to learn that [honoring each child's preferences] with my own twins." Ashli described the themed refreshments: Cheshire Cat–shaped cookies, heart-shaped peanut-butter-and-jelly tea sandwiches, and Queen of Hearts jam tarts for *Alice in Wonderland*; hot (Jabba the "Hutt") dogs, obi ("Obi-Wan Kenobi") kabobs, and seven-layer ("Leia") cake for *Star Wars*. As I described in chapter 7, a reptile display is a popular event at children's parties, and one took place in the family's backyard. The children handled a six-foot snake, tortoises, and various other creatures. Ashli also applauded the diversity of the guests who were invited—boys and girls, friends and siblings, gay parents and straight parents.

The twins' grandparents sent the boys birthday gifts from their homes in Florida and Tel Aviv. Ann gave them "lots and lots of one-dollar bills to be spent at the dollar store, where the twins could feel like millionaires!" It was the first birthday she missed, but she would see them for Thanksgiving. Moti and Tovi spoke to their grandsons by

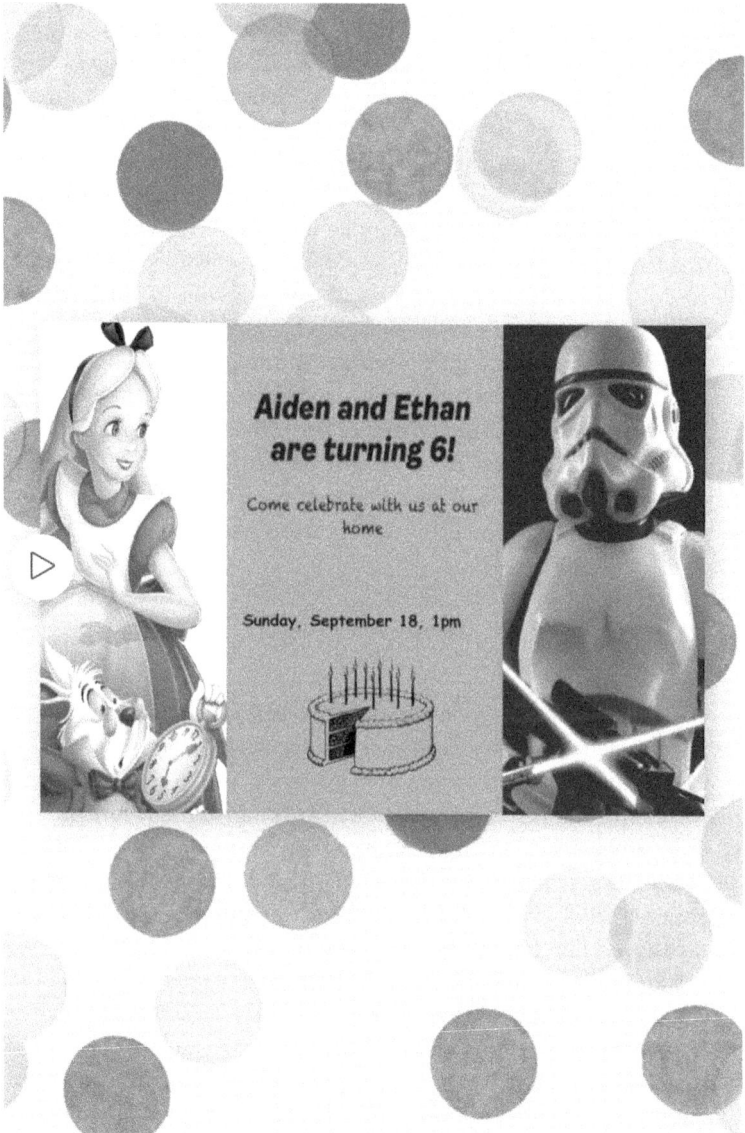

The twins' sixth birthday party invitation that captured the two themes of their celebration—*Alice in Wonderland* and *Star Wars*, 2022. The invitation was designed by Stephen Levin. *Source*: Photo courtesy of Andrew and Elad Dvash-Banks.

telephone from Tel Aviv and sent the children a Nintendo Switch—a popular handheld device that offers a huge library of games, such as *Super Mario Odyssey* and *The Legend of Zelda*.[14] According to Elad, this was something the boys "really wanted." I sent the twins two different e-cards that delivered personalized Donny Osmond and Dolly Parton birthday songs. Each card included both names, but in reverse order in the interest of equality. Elad replied, "Thank you so much for the cards, Nancy. The kids loved both of them and laughed so hard!!! 😂😂."

Ashli left the birthday party early for a scheduled photo shoot. Before doing so, she overheard a small five-year-old blond boy say to Andrew, "Aiden looks just like you—and Ethan looks just like Elad." The grown-ups standing nearby laughed and smiled.

On October 24, 2022, the twins and their parents attended a Diwali celebration at the home of one of the children's classmates. Recall that the twins are one-quarter Punjabi, since their egg donor had one Punjabi parent. Punjab is a state in Northern India where the Diwali festival is a time to rejoice—and to anticipate a bright future.[15]

JUST THE TWINS AT PLAY

My research on young twin children's relationships with each other shows that identical twins cooperate more, smile more, and generally enjoy each other more than fraternal twins do. These tendencies were evident in my filmed analysis of twins working together on puzzles.[16] But these are average findings, because there is overlap in how the two types of twins get along. The play scenes Elad described during the family's summer 2022 trip to Israel included elements of both. Aiden and Ethan behaved like typical fraternal twin brothers.

According to Elad, Aiden and Ethan both "feed off each other" when it comes to mischievous behavior. Elad's father, Moti, had put a big blow-up pool in the backyard for them. "At first, they were just going in and swimming—then Ethan took one of the water guns that my parents gave them and started spraying us. We were all sitting on a patio next to the pool. Then Ethan looked at Aiden, they kind of looked at each other, and both picked up the water guns and started spraying everywhere. My mom had laundry drying outside, and it started getting wet and everyone was yelling, 'No, stop it, stop it.' Then we tried to grab them [the water guns] and Ethan was like, 'Aiden come here, come here.' Ethan was trying to help his brother get to one corner of the pool, away from us. It was really funny, that interaction between the two of them."

Moti also arranged for his grandsons to visit a farm where he helps horses and donkeys that were abused. "There was one donkey named Pikachu that my dad works with.[17] He took the donkey out and let the kids feed the donkey and play with him—it was beautiful to see how they were both kind of scared of the donkey, but also pushing each other to feed the donkey. They were kind of talking among themselves. Aiden shouted, 'No, no, stay back. The donkey could kick you.' Ethan was walking behind the donkey, and Moti said, 'You're not supposed to walk behind the donkey.' But Ethan was sure the donkey liked it. The interaction was really cute, the two of them kind of taking care of each other and also having fun."[18]

"WE ARE SO BORING"

Reflecting on family life, Andrew said, "All we literally do is watch Netflix at night and go to Disneyland with our kids."

Of course, that's not all they do. Andrew and Elad escort their children to school, Hebrew lessons, swim lessons, and play dates. And they carefully follow a set routine for managing Aiden's special needs. While Elad (mostly) is responsible for making meals during the week, as well as some weekends, the family's Saturday lunches after synagogue are often at local restaurants. Occasionally on a Saturday afternoon they go shopping at Costco—"The kids love going to Costco. It's like an adventure for them"—or they visit the zoo where the family has a membership.

On most Sundays, Andrew or Elad do artwork with their children in the morning—Aiden likes working with Play-Doh—or Aiden and Ethan play in the backyard. They may watch TV, then have a late breakfast or brunch before swimming class at noon. "After that, we find another activity for the afternoon. If we don't have planned activities or play dates, it's not fun, since we're at home with them and they're going crazy."

I am writing the present paragraph on Halloween, October 31, 2022. Elad and Andrew are taking their children trick-or-treating tonight and have promised to send me pictures of the twins in their costumes. True to their birthday themes, Aiden is dressing up as the rabbit from *Alice in Wonderland*, and Ethan will dress as the Mandalorian, a lead character and warrior in the *Star Wars* series.

Andrew and Elad sound like many other involved parents I have known who are raising children and facing challenges, but also enjoying life. Ethan's citizenship is no longer in question, a relief to everyone—and Elad became a US citizen in 2022, an achievement of which he is very proud. Tovi pronounces her son Elad "perfect" and wishes that every parent could "have a child like mine." And Andrew's mother Ann praised her son for "lovingly" allowing the twins to FaceTime with her nearly every night. Andrew and Elad's shared passion for travel takes the family to interesting places, both locally and overseas. In the fall of 2022, they went to the Underwood Family Farm in Ventura County, California, where visitors pick their own fruits and vegetables. They also took a Caribbean cruise with Elad's parents to celebrate Tovi's sixtieth

On vacation in October 2022 with Elad's parents, Moti and Tovi; Moti (L), the twins' grandfather, is chasing after Ethan at the New Jersey cruise terminal; Tovi (R), the twins' grandmother, is seated next to Aiden, with Ethan next to him. They are in Nassau, in the Bahamas. *Source*: Photo courtesy of Andrew and Elad Dvash-Banks.

birthday and the twins' sixth. They can travel safely now, knowing Ethan has a US passport.

Andrew and Elad will most likely encounter the unforeseen trials regarding work, school, and health that all families face from time to time—think of the line from the Grateful Dead's 1969 song, "Uncle John's Band": "When life looks like Easy Street there is danger at your door." The Supreme Court's June 2022 overturning of *Roe v. Wade*, denying women the right to choose, and the possible implications of that decision for same-sex marriage and surrogacy, may pose significant societal difficulties specific to some families—like the Dvash-Bankses. But for now, both Andrew and Elad agree that "a point we would love to get across is we are pretty much as normal as they come."[19]

Now, and in the years to come, Andrew, Elad, Aiden, and Ethan will be a family—together as one. Recall that earlier in this chapter Aiden described his swimming lesson as not good, but "great." The words of this young boy also define the conclusion to Andrew and Elad's landmark case—not good, but great.

Five Years and Four Lawsuits: Now—and Next Time?

$\mathcal{A}$ndrew's high school friend, Jen Sikov, and her husband joined Andrew, Elad, and their twins during a vacation to Miami in January 2017. The two families decided to visit the Florida Keys. They never completed the 115-mile drive, but they did stop at a Cracker Barrel restaurant for a meal. Seated at a table, they were approached by an older couple who commented on how cute the boys were and asked Jen if they were twins. "They just assumed I was the mom since there couldn't be two dads. This is a typical assumption of people living outside a big city. I probably said, 'I'm not the mom'—that's something I would say. [The older couple] didn't seem thrilled by my answer."

The frequency of same-sex couples having children through assisted reproduction is now acceptable in some social circles. But many people recognize only traditional family structures, so these families appear novel, unnatural, and untested—even unheard of, as evidenced by the older Florida couple. The joy these children bring to same-sex couples is certainly equal to that of heterosexual couples who conceive naturally or by assisted means. Gay parents can be excellent mothers and fathers who raise happy, well-adjusted children, as I indicated earlier.

Andrew and Elad were fortunate that, in 2010, Canada gave them the freedom to marry the person they loved and, in 2016, to have the children they desired. At that time (with some exceptions), same-sex couples living in the United States were prohibited from getting married, a restriction that was lifted in 2015 with *Obergefell v. Hodges*.[1] However, since the Dvash-Banks case settled in 2020, social events and political developments have threatened many educational and reproductive rights. Between July of 2021 and March of 2022, books that addressed racial discrimination, gender identity, and other seemingly questionable content were banned in twelve states, with Texas leading the count, and Pennsylvania coming in second.[2] In March 2022, the Florida legislature passed a bill restricting the classroom instruction of sexual orientation and gender identity issues.[3] And on June 24, 2022, the United States Supreme Court overturned *Roe v. Wade*, the 1973 case that gave women the constitutional right of freedom to choose.[4] Within hours of that decision, more than twenty states were poised to restrict or ban abortions.

Events have consequences. Supreme Court justice Clarence Thomas argued that the reasoning behind the overturning of *Roe v. Wade* applied to same-sex couples with regard to contraception, consensual relationships, and marriage.[5] Thomas made these assertions despite Justice Samuel A. Alito's claim that the abortion rights decision would not affect rulings in these other areas; Alito authored the decision regarding *Roe v. Wade*. At the time of this writing, same-sex marriage has not been overturned. In fact, in July 2022, bipartisan support in the House of Representatives for the Respect for Marriage Act was demonstrated in response to Thomas's remarks.[6] The bill would require state and federal governments to recognize both same-sex marriages and interracial marriages performed under state law. It was introduced in the Senate, but a vote had not been taken.

However, the situation changed dramatically as this book was going into production, which I explain below.

SAME-SEX MARRIAGE—AND MORE— IN POSSIBLE DANGER

Future threats to same-sex marriage, egg donation, and surrogacy were real in light of the 2022 abortion decision.[7] Justice Thomas called for the reexamination of outcomes in three previous cases: *Griswold v. Connecticut* (1965), which allowed married couples to use contraception;[8] *Lawrence v. Texas* (2003), which overturned a Texas law criminalizing sexual relations between same-sex couples;[9] and *Obergefell v. Hodges* (2015), which gave marital rights to same-sex couples in every state.[10] The LGBTQ community and its supporters were shocked, outraged, and horrified by Thomas's words. They feared they would be denied the freedom to marry, face obstacles to health care, and even have their children taken from them. Still, they vowed to resist attempts to threaten the rights they have fought so vigorously to obtain. In a joint dissent, three liberal Supreme Court justices wrote that the decision would bring "sorrow" to American women, who would lose a "50-year-old constitutional right."[11]

Daniel Head and Darek Sady, fathers of opposite sex-twins Darby and Darwin, were concerned. Daniel admitted that when he first heard about the overturning of *Roe v. Wade*, "I didn't think about it. But then it was like, 'How fragile is our family after all?' We're not panicking [now], but it caused moments of questioning, such as, 'Do we need to hire a lawyer?'"[12]

George Washington University law professor Catherine Ross, one of sixty-five professors who endorsed the professors' brief (referenced in chapter 8), affirmed Daniel's fear. "By throwing out the precedents that supported *Roe*, they've [the Supreme Court justices] seriously undermined the line of authority behind family privacy, placing it in serious jeopardy. At least several justices have made their intentions clear—it's a very activist court. That's not to say same-sex marriage will be gone next year, but it is quite thinkable."[13]

Law professor Courtney Joslin alluded to the "vulnerability" of a number of current precedents, including the *Obergefell* decision that established a constitutional right to marriage for same-sex couples. "The joint dissent [by the three liberal Supreme Court justices] in the *Dobbs* decision [*Dobbs v. Jackson Women's Health Organization*] overturning *Roe v. Wade* explains that there is reason to be concerned; it seems impossible to restrain the majority's reasoning and approach."[14]

It is not unreasonable to imagine other scenarios triggered by the overturning of *Roe v. Wade*. Women who underwent abortions and the health-care professionals they worked with might be retroactively penalized. Same-sex marriages that were in place for years could be annulled and their children considered born out of wedlock; the citizenship rights of children born abroad might be placed in jeopardy. Even if same-sex marriages were allowed, such couples might be denied access to egg donation and surrogacy for creating the families they always wanted. Health benefits tied to employment and to children's well-being might be denied.

These outcomes may seem extreme, but once an action is taken, it sets a process in motion, leading to unexpected events—like Thomas instantly extending the logic of overturning *Roe v. Wade* to other areas. Catherine Ross emphasized that in the absence of clear federal laws, individual and family rights may vary, based on geographical location and divisions among federal appellate courts. Policies established by statute or regulation that support individual and family rights can be easily reversed by subsequent administrations. Eliminating freedoms is easier than granting them.

Andrew's mother, Ann, is incredulous that in her state of Florida, it is no longer permissible to say "gay" in primary schools.[15] She is also concerned about restrictions on the discussion of other controversial topics in schools around the country. "Isn't the classroom the place where these discussions are supposed to take place?" she asked. "And women thought *Roe v. Wade* would never become an issue again."

According to Catherine Ross, the late Supreme Court justice Antonin Scalia said years ago that eliminating abortion rights was his intent. When the Supreme Court held that criminalization of same-sex intimate relationships violated constitutional rights—reversing a recent precedent—Justice Scalia made clear that the same reasoning supported his intent to go after abortion rights—and that if same-sex marriage was legalized, the Supreme Court would be going after abortion.[16]

Sasha Hochman, the Barnard undergraduate student whose work I referenced in chapter 8, was also uneasy. We spoke during her semester abroad in Santiago, Chile: "As someone who wants to be a historian, I do like to think that in our little recent slice of history, our immigration and family laws are becoming more inclusive, more equal. It's scary to think that with a more conservative court and a more conservative turn away from equality in marriage rights and family recognition, that nothing is set in stone."[17]

But during the waning days of the Democrat-controlled Congress, some surprising things happened, and they happened fast.

BACKFIRE

Justice Thomas's assertion that overturning *Roe v. Wade* extended to same-sex marriage had an unintended effect. Societal trends had changed; by the end of 2022, the number of same-sex households exceeded one million, reflecting the public's general approval of same-sex unions.[18] On November 29, 2022, the Senate passed a bill mandating federal recognition of marriages between two men and between two women. The bill repealed the 1996 Defense of Marriage Act that had denied federal benefits to same-sex couples and prevented states from negating the validity of same-sex marriages performed in other states. The bill was then passed by the House of Representatives on December 8. President Biden signed the newly passed Respect for Marriage Act into law on December 13, 2022.[19]

This legislative achievement was understandably applauded by its supporters and embraced by the LGBTQ community. While it was not perfect—in order to vote in favor of the bill, Republicans insisted that religious organizations be free to deny services to members of same-sex couples without penalty—nevertheless, this landmark legislation brought immediate relief to the individuals most directly affected.

WHAT'S NEXT?

Yale University law professor Douglas NeJaime thinks the next set of questions will center on whether unmarried people using assisted reproduction to have children will be afforded the same respect given to married people who also become parents through assisted means.[20] He asserted that even if Andrew and Elad were not married, "we should be treating their child as *their child* [my emphasis] because they're the intended parents of the child. . . . This [becoming a parent in such circumstances] should not turn on the marital connection."

Like the State Department official (SDO) I cited in chapter 8, NeJaime believes a future legal framework should have *intent* as a basis for parentage. He advocates access to *prebirth orders* or *prebirth judgments* of parentage that would serve as a declaration of intent. If a child is conceived by surrogacy, a state or family court could issue an order stating that when the child is born, the intended parents (regardless of marital status) are the legal parents. Another option is securing an acknowledgment of parentage that establishes a man's paternity as the legal father right after the birth of the child. And in his view (while noting that his expertise is in family law, not immigration law), citizenship would flow presumably from parentage. NeJaime believes that "federal regulation should mirror what the relevant parentage law is."

Related issues concern the treatment of the unrelated gay parent in a surrogacy arrangement. In some states this parent is not regarded as a legal parent if they haven't adopted the child. "I don't think people should have to adopt their own children," he insisted. These remarks echo Ross's concern with the possible inequity of viewing the children of married and unmarried couples differently, based on state laws. In an ambitious undertaking, NeJaime and Joslin are looking at case law in all fifty states that protects non-biological parent-child relationships. Little is known about these "functional parental doctrines" and how they work in practice—and not all states have clarified the circumstances in which these relationships would be protected. Their findings will have implications not only for families formed through assisted reproduction, like the Dvash-Banks family, but for the large number and varied types of families today "that include non-biological parents and their children."[21]

NeJaime predicts that the overturning of *Roe v. Wade* "will certainly change assisted reproduction in states that are restricting abortion." One such change would involve the selective reduction of embryos. (Selective reduction, also known as selective termination, is the elimination of embryos in multiple pregnancies done to foster the healthy development of the embryos that remain.) It is expected that this practice would be affected by the Supreme Court's decision because selective reduction could conceivably be viewed as abortion. However, selective reduction can be an important medical procedure for eliminating an embryo with a serious defect or malformation, improving the chance of a successful birth and/or serving the health interests of the mother. Pregnant women in their mid-thirties and beyond are (and will be) at greater risk because chromosomal anomalies, like Down's syndrome, increase with maternal age.[22] In Connecticut, where NeJaime lives, and in New York, surrogates have been given rights to decide if they want to carry a multiple pregnancy or whether to terminate a pregnancy. It is likely that such rights will be removed in states restricting abortion.

NeJaime's final thoughts: What about people who don't get married? Should it make any difference, in terms of parentage? What if neither parent has a genetic connection to the child? A future question is going to be: Is that so important?

I would like to see increased efforts by developmental psychologists toward understanding the nature of same-sex parenting. As discussed in chapter 7, the few available studies show that these couples make excellent parents and raise children with very good outcomes. Same-sex couples would benefit from wider dissemination of these findings, helping them to enter the family mainstream until the time when most people will no longer take notice. I also favor examining the quality of twin and sibling relationships in these families. Sibling relationships evolve within family settings and are significantly affected by children's perceptions and experiences.[23] Family law has also focused more narrowly on marriage and parenthood, with scant attention paid to twins and siblings.[24]

"WE ARE SO NOT DONE"

Reflecting on the past few years, Elad is grateful that gay marriage "is here—it's federally recognized, we're done.[25] But we are so not done, because there [are] so many issues that have not been resolved for same-sex families." And he now knows that the legality of gay marriage may still be threatened.[26] "Are we in prehistoric times?" he asked. Andrew recalled how confident both he and Elad were feeling, truly believing that everything would be "fine" by moving to Los Angeles—after all, they had been a married couple living in Toronto and had conceived twin sons through legal means. "But we were not fine. And we don't know what the next hurdle will be—I hope there won't be any more. Who would have thought we would encounter all that difficulty with Ethan's citizenship?"[27]

Several weeks after his swearing-in ceremony, Elad spoke more about the meaning of becoming a United States citizen. "I feel that now I can make a difference by voting, by participating in civil society, and really make a difference in this country. I think this country has so much potential, but unfortunately, it's being misused many times by politicians and other interest groups. I love this country, and I think that's why we always wanted to move here. . . . This country is about families, right? From the most ancient times, the family was the most important unit, which is how people were able to work, have food, and raise kids. So why, when a same-sex couple wants to live that principle and have a family, why are you not advocating for them and making it easy for them to do that? I hear some politicians say, 'Family First.' I agree, 'Family First,' but *all families first* [my emphasis]. Not just your family first. All families."

Continuing this theme, Andrew admitted that it is hard not to be political about his own situation and the recent restrictions on personal freedoms. "We are [Elad and I] both very politically charged. Our lawyers had us stay away from politics [during the lawsuit] because they felt, and I agreed with them, that our story could really resonate with Middle America. We're a monogamous, happily married couple with kids. We just happen to be same-sex, but we are a family unit and we're whole, and that is something that Middle America—Republican or Democrat—can relate to. I really hope that's true—I mean, I think it's true."

Andrew's motivation to correct things he feels are unjust remains high. He believes there is work to be done for the LGBTQ and immigrant communities and that it is vital to add a face to these groups to help move the conversation forward in America. As Elad said, "Andrew got out the boxing gloves." Looking back, Andrew believes that he and thousands of others in the gay community were successful because they had dinner-table conversations with their families and friends. Just ordinary people.

ORDINARY PEOPLE

Ordinary People is a 1980 dramatic film about the Jarrett family's attempts to return to normalcy after the accidental death of their older son, Buck, and the release of their younger son, Calvin, from psychiatric treatment.[28] Their lives are in disarray until a perceptive psychiatrist helps Calvin realize he is not responsible for Buck's loss.

(L) Ethan is examining a mussel he found on the beach as his twin brother, Aiden, looks on; (R) A family run on the beach. Both pictures were taken in October 2017 at a beach in Malibu, California. *Photo credit*: Images of Life by Ashli.

Andrew and Elad are ordinary people. Like the Jarrett family experienced, their carefully orchestrated future was derailed for a time by events beyond their control. But with help from a cadre of skilled attorneys, they are leading a normal life. The only thing setting them apart from most other families is that their twins have two fathers. However, that's not what you see when you spend time with them. Instead, all you see are two parents doing what all parents do—teaching, entertaining, and supervising their children. I believe that people who reject such alternative family structures have probably never experienced them personally; as Andrew said, casual dinner-table conversations are powerful ways to show, not tell, reluctant others that all families are variations on the same theme. The wonderful thing about being human is that we can thrive in many settings and under varied conditions, given that the basic needs of love, nutrition, and safety are secure.

Most people will continue to cling to their biases, but it is possible to do so without interfering in the lives of others. Accepting alternative lifestyles, even while rejecting them at a personal level, would allow everyone the freedom to be themselves. I am unaware of any gay movements that denigrate the life choices of heterosexual couples or try to take away their rights to marry and have children. Same-sex couples just want to be treated like everyone else. And they want their children to be entitled to the same respect and opportunities as the children of heterosexual couples.

THE LAST LINE

Authors focused on finding great titles, catchphrases, or closing words can be disappointed, because these gems arise unexpectedly. But they are recognizable. The first time I met Andrew in person, he recited a line that I knew I would use for either the opening or closing of this book, because his words captured the tone of everything he and Elad have gone through together:

> "It's a Gordian knot of investors who would never do this to a heterosexual couple."
>
> —Andrew, December 12, 2021

Notes

PREFACE

1. Alene Tchekmedyian, "These Twins Were Born 4 Minutes Apart. But Only One is a U.S. Citizen," *Los Angeles Times*, January 27, 2018, https://www.latimes.com/local/lanow/la-me-ln-twins-citizenship-20180127-story.html.

2. Legal Information Institute, Cornell Law School, "Defense of Marriage Act (DOMA)," https://www.law.cornell.edu/wex/defense_of_marriage_act_(doma), accessed January 27, 2022. The act allowed states to refuse to recognize same-sex marriages granted under the laws of other states.

3. "Dvash-Banks Family," Immigration Equality, https://immigrationequality.org/andrew-elad-and-ethan-dvash-banks/, 2018. In February 2011, the Obama administration announced it would no longer defend DOMA, and that laws affecting gays and lesbians deserved "heightened scrutiny" by the courts. However, only Congress could overturn the law. E. J. Graff, "Is DOMA Dead?," *The Nation*, https://www.thenation.com/article/archive/doma-dead/, February 24, 2011. A key provision of DOMA that denied federal benefits to legally married same-sex couples was struck down by the US Supreme Court in 2013. Stephanie Condon, "Supreme Court Strikes Down Key Part of DOMA, Dismisses Prop 8 Case," CBS News, https://www.cbsnews.com/news/supreme-court-strikes-down-key-part-of-doma-dismisses-prop-8-case/, June 26, 2013. Same-sex marriage was legalized on June 26, 2015, in the outcome of *Obergefell v. Hodges*.

4. Andrew had a Canadian passport before acquiring a United States passport, because his parents were from Canada.

5. Dietmar Spitzer, R. Haidbauer, C. Corn, J. Stadler, B. Wirleitner, and N. H. Zech, "Effects of Embryo Transfer Quality on Pregnancy and Live Birth Delivery Rates," *Journal of Assisted Reproduction and Genetics* 29, no. 2 (2012): 131–35.

6. Jackie Yodashkin is currently a self-employed organization development and strategic communications consultant. *LinkedIn*, https://www.linkedin.com /in/jackie-yodashkin-a70a42/.

7. Nancy L. Segal, *Deliberately Divided: Inside the Controversial Study of Twins and Triplets Adopted Apart* (Lanham, MD: Rowman & Littlefield, 2021).

8. Spencer Tilger is currently media relations manager at the International Refugee Assistance Project in New York City. *LinkedIn*, https://www.linkedin .com/in/spencer-tilger-44760445/.

INTRODUCTION

1. "Pros and Cons of Preimplantation Genetic Screening PGGS," Pacific Fertility Center, Los Angeles, https://www.pfcla.com/blog/preimplantation -genetic-screening-pgs-pros-and-cons, April 15, 2021.

2. California offers transitional-kindergarten (TK) classes for children born in September or later. Aiden and Ethan were born on September 16, so they had to wait a year before entering the regular kindergarten class.

3. "Home and Neighborhood Details," *Zillow*, https://www.zillow.com/, 2006–2022.

4. The separate adoptions of Michele and Allison, other twin pairs, and a set of triplets happened because of a misguided policy implemented by Louise Wise Services. My 2021 book, *Deliberately Divided*, tells the story of these multiple-birth babies and the investigators who secretly studied them. Michele and Allison's reunion can be seen at the following link: https://www.theatlantic.com /video/index/571867/two-identical-strangers/.

CHAPTER 1

1. Andrew Dvash-Banks, Brian Banks, interviews with Nancy L. Segal, 2022.

2. Ann Banks, interview with Nancy L. Segal, 2022.

3. James Banks, interview with Nancy L. Segal, 2022.

4. Ann Banks, Andrew Dvash-Banks, interviews with Nancy L. Segal, 2022. Jennifer was raised mostly by her biological mother in Encino, California.

5. Andrew Dvash-Banks, Ann Banks, interviews with Nancy L. Segal, 2022, 2023.

6. Identical twinning, once thought to be a matter of random chance, may be genetically transmitted in some families, although this idea remains con-

troversial. Particular genes associated with identical twinning in humans and non-humans have been reported but require further study. Jeffrey J. Beck, Susanne Bruins, Hamdi Mbarek, Gareth E. Davies, and Dorret I. Boomsma, "Biology and Genetics of Dizygotic and Monozygotic Twinning," in *Twin and Higher-Order Pregnancies*, Asma Kahlil, Liesbeth Lewi, and Enrico Lopriore, eds. (Springer Nature, Cham: Switzerland AG, 2021, 31–50); also see Nancy L. Segal, *Twin Mythconceptions: False Beliefs, Fables, and Facts about Twins* (San Diego, CA: Academic Press, 2017) and Hanan A. Hamamy, Heitham K. Ajlouni, and Kamel M. Ajlouni, "Familial Monozygotic Twinning: Report of an Extended Multi-Generation Family," *Twin Research* 7, no. 3 (2004): 219–22.

7. "Goldblum Among 6 Sentenced to Jail in Equity Funding Case," *New York Times*, https://www.nytimes.com/1975/03/19/archives/goldblum-among-6-sentenced-to-jail-in-equity-funding-case.html, March 19, 1975.

8. Brian Banks, interview with Nancy L. Segal, 2022; also Ronald E. Soble and Robert E. Dallos, *The Impossible Dream: The Equity Funding Story, the Fraud of the Century* (New York: G. P. Putnam's Sons, 1975) and *Billion Dollar Bubble*, BBC television series (1976). Jim Banks was part of a lesser group of lawbreakers (the "little six"), compared with the "big three."

9. Andrew Dvash-Banks, interview with Nancy L. Segal, 2022.

10. Brian Banks, interview with Nancy L. Segal, 2022.

11 Andrew Dvash-Banks, interview with Nancy L. Segal, 2022.

12. Jewish boys have a bar mitzvah at age thirteen to celebrate their passage into adulthood, or coming of age.

13. Bill Carter, "ABC Is Canceling 'Ellen,' " *New York Times*, https://www.nytimes.com/1998/04/25/arts/abc-is-canceling-ellen.html, April 25, 1998.

14. Ellen DeGeneres may be better known for *The Ellen DeGeneres Show*, which she launched in 2003. She ended that series in 2022 amid allegations of a toxic workplace. Lauren Samer, "Behind the Comedic Rise—and Controversial Fall—of Ellen DeGeneres," *New York Post*, https://nypost.com/2021/05/12/how-ellen-degeneres-spectacular-downfall-happened/, May 12, 2021.

15. Dr. Elaine Leader, interview with Nancy L. Segal, 2022; letter from Beverly Hills High School counselor Marlene Mish to principal Ben Bushman, April 19, 1999.

16. Gerulf Rieger, Tuesday M. Watts-Overall, Luke Holmes, and Dragos C. Gruia, "Gender Nonconformity of Identical Twins with Discordant Sexual Orientations: Evidence from Video Recordings," *Archives of Sexual Behavior* 49, no. 7 (2020): 2469–79.

17. Teen Line operates out of Cedars-Sinai Medical Center in Los Angeles, https://www.teenline.org/, 2021; Dr. Elaine Leader, interview with Nancy L. Segal, 2022.

18. Andrew Dvash-Banks, interview with Nancy L. Segal, 2022.

19. Ann Banks, interview with Nancy L. Segal, 2022.

20. James Banks, interview with Nancy L. Segal; 2022. Research shows that sexual orientation and gender identity are influenced by genetic factors, but specific genes linked to these characteristics have not been identified. Alessandra D. Fisher, Jiska Ristori, Girolamo Morelli, and Mario Maggi, "The Molecular Mechanisms of Sexual Orientation and Gender Identity," *Molecular and Cellular Endocrinology* 467 (2018): 3–13.

21. Brian Banks, interview with Nancy L. Segal, 2022.

22. Brian Banks, interview with Nancy L. Segal, 2022.

23. Laurel Mintz, interview with Nancy L. Segal, 2022.

24. Andrew Dvash-Banks, interview with Nancy L. Segal, 2022.

25. StudyPortals, "Ca'Foscari University of Venice," https://www.masters portal.com/universities/750/ca-foscari-university-of-venice.html, 2022. Andrew studied in Venice during his sophomore year in college, which was somewhat unusual—most students study abroad during their junior year.

26. The Birthright Israel Foundation was founded in 1999 to allow young Jewish adults to visit Israel for purposes of identity and education, https://birth rightisrael.foundation/approach/, 2022.

27. Andrew Dvash-Banks, interview with Nancy L. Segal, 2022.

28. Jessica Yousem, interview with Nancy L. Segal, 2022.

29. Laurel Mintz, interview with Nancy L. Segal, 2022.

30. Gay and bisexual men were restricted from donating blood beginning in the 1980s. In November 2022, blood shortages in the United States reduced the deferral period (length of celibacy) from twelve months to three months (https://abcnews.go.com/US/gay-men-face-hurdles-donate-blood-amid -national/story?id=82197317). As of 2021, the Canadian Blood Services allows gay men to donate plasma, as long as they have not had a new sexual partner or their partner has not had another sexual partner for three months (https://www.ctvnews.ca/health/canadian-blood-services-eases-restrictions -for-some-gay-men-in-alta-ont-1.562050).

31. Andrew Dvash-Banks, interview with Nancy L. Segal, 2022.

32. "Kibbutz: Israeli Commune," *Encyclopedia Britannica*, https://www.bri tannica.com/topic/kibbutz, 2022.

33. The 2006 Lebanon War began when Hezbollah ambushed an Israeli military patrol in a raid across the border. It is known as the July War in Lebanon and the Second Lebanon War in Israel. Three Israeli soldiers were killed and two were kidnapped. Just Vision, https://justvision.org/glossary/2006 -lebanon-war, 2022.

34. "Hezbollah" is the Arabic term for "Party of God." It is a Shi'a Muslim political group with a military wing. https://justvision.org/glossary/hezbollah, 2022.

35. Ann Banks, interview with Nancy L. Segal, 2022.

36. Jessica Yousem, interview with Nancy L. Segal, 2022.

37. "Rosa Louise Parks Biography," Rosa and Raymond Parks Institute for Self Development, https://www.rosaparks.org/biography/, 2022.

38. Ann Banks, Jennifer (Stone) Sikov, interviews with Nancy L. Segal, 2022.

39. Segal, *Twin Mythconceptions*.

40. "Children of Alcoholics," *Alcohol.org*, https://www.alcohol.org/helping -an-alcoholic/children-of-alcoholics/, 2022.

41. Tinca J. C. Polderman, Beben Benyamin, Christiaan A. De Leeuw, Patrick F. Sullivan, Arjen Van Bochoven, Peter M. Visscher, and Danielle Post-huma, "Meta-Analysis of the Heritability of Human Traits Based on Fifty Years of Twin Studies," *Nature Genetics* 47, no. 7 (2015): 702–09.

42. Ann Banks, Brian Banks, interviews with Nancy L. Segal, 2022.

43. Andrew-Dvash Banks, interview with Nancy L. Segal, 2022.

44. "Elon Musk's Kids: Meet His Six Kids from Oldest to Youngest, & Their Moms," *New York Press News*, https://nypressnews.com/news/entertainment /elon-musks-kids-meet-his-6-kids-from-oldest-to-youngest-their-moms/, September 14, 2021.

45. James Banks, interview with Nancy L. Segal, 2022.

CHAPTER 2

1. My late colleague, David T. Lykken, applied this idea to happiness. Twin studies showed that a lucky bet or a severe misfortune can raise or lower one's characteristic happiness level, but the effect is fleeting; eventually we drift back to what Lykken called "the happiness set point." See David T. Lykken and Auke Tellegen, "Happiness is a Stochastic Phenomenon," *Psychological Science* 7, no. 3 (1996): 186–89.

2. Cheryl Dickow, "Firstborn Sons," *Catholic Exchange*, https://catholic exchange.com/firstborn-sons/#:~:text=First-born%20sons%20have%20 always%20held%20a%20place%20of,mother%E2%80%99s%20womb%2C %E2%80%9D%20is%20said%20to%20belong%20to%20God, August 17, 2010; Dovid Rosenfeld, "Firstborn (Bechor) Privileges," *Aish*, https://aish.com/first born-bechor-privileges/, December 2, 2016; Elisha Klirs, e-mail correspon-dence with Nancy L. Segal, 2022.

3. Yarden Dvash, interview with Nancy L. Segal, 2022.

4. Rebecca Weiner, "Judaism: Sephardim," *Jewish Virtual Library*, https:// www.jewishvirtuallibrary.org/sephardim, 2022. The terms *Sephardi* and *Mizrahi* are often used interchangeably but refer to people from different Jewish dias-poras; see Dina Danon, "What Do You Know? Sephardi vs. Mizrahi," Katz Center, University of Pennsylvania, https://katz.sas.upenn.edu/resources/blog

/what-do-you-know-sephardi-vs-mizrahi, December 5, 2018. Mizrahi ("Easterners") refers to many Jewish subcultures across the Middle East, North Africa, and Central Asia.

5. Eran Razin, "Tel Aviv-Yafo," *Britannica*, https://www.britannica.com /place/Tel-Aviv-Yafo, accessed 2022. Tel Aviv means "Hill of Spring." It is located forty miles northwest of Jerusalem.

6. Elad Dvash-Banks, Tovi Dvash, interviews with Nancy L. Segal, 2022.

7. Elad Dvash-Banks, interview with Nancy L. Segal, 2022.

8. Elad Dvash-Banks, interview with Nancy L. Segal, 2022, 2023.

9. Shabbat is the day of rest and enrichment for Jewish people. It lasts from sundown on Friday until sundown on Saturday. "Shabbat: What is Shabbat?," Jewish Virtual Library, https://www.jewishvirtuallibrary.org/what-is-shabbat -jewish-sabbath, 2008.

10. Nathan Guttman, "Pew Level: Meet the Mazorti, Israel's 'Tradition' Tribe," *Forward*, https://forward.com/news/335410/pew-report-meet-the -masorti-israels-traditional-tribe/, 2022. Elad's paternal grandparents recited prayers and did not use electrical appliances or drive on Shabbat, but they were not strictly kosher.

11. "Arison Campus of the Arts," Tel-Aviv Foundation, https://telaviv foundation.org/initiatives/arison-campus-of-the-arts/, 2021; Elad Dvash-Banks, interview with Nancy L. Segal, 2022.

12. Tovi Dvash, interview with Nancy L. Segal, 2022.

13. Nancy L. Segal, *Twin Mythconceptions: False Beliefs, Fables, and Facts about Twins* (San Diego: Academic Press, 2017).

14. Elad drew an analogy between Givatayim and Beverly Hills. Beverly Hills, while part of Los Angeles, is a city all its own. Givatayim, situated inside Tel Aviv, also has a unique status in the metropolitan area that includes Tel Aviv. Givatayim's educational opportunities, environmental protections, and 2003 recognition as "the best cared for city in Israel" make it a highly sought residential area. Elad Dvash-Banks, interview with Nancy L. Segal, 2022; "Givatayim," *Jewish Virtual Library*, https://www.jewishvirtuallibrary.org/giva tayim, 2008; "About the City," *The City of Givatayim*, http://www.givatayim .muni.il/, 2008.

15. Moti Dvash, interview with Nancy L. Segal, 2022.

16. Elad Dvash-Banks, Rotem Cohen, interviews with Nancy L. Segal, 2022. The name Rotem means "flowering bush."

17. Rotem Cohen, interview with Nancy L. Segal, 2022. One Israeli shekel was worth about one-third of a US dollar (36 cents) in 1995, when Elad was in elementary school.

18. Elad Dvash-Banks, interview with Nancy L. Segal, 2022.

19. Childhood gender nonconformity has been associated with later homosexual orientation. Gerulf Rieger, Joan A. W. Linsenmeier, Lorenz Gygax, and

J. Michael Bailey, "Sexual Orientation and Childhood Gender Nonconformity: Evidence from Home Videos," *Developmental Psychology* 44, no. 1 (2008): 46–58. However, not every child who displays behaviors typical of the opposite sex are homosexual as adults.

20. Yarden Dvash, interview with Nancy L. Segal, 2022.

21. Elad Dvash-Banks, interview with Nancy L. Segal, 2022.

22. The first country to legalize gay marriage was the Netherlands, in 2001. Gay marriage was legalized in Canada in 2005 and in the United States in 2015. Israel does not perform marriages for gay couples but recognizes gay marriage if the ceremony occurred elsewhere; however, such couples cannot obtain a marriage license. "The First Countries to Legalize Gay Marriage," *World Atlas*, https://www.worldatlas.com/articles/first-countries-to-recognize -same-sex-marriages-nationally.html, 2022; Liam Hoare, "Israel Won't Legalize Gay Marriage. Here's Why," *Slate*, https://slate.com/human-interest/2013/11 /israel-wont-legalize-gay-marriage-heres-why.html, November 21, 2013.

23. "What is IKAR?" IKAR, https://ikar.org/ask/what-is-ikar/, 2022.

24. Males in Israel complete three years of required army service between high school graduation and college entry. Females serve for two years.

25. Seth Adler, "Inside the Elite Israeli Military Unit 8200," *Cyber Security Hub*, https://www.cshub.com/threat-defense/articles/inside-the-elite-israeli -military-unit-8200, June 11, 2020.

26. *The Amazing Race* recruits teams of two to travel to different destinations around the world. At each destination they must complete certain tasks before moving to the next one; see https://www.cbs.com/shows/amazing_race/, 2022.

27. Ilona Krashanny, interview with Nancy L. Segal, 2022.

28. Elad Dvash-Banks, interview with Nancy L. Segal, 2022.

29. MasterClass Staff, "What Is Intertextuality? How to Apply Literary In-spiration to Your Writing," *MasterClass*, https://www.masterclass.com/articles /how-to-apply-literary-inspiration-to-your-writing, August 23, 2021.

30. "Intertextuality," *Literary Devices*, https://literarydevices.net/inter textuality/, 2022.

31. This work was a capstone project, an opportunity to conduct indepen-dent group research for the purpose of devising an innovative solution for a real-world problem. Stephanie L., "What is a Capstone Project? And Why is it Important? *Top Universities*, https://www.topuniversities.com/student-info /careers-advice-articles/what-capstone-project-why-it-important, January 14, 2022.

32. Sephardic and Mizrahi Jews have a separate heritage, but they have many religious customs in common. Rachel M. Solomin, "Sephardic, Ashkenazic, Mizrahi and Ethiopian Jews," *My Jewish Learning*, https://www.myjewishlearn ing.com/article/sephardic-ashkenazic-mizrahi-jews-jewish-ethnic-diversity/, 2022.

33. Elad Dvash-Banks, interview with Nancy L. Segal, 2022.

34. Or Kashti, "Israel Recognizes Middle Eastern Jewry Studies as Independent Academic Discipline," *Haaretz*, https://www.haaretz.com/israel-news/.premium-israeli-council-recognizes-middle-eastern-jewry-studies-as-independent-discipline-1.10628246, February 22, 2022.

35. David Shasha, "Sephardim, Ashkenazim, and Ultra-Orthodox Racism in Israel," *Huffington Post*, https://www.huffpost.com/entry/sephardim-ashkenazim-and_b_615692, June 21, 2010.

36. Elad Dvash-Banks, interview with Nancy L. Segal, 2022.

37. Elad Dvash-Banks, Kari Zalik, interviews with Nancy L. Segal, 2022. Hawthorne, California, is home to where Andrew works.

38. This phrase is most often attributed to the late Beatles singer and songwriter, John Lennon. It was a line in his song "Beautiful Boy (Darling Boy)," released in 1980. However, its origin has been traced to several other individuals. "Life Is What Happens to You While You're Busy Making Other Plans," *QuoteInvestigator*, https://quoteinvestigator.com/2012/05/06/other-plans/, May 6, 2012.

CHAPTER 3

1. "Modern Love," *New York Times*, https://www.nytimes.com/column/modern-love, 2022; "Sunday Styles," https://archive.nytimes.com/www.nytimes.com/pages/fashion/sundaystyles/index.html, 2022.

2. Studies have shown show that romantic partners match to a greater degree on behavioral traits than physical characteristics, known as assortative mating; see Yoon-Mi Hur, "Assortative Mating for Personality Traits, Educational Level, Religious Affiliation, Height, Weight, and Body Mass Index in Parents of a Korean Twin Sample," *Twin Research* 6, no. 6 (2003): 467–70; Brendan P. Zietsch, Karin J. H. Verweij, Andrew C. Heath, and Nicholas G. Martin, "Variation in Human Mate Choice: Simultaneously Investigating Heritability, Parental Influence, Sexual Imprinting, and Assortative Mating," *American Naturalist* 177, no. 5 (2011): 605–16.

3. Elad Dvash-Banks, interview with Nancy L. Segal, 2022.

4. Elad was a counselor for undergraduate foreign students.

5. Nancy L. Segal, "Unusual Behavioral Similarities in Twins Reared Apart: Genetic Effects, Random Chance or Both?," *Japanese Journal of Twin Studies* 1, no. 1 (2022): 1–11.

6. Chabad-Lubavitch Media Center, "What is Purim?" *Chabad.org*, https://www.chabad.org/holidays/purim/article_cdo/aid/645309/jewish/What-Is-Purim.htm, 2022.

7. "What is the Jewish Festival of Purim Otherwise Known As?," *Chicago Jewish News*, https://www.chicagojewishnews.com/what-is-the-jewish-festival-of-purim-otherwise-known-as/, 2022; Gavriel Fiske, "Purim: Part on Hevre," *Jerusalem Post*, https://www.jpost.com/Local-Israel/In-Jerusalem/Purim-Party-on-hevre, March 13, 2008. The holiday is based on the Book of Esther from the Hebrew Scriptures, and modern scholars agree as to its historical authenticity. Foods eaten in Purim vary across countries and cultures.

8. Jonathan Banks, interview with Nancy L. Segal, 2022.

9. Bad Parade, https://www.badparade.com/, 2021.

10. Hur, "Assortative Mating for Personality Traits," 467–70; J. Philippe Rushton and Trudy Ann Bons, "Mate Choice and Friendship in Twins: Evidence for Genetic Similarity," *Psychological Science* 16, no. 7 (2005): 555–59; Brendan P. Zietsch, Karin J. H. Verweij, Andrew C. Heath, and Nicholas G. Martin, "Variation in Human Mate Choice: Simultaneously Investigating Heritability, Parental Influence, Sexual Imprinting, and Assortative Mating," *The American Naturalist* 177, no. 5 (2011): 605–16.

11. Dorit Sasson, "The American and Israeli Cultural Differences between Big and Small," *The Times of Israel*, https://blogs.timesofisrael.com/the-american-and-israeli-cultural-differences-between-big-and-small/, January 15, 2016.

12. Rotem Cohen, interview with Nancy L. Segal, 2022.

13. Legal Information Institute, "Defense of Marriage Act (DOMA)," Cornell University, https://www.law.cornell.edu/wex/defense_of_marriage_act_%28doma%29, 2020.

14. "California Proposition 8, Same-Sex Marriage Ban Initiative (2008)," *Ballotpedia.org*, https://ballotpedia.org/California_Proposition_8,_Same-Sex_Marriage_Ban_Initiative_ (2008); History, "Same-Sex Marriage is Made Legal Nationwide with *Obergefell v. Hodges* Decision," *History.com*, https://www.history.com/this-day-in-history/obergefell-v-hodges-ruling-same-sex-marriage-legalized-nationwide, 2022. A comprehensive account of the history of gay marriage in America is available in Sasha Issenberg, *The Engagement: America's Quarter-Century Struggle Over Same-Sex Marriage* (New York: Penguin Books, 2021).

15. Andrew Dvash-Banks, interview with Nancy L. Segal, 2022.

16. The names on the marriage license are Andrew Mason Banks and Elad Dvash. Andrew's middle name (Mason) is his mother's maiden name. Elad added a middle name (Austin) after he and Andrew were married, chosen because he liked the way it sounded. Marriage License, Ontario Ministry of Government Services, *PACER, Case 2:18-cv-00523-JFW-JC, Document 1-2*, August 19, 2010; Andrew and Elad Dvash-Banks, e-mail correspondence with Nancy L. Segal, 2022.

17. "Estates of Sunnybrook," *Venue Report*, https://www.venuereport.com/venue/estates-of-sunnybrook/profile/, 2022.

18. Ann Banks, interview with Nancy L. Segal, 2022.

19. Caillianne and Samantha Beckerman, interview with Nancy L. Segal, 2023.

20. *Beverly Hills, 90210* was a television series that aired between 1990 and 2000. It focused on a group of friends in Beverly Hills as they transitioned from school age to adulthood, https://www.imdb.com/title/tt0098749/.

21. Elad Dvash-Banks, interview with Nancy L. Segal, 2022.

22. Kari Zalik, interview with Nancy L. Segal, 2022.

23. Jacob Samsian, "The Unexpected History Behind Why the Couple Stomps on a Piece of Glass in a Jewish Wedding," *Insider.com*, https://www .insider.com/jewish-wedding-glass-break-tradition-2017-4, April 14, 2017; Kim Forrest, "14 Jewish Wedding Traditions and What They Mean," https:// www.weddingwire.com/wedding-ideas/jewish-wedding-traditions, June 13, 2018.

24. Elad and Andrew Dvash-Banks, interview with Nancy L. Segal, 2021.

25. "All You Need is Love: Weddings," *Weddingwire.ca*, https://www.wed dingwire.ca/wedding-officiants/all-you-need-is-love-~-weddings--e8139, 2022.

26. Andrew Dvash-Banks, interview with Nancy L. Segal, 2022.

27. Elad worked at the Egmont Group in Toronto for three and a half years as an intern, part-time consultant, and senior officer. A financial intelligence unit (FIU) is an investigative body established by different countries to centralize the gathering of suspicious activity related to criminal financial activity. News Corp, "What Are Financial Intelligence Units?" *Dow Jones*, https://www.dowjones .com/professional/risk/glossary/financial-crime/financial-intelligence-units/, 2022. Recall from chapter 2 that Elad's master's thesis was based on information gathered during his time there.

CHAPTER 4

1. A parent has a 50 percent chance of transmitting a given gene to child 1 and a 50 percent chance of transmitting the given gene to child 2. The chance that the two children would inherit the same gene is: $0.50 \times 0.50 = 0.25$, or 25 percent. These two events are independent.

2. John Archer, "Facts Illustrating a Disease Peculiar to the Female Children of Negro Slaves," *The Medical Repository of Original Essays and Intelligence, Relative to Physic, Surgery, Chemistry, and Natural History (1800–1824)* 1 (1810): 319–23.

3. Okamura Kunihiro, Jun Murotsuki, Mitsuru Iwamoto, Hidetaka Endo, Takanori Watanabe, Kazuo Ohashi, and Akira Yajima, "A Probable Case of Superfecundation," *Fetal Diagnosis and Therapy* 7, no. 1 (1992): 17–20.

4. Nancy L. Segal, *Twin Mythconceptions: False Beliefs, Fables, and Facts About Twins* (San Diego, CA: Academic Press, 2017). Another reproductive process, superfetation, could also yield twins with different fathers. In this case, a woman would release a second egg several weeks after already conceiving. If the woman had different partners, these superfetated twins would be genetic half-siblings, just like superfecundated twins. They would share their birthdays but would be developmentally discrepant, given that one twin was conceived several weeks before the other twin.

5. Amsalem Hagai, Rimona Tsvieli, Bat Sheva Zentner, Simcha Yagel, Stella Mitrani-Rosenbaum, and Arye Hurwitz, "Monopaternal Superfecundation of Quintuplets after Transfer of Two Embryos in an In Vitro Fertilization Cycle," *Fertility and Sterility* 76, no. 3 (2001): 621–23.

6. Nancy L. Segal and Joseph L. Nedelec, "Heteropaternal Twinning: Unique Case of Opposite-Sex Twins with Different Fathers," *Forensic Science International* 327 (2021): 110948.

7. R. E. Wenk, T. Houtz, M. Brooks, and F. A. Chiafari, "How Frequent Is Heteropaternal Superfecundation?" *Acta Geneticae Medicae et Gemellologiae: Twin Research* 41, no. 1 (1992): 43–47.

8. Nancy L. Segal, Jeffrey M. Craig, and Mark P. Umstad, "Challenge to the Assumed Rarity of Heteropaternal Superfecundation: Findings from a Case Report," *Australian Journal of Forensic Sciences* 52, no. 5 (2020): 547–52.

9. National Survey of Family Growth, "Number of Sexual Partners in Lifetime," *Centers for Disease Control and Prevention*, https://www.cdc.gov/nchs/nsfg /key_statistics/n-keystat.htm#numberlifetime, November 8, 2021. Data were gathered in 2015–2018.

10. W. H. James, "Coital Frequency and Twinning: A Comment," *Journal of Biosocial Science* 24, no. 1 (1992): 135–36; B. Bønnelykke, J. Olsen, and J. Nielsen, "Coital Frequency and Twinning," *Journal of Biosocial Science* 22, no. 2 (1990): 191–96.

11. J. J. Goedert, R. J. Biggar, C. I. Amos, A. M. Duliège, and S. Felton, "High Risk of HIV-1 Infection for First-born Twins," *The Lancet* 338, no. 8781 (1991): 1471–75; see also Nancy L. Segal, *Entwined Lives: Twins and What They Tell Us About Human Behavior* (New York: Plume, 2000).

12. The 2017 rate of same-sex marriage among cohabiting same-sex couples was 10.2 percent. This was an increase from the 7.9 percent reported prior to the Supreme Court's 2015 decision that states could not prohibit unions of same-sex couples. Jeffrey M. Jones, "In U.S. 10.2% of LGBT Adults Now Married to Same-Sex Spouse," *Gallup*, https://news.gallup.com/poll/212702/lgbt -adults-married-sex-spouse.aspx?utm_source=alert&utm_medium =email&utm_content=morelink&utm_campaign=syndication, 2022.

13. Jimmy Nsubuga, "Baby 'Twins' Born with Two Different Dads after Gay Parents Have IVF," Associated Newspapers (*Metro*), https://

metro.co.uk/2019/01/28/baby-twins-born-two-different-dads-gay-parents-ivf-8399648/, January 28, 2019.

14. David Dodge, " 'A Family Like Ours': Portraits of Gay Fatherhood," *New York Times*, https://www.nytimes.com/2021/06/16/well/family/gay-fatherhood-photos.html, June 16, 2021.

15. Nicole Acevedo, "Pete Buttigieg and Husband, Chasten, Welcome Two Children Into Their Family," *NBC News*, https://www.nbcnews.com/feature/nbc-out/pete-buttigieg-husband-chasten-welcome-two-children-their-family-n1278512, September 4, 2021.

16. Nancy L. Segal, "Behavioral Aspects of Intergenerational Cloning: What Twins Tell Us," *Jurimetrics* 38 (1997), 57–67; Nancy L. Segal, "Human Cloning: A Twin-Research Perspective," *Hastings Law Journal* 53 (2002), 1073–84; Nancy L. Segal, "Psychological Features of Human Reproductive Cloning: A Twin-Based Perspective" (invited paper), *Psychiatric Times* XXIII (2006), 20, 22.

17. News Roundup, "Black Twins Are Born to White Parents after Infertility Treatment," *British Medical Journal* (2002): 325; *Dateline*, NBC-TV, November 16, 1996.

18. Yu Neng, Margot S. Kruskall, Juan J. Yunis, Joan H. M. Knoll, Lynne Uhl, Sharon Alosco, Marina Ohashi, et al., "Disputed Maternity Leading to Identification of Tetragametic Chimerism," *New England Journal of Medicine* 346, no. 20 (2002): 1545–52; Alexis Darby, "The Case of Lydia Fairchild and Her Chimerism," *Embryo Project Encyclopedia*, https://embryo.asu.edu/pages/case-lydia-fairchild-and-her-chimerism-2002, June 1, 2021.

19. Peter Pan was a central character in J. M. Barrie's 1911 novel, *Peter and Wendy*. There are no formal symptoms associated with the Peter Pan syndrome, although behaviors such as failing to make important decisions and/or spending money unwisely (neither of which characterize Andrew) have been mentioned. The term was first used in 1983 by Dan Kiley in his book *Peter Pan Syndrome: Men Who Have Never Grown Up*. Crystal Raypole, "Peter Pan Syndrome: When People Just Can't Grow Up," *Healthline*, https://www.healthline.com/health/peter-pan-syndrome, October 21, 2021.

20. ReproMed, "Fee Schedule: Donor Semen Specimens," https://www.repromed.ca/UserFiles/File/RML_Fee_Schedule_2021.06.01.pdf, June 1, 2021. In 2015 the Canadian dollar (CAD) was equivalent to $1.16 US dollars, explaining why many Americans traveled across the border for reproductive services. Elad and Andrew spent an estimated $91,500 CAD in total.

21. Michelle Flowerday, interview with Nancy L. Segal, 2022. Canada's Assisted Human Reproduction Act of 2004 established the category of expenses that donors and surrogates can claim and the process by which these expenses can be recovered,

22. Elad estimated the following costs for the couple's entire process of egg donation and surrogacy in Canadian dollars (CAD): donor agency fee ($1,500);

Canadian Surrogacy Options ($10,000); in vitro fertilization, insemination, sperm collection, preimplantation genetic screening (PGS), medications, and related expenses ($35,000); legal fees ($20,000); and surrogate's personal expenses ($25,000). The total amount was $91,500 (CAD), equivalent to $78,324 USD, based on the 2015 exchange rate when they began the process.

23. Little Miracles, https://little-miracles.ca/, 2022.

24. ReproMed (Toronto Institute for Reproductive Medicine), https://www.repromed.ca/, 2022.

25. Michelle Flowerday, "Legal Services of Flowerday Fertility Law," Flowerday Fertility Law, https://www.familysurrogacylawyer.com/, 2011.

26. Michelle Flowerday, interview with Nancy L. Segal, 2022.

27. Eran Amir, "An Overview of Egg Donation Costs," *GoStork*, https://www.gostork.com/blog/eggdonor/egg-donation-costs/#:~:text=The%20cost%20of%20egg%20donation%20varies%2C%20as%20it,add%20up%20to%20anywhere%20from%20%2435%2C000%20to%20%2465%2C000, accessed 2022. The cost was most likely somewhat lower in 2015 when Andrew and Elad began the process.

28. Canada is moving toward more open relationships among prospective parents and donors. Canada lacks donor sibling registries but does provide parents with information about date of birth, city of birth, and biological sex of their children's half-siblings to prevent romantic relationships between them. Michelle Flowerday, interview with Nancy L. Segal, 2022.

29. The complex genetics of hair color have not been definitively established, but it is believed that a number of genetic variants are involved. Michael D. Morgan, Erola Pairo-Castineira, Konrad Rawlik, Oriol Canela-Xandri, Jonathan Rees, David Sims, Albert Tenesa, and Ian J. Jackson, "Genome-Wide Study of Hair Colour in UK Biobank Explains Most of the SNP Heritability," *Nature Communications* 9, no. 1 (2018): 1–10.

30. The Punjabi people are one of the largest ethnic groups in the world, found mostly in Northern India and Pakistan. "Who Are the Punjabi People?" *World Atlas*, https://www.worldatlas.com/articles/who-are-the-punjabi-people.html, 2022.

31. Currently, Canada rarely performs double embryo transfer that would result in twins, given the risks to the mother and fetuses. In addition, Canada's 2004 Assisted Human Reproduction Act prohibits embryo selection for sex; however, prenatal screening is allowed if a sex-linked disorder is possible, based on family history. Michelle Flowerday, interview with Nancy L. Segal, 2022.

32. "Factors Affecting IVF Outcome," Los Angeles In Vitro Fertility Clinic (LAIVF), https://laivfclinic.com/in-vitro-fertilization-ivf/, accessed 2022.

33. Andrea Rodrigo, Mark P. Trotice, Silvio Azaña Gutiérrez, Victor Montalvo Pallés, and Cristina Algarra Goosman, "How Many Eggs Do You

Need to Obtain to Perform IVF?" *inviTRA,* https://www.invitra.com/en /number-of-eggs-obtained/, February 21, 2022.

34. Rodrigo et al., "How Many Eggs Do You Need to Obtain to Perform IVF?"

35 The first successful in vitro fertilization (IVF) procedure took place in Great Britain in 1978. The first IVF babies born in the United States and Canada occurred in 1981 and 1983, respectively. IVF Worldwide, "The History of IVF—The Milestones," *Research and Education,* https://ivf-worldwide.com /ivf-history.html, 2008.

36. Rodrigo et al., "How Many Eggs Do You Need to Obtain to Perform IVF?"; Mindy Christianson, "Freezing Embryos," *John Hopkins Medicine,* https:// www.hopkinsmedicine.org/health/treatment-tests-and-therapies/freezing -embryos#:~:text=When%20thawed%2C%20the%20fertilized%20eggs%20 %E2%80%94%20embryos%20%E2%80%94,successful%20procedure%20 took%20place%20in%20the%20late%201980s, 2022. Pregnancy rates are sometimes higher with frozen embryos than with embryos that are not frozen.

37. PGS testing involves removing a few cells from the embryo and examining them for genetic defects. Coastal Fertility Medical Center, "How Does Preimplantation Genetic Screening (PGS) Work and What Are the Risks Associated With It?" https://coastalfertility.com/pgs-testing-and-risks/, February 18, 2021.

38. Preimplantation genetic testing (PGT) can reveal the sex of an embryo. This procedure would be advisable if a serious sex-related disorder, such as hemophilia, was present in the family. Some couples request PGT if they wish to add a boy or a girl to their family, but Canada prohibits this practice. Most couples, like Andrew and Elad, learn the sex of their fetus by ultrasound at eighteen to twenty-one weeks' gestation. See Healthline, "How Soon Can You Find Out the Sex of Your Baby?," https://www.healthline.com/health/pregnancy /when-can-you-find-out-sex-of-baby#medical-tests, 2022.

39. Paul Dingsdale, "Double Duty: Twin Surgeons Perform Kidney Transplant on Twin Patients," *USC News,* https://news.usc.edu/9409/Double-duty -Twin-surgeons-perform-kidney-transplant-on-twin-patients/, January 29, 1999.

40. Altruism can be understood at two levels: proximal (life history) and distal (evolutionary). These perspectives are both relevant to understanding altruistic behavior. Evolutionary psychologists would assert that we are predisposed to act more altruistically toward close relatives, with whom we share high proportions of genes, compared with distant relatives, as a way of transmitting our genes to future generations. Of course, this does not occur consciously. In terms of everyday behavior, acting for the benefit of another brings us pleasure, thereby maintaining that behavior. Generosity toward strangers may be understood with reference to reciprocal altruism—the idea that favors we perform for non-

relatives may be directed toward us in the future; see David M. Buss, *Evolutionary Psychology: The New Science of the Mind* (London: Routledge, 2019).

41. When I heard from Amanda in May 2022, she was devastated to learn that a distant relative would be fostering the little boy she had grown to love.

42. Mayo Clinic Staff, "Uterine Prolapse," *Mayo Clinic*, https://www.mayoclinic.org/diseases-conditions/uterine-prolapse/symptoms-causes/syc-2035 3458, accessed 2022.

43. The success rates for singleton births and live births from egg retrieval (all embryo transfers) are 51 percent and 55 percent, respectively, for women under thirty-five years of age. Society for Assisted Reproductive Technology (SART), "Final National Summary Report," https://www.sartcorsonline.com /rptCSR_PublicMultYear.aspx?reportingYear=2019, 2022. These figures vary depending upon maternal age, early or later embryo transfer, and other factors.

44. Nancy L. Segal, *Twin Mythconceptions: False Beliefs, Fables, and Facts About Twins* (San Diego, CA: Academic Press, 2017).

45. Kari Zalik, interview with Nancy L. Segal, 2022.

46. Intrauterine growth restriction can result from various factors, such as problems with the placenta, which delivers nutrition and oxygen to the fetus and blood flow from the umbilical cord. "Intrauterine Growth Restriction (IUGR)," *Johns Hopkins Medicine*, https://www.hopkinsallchildrens.org /Patients-Families/Health-Library/HealthDocNew/Intrauterine-Growth -Restriction-(IUGR), 2021.

47. A level 3 neonatal intensive care unit (NICU) is designed to assist babies who are born before thirty-two weeks; weigh less than three pounds, five ounces; and require special medical care. Level 4 NICUs treat extremely ill newborns. Ryne Dunkelberger, "What It Means to Be a Level 3 or Level 4 NICU," *Norton Children's*, https://nortonchildrens.com/news/what-it-means -to-be-a-level-3-nicu-or-level-4-nicu/, November 20, 2018.

48. María José Benítez-Marín, Jesús Marín-Clavijo, Juan Antonio Blanco-Elena, Jesús Jiménez-López, and Ernesto González-Mesa, "Brain Sparing Effect on Neurodevelopment in Children with Intrauterine Growth Restriction: A Systematic Review," *Children* 8, no. 9 (2021): 745. Brain sparing has been considered an adaptive response on the part of the fetus to overcome the lack of oxygen and nutrition. However, it may not be fully protective against neurological deficits.

49. Stephen Soong, Ristan M. Greer, Glenn Gardener, Vicki Flenady, and Sailesh Kumar, "Impact of Mode of Delivery after 32 Weeks' Gestation on Neonatal Outcome in Dichorionic Diamniotic Twins," *Journal of Obstetrics and Gynaecology Research* 42, no. 4 (2016): 392–98.

50. Ashlee K. Koch, Renée J. Burger, Ewoud Schuit, Julio Fernando Mateus, Maria Goya, Elena Carreras, Sckarlet E. Biancolin, et al., "Timing of Delivery for Twins with Growth Discordance and Growth Restriction: An

Individual Participant Data Meta-Analysis," *Obstetrics & Gynecology* 139, no. 6 (2022): 1155–67.

51. The average weight of male twins born at thirty-two weeks is four pounds, 1 ounce. See Soong et al., "Impact of Mode of Delivery after 32 Weeks' Gestation."

52. Amanda Adams, interview with Nancy L. Segal, 2022.

53. The twins eventually transitioned to formula in preparation for a visit to Israel when they were eight months old. The Center for Disease Control (CDC) advises that age at weaning is an individual decision for each family. Guidelines are offered for parents who wean their infants before and after twelve months of age. US Department of Health and Human Services, "Weaning," *CDC*, https://www.cdc.gov/nutrition/InfantandToddlerNutrition/breastfeed ing/weaning.html, accessed 2022.

54. Sarah J. Buckley, "Executive Summary of Hormonal Physiology of Childbearing: Evidence and Implications for Women, Babies, and Maternity Care," *Journal of Perinatal Education* 24, no. 3 (2015): 145–53.

55. Andrew Dvash-Banks, interview with Nancy Segal, May 3, 2022. Andrew described Elad as "super smart." *Strategic foresight* aims to identify solutions and responses that are likely to suit an evolving mission and/or organization. Office of Personnel Management, "Policy, Data, Oversight: Human Capital Management," *OPM.gov*, https://www.opm.gov/policy-data-oversight/human -capital-management/strategic-foresight/, accessed 2022.

56. "The Name Aiden: A Germanic Name with Irish Origins," https://www .ilovelanguages.com/what-does-the-name-aiden-mean-in-english, accessed November 21, 2021; Elad Dvash-Banks, interview with Nancy L. Segal, 2021.

57. "Sandak," *The Jewish Chronicle*, https://www.thejc.com/judaism/jewish -words/sandak-1.4005, July 18, 2008.

58. "The Brit Milah (Bris): What You Need to Know," *My Jewish Learning*, https://www.myjewishlearning.com/article/the-brit-milah-bris-ceremony/, 2022.

59. Twin-to-twin interactions in the womb have been recorded and studied by several investigators; see Segal, *Twin Mythconceptions*.

CHAPTER 5

1. Elad Dvash-Banks, Andrew Dvash-Banks, interviews with Nancy L. Segal, 2022.

2. "Life is what happens to you while you're busy making other plans." This line was made famous by John Lennon's 1980 song "Beautiful Boy (Darling

Boy)," but it appeared in a number of earlier sources. *Quote Investigator,* https://
quoteinvestigator.com/2012/05/06/other-plans/, accessed June 18, 2022.

3. Andrew Dvash-Banks, interview with Nancy L. Segal, 2022.

4. Andrew and Elad visited the US consulate in Toronto on Tuesday, January 24, 2017, just four days after President Barack Obama had left office and Donald Trump had been sworn in as his successor.

5. Aaron C. Morris, interview with Nancy L. Segal, 2022. Morris is the executive director of Immigration Equality, based in New York City.

6. "Excerpts from the Deposition of Andrew Mason Dvash-Banks in Support of Plaintiff's Motion 7, 2019" and "Excerpts from the Deposition of Terri Nathine Frances Day in Support of Plaintiff's Motion for Partial Summary Judgement," *PACER, Case 2:18-cv-00523-JFW-JC, Document 84,* January 19, 2019.

7. Elad Dvash-Banks, Andrew Dvash-Banks, interviews with Nancy L. Segal, 2022.

8. Maxxam Analytics rebranded to Bureau Veritas in 2019: https://www.bvna.com/insight/maxxam-analytics-has-rebranded-bureau-veritas.

9. DNA testing of baby and surrogate is no longer required in Canada. Lawyers appearing in court on behalf of clients to secure a declaration of parentage can now submit a letter stating how the embryo was created. Michelle Flowerday, interview with Nancy L. Segal, 2022. Flowerday was among the group of attorneys responsible for changing this practice, which now saves clients $1,000 (CAD).

10. Elad Dvash-Banks, Andrew Dvash-Banks, interviews with Nancy L. Segal, 2022.

11. Michelle Flowerday, interview with Nancy L. Segal, 2022.

12. Kristin Collins, interview with Nancy L. Segal, 2022. Professor Collins was a faculty member at the Boston University School of Law at the time of our interview. Meagan Flynn, "One Twin Was a Citizen, the Other Undocumented: A Victory in Court for Their Same-Sex Parents Rebukes the State Department," *Washington Post,* https://www.washingtonpost.com/nation/2019/02/22/one-twin-was-citizen-other-undocumented-victory-court-their-same-sex-parents-rebukes-state-dept/, February 22, 2019. The State Department does not follow the formal rule-making process of most agencies; according to Judge John F. Walter, the *Foreign Affairs Manual* included a poor interpretation of statutes in the Immigration and Nationality Act.

13. Cristina Rodríguez, interview with Nancy L. Segal, 2022.

14. US Department of State, *Foreign Affairs Manual,* 8 FAM 101.1-2, "Introduction to Consular Reports of Birth Abroad," https://fam.state.gov/FAM/08FAM/08FAM010101.html, October 20, 2020.

15. US Department of State, "Acquisition of U.S. Citizenship at Birth by a Child Born Abroad," *Bureau of Consular Affairs,* https://travel.state.gov

/content/travel/en/legal/travel-legal-considerations/us-citizenship/Acquisi tion-US-Citizenship-Child-Born-Abroad.html, accessed June 2022. The document states that "for birth on or after November 14, 1986, the U.S. citizen parent must have been physically present in the United States or one of its outlying possessions for five years prior to the person's birth, at least two of which were after the age of 14." Andrew satisfied that requirement as stated, although he had left the United States to study in Israel in 2007; it appears that the five years of physical presence in the United States do not need to occur immediately prior to the child's birth.

16. US Department of State, "Acquisition of U.S. Citizenship at Birth by a Child Born Abroad."

17. Andrew and Elad later learned that Secretary of State Rex Tillerson looked favorably upon their case, unlike Mike Pompeo, who eventually replaced him.

18. Elad Dvash-Banks, Andrew Dvash-Banks, interviews with Nancy L. Segal, 2022.

19. "United States District Court: Civil Minutes—General," *Case 2:18-cv-00523-JFW-JC, Document 123*, February 21, 2019.

20. Frank Gogol, "How Long Can a Canadian Citizen Stay in the U.S.?" https://www.stilt.com/blog/2020/09/how-long-can-a-canadian-stay-in-the -u-s/#How_Long_Can_Canadians_Stay_in_the_United_States, 2022.

21. Nefesh B'Nefesh, "What is Aliyah?" https://www.nbn.org.il/what-is -aliyah/, accessed 2022.

22. Terri N. Day, letter to Andrew Dvash-Banks, *PACER: Case 2:18-cv-00523-JFW-JC, Document 1-3,* March 2, 2017. The Immigration and Nationality Act (INA) of 1952 is often known as the McCarran-Walter Act, following its reorganization and revision by its congressional sponsors. Adam B. Cox and Cristina M. Rodríguez, *The President and Immigration Law* (Oxford: Oxford University Press, 2020). The INA continues to provide the framework for immigration policy in the United States.

23. Research shows that fathers in both opposite-sex and same-sex relationships who take paternity leave develop greater sensitivity to their infants than those who do not. Darbe Saxbe and Sofia Cardenas, "What Paternity Leave Does for a Father's Brain," *New York Times*, https://www.nytimes.com/2021 /11/08/opinion/paid-family-leave-fathers.html#:~:text=One%20reason %20paternity%20leave%20might%20boost%20fathers%E2%80%99%20 relationships,brains%20reflect%20the%20transition%20to%20parenthood%20 as%20well, November 8, 2021.

24. Ann Banks, Andrew Dvash-Banks, interviews with Nancy L. Segal, 2022.

25. Elad Dvash-Banks, Andrew Dvash-Banks, interviews with Nancy L. Segal, 2022.

26. Cox and Rodríguez, *The President and Immigration Law*. Cox and Rodríguez referenced six Muslim countries for which President Trump imposed a ban against entry into the United States. However, other sources have named seven countries: Iran, Iraq, Libya, Somalia, Syria, Sudan, and Yemen; see Aaliyah Brandon, "What Muslim Countries Did Trump Ban?" https://whatcountries.com/what-muslim-countries-did-trump-ban/, 2021.

27. BBC News, "Trump Migrant Separation Policy: Children 'in Cages' in Texas," https://www.bbc.com/news/world-us-canada-44518942, June 18, 2018.

28. Immigration Resources, "The Green Card Explained," *Boundless .com*, https://www.boundless.com/immigration-resources/the-green-card-explained/#:~:text=A%20green%20card%20allows%20a%20non-U.S.%20citizen%20to,for%20U.S.%20citizenship%20after%20three%20or%20five%20years, accessed 2022. Children may obtain a Green Card at any age via sponsorship through a parent, but the individual must be under the age of twenty-one and unmarried. Immigration rights attorney, personal communication, 2022.

29. US Department of State, "FAQ: Child Citizenship Act of 2000," Bureau of Consular Affairs, https://travel.state.gov/content/travel/en/Intercountry-Adoption/adopt_ref/adoption-FAQs/child-citizenship-act-of-2000.html, accessed 2022.

30. This line is from the Beatles' 1967 song "With a Little Help from My Friends," included on their album *Sgt. Pepper's Lonely Hearts Club Band*.

31. Jonathan Banks, interview with Nancy L. Segal, 2022.

32. Ashli Shapiro, interview with Nancy L. Segal, 2022.

33. Jennifer Levinson, interview with Nancy L. Segal, 2022. I found the CBS reporter, but she informed me that she no longer works for the station and did not respond to my follow-up messages.

34. Elad Dvash-Banks, interview with Nancy L. Segal, 2022.

CHAPTER 6

1. Fiona Hill, *There Is Nothing for You Here: Finding Opportunity in the Twenty-First Century* (New York: Mariner Books, 2021).

2. Jose Luis Gonzalez and Anthony Esposito, "In Mexico, Trump's Child Separations Trigger Wrenching Decisions," *Reuters*, https://www.cnn.com/2020/12/02/politics/family-separation-us-border-children/index.html, June 19, 2018.

3. Carlos Hernandez, Letter to Congressman Ted Lieu, c/o Ashley Fumiko Dominguez, *PACER, Case 2:18-cv-00523-JFW-JC, Document 10-4*, October 2, 2017.

4. "What We Do," Immigration Equality, https://immigrationequality.org /about-us/what-we-do/, accessed 2022. Immigration Equality has been in operation for twenty-five years; their success rate is 99 percent; see Jackie Yodashkin, "Immigration Equality and Sullivan & Cromwell LLP File Two Lawsuits Against U.S. State Department for Discriminating Against Married Same-Sex Couples and Their Children," Immigration Equality (Press Release), January 22, 2018.

5. "Contact Our Legal Team," Immigration Equality, https://immigration equality.org/contact-our-legal-team/; "Couples and Families." Three categories of inquiry are listed under this designation: Foreign-Born Children of Same-Sex Couples, Dual Foreign-National Couples, and Bi-National Couples. Resources are also provided; to be eligible for pro bono legal assistance, income cannot exceed $31,000; accessed August 22, 2022.

6. A BIA-accredited representative helps prepare immigration documents and provides legal advice regarding options for receiving immigration benefits. "Immigration: BIA Accredited Representatives," AVVO, Inc., https://www .avvo.com/legal-guides/ugc/immigration-bia-accredited-representatives, 2022. AVVO is derived from *avvocato*, the Italian word for lawyer. AVVO, Inc., "AVVO Q&A," https://www.avvo.com/legal-answers/what-does-avvo-stand -for—1885836.html, 2022.

7. Akin Gump Strauss Hauer & Feld LLP, "Regulatory: Immigration Law and Policy," https://www.akingump.com/en/experience/practices/regulatory /immigration-law-and-policy.html, 2022.

8. Yodashkin, "Immigration Equality and Sullivan & Cromwell LLP File Two Lawsuits Against U.S. State Department for Discriminating Against Married Same-Sex Couples and Their Children."

9. Kristen Thompson, interview with Dr. Nancy L. Segal, 2022.

10. Aaron C. Morris, e-mail communication to Nancy L. Segal, June 2022. I had not suggested Monday night when I initially wrote to Morris. During our conversation, he expressed concern about his family vacation, due to severe flooding at Yellowstone.

11. "Our Staff," Immigration Equality, https://immigrationequality.org /about-us/who-we-are/our-staff/, 2022.

12. During President Obama's administration, the State Department altered a requirement, thereby allowing a parent to establish a biological connection to a child by giving birth, as well as by providing the egg or sperm. This allowed lesbian couples to have a child in wedlock if one parent supplied the egg and the other parent carried the pregnancy. However, same-sex male couples do not have this option. Sarah Mervosh, "Democrats Urge Pompeo to End Policy Used to Deny Citizenship to Children of Gay Couples," *New York Times*, https://www.nytimes.com/2019/06/06/us/citizenship-immigrants-lgbtq.html, June 6, 2019. Also see "*Windsor v. United States*," American Civil Liberties

Union, https://www.aclu.org/cases/lesbian-and-gay-rights/windsor-v-united
-states, 2013; *"Obergefell v. Hodges,"* Legal Information Institute, https://www
.law.cornell.edu/supremecourt/text/14-556, 2015.

13. "Administrative Advocacy," Harvard Law School, https://hls.harvard
.edu/dept/opia/what-is-public-interest-law/public-interest-work-types
/administrative-advocacy/, 2022.

14. Aaron C. Morris, interview with Nancy L. Segal, 2022.

15. "Same Sex Marriage Becomes Law," *Gov.UK*, https://www.gov.uk
/government/news/same-sex-marriage-becomes-law, July 17, 2013.

16. "Zaccari-Blixt Family," Immigration Equality, https://immigration
equality.org/allison-stefania-and-lucas-zaccari-blixt/, 2022; Allison Blixt, "Will
the State Department Stop Discriminating Against My Family?" https://im
migrationequality.org/about-us/what-we-do/impact-litigation/will-the-state
-department-stop-discriminating-against-my-family/, 2022.

17. "Mize-Gregg Family," Immigration Equality, https://immigration
equality.org/derek-jonathan-and-simone-mize-gregg/, 2022; Sarah Mervosh,
"Gay U.S. Couple Sues State Dept. for Denying Their Baby Citizenship,"
New York Times, https://www.nytimes.com/2019/07/23/us/state-department
-assisted-reproductive-citizenship.html, July 23, 2019. The lawyer for this family argued that the residency requirement would not have applied if they had
been treated as a married couple.

18. "Federal Court Hears Oral Argument in Case of Child of Gay Maryland
Couple Denied Recognition as U.S. Citizen," Immigration Equality, https://
immigrationequality.org/press/press-releases-2/federal-court-hears-oral-argu
ment-in-case-of-child-of-gay-maryland-couple-denied-recognition-as-u-s-citi
zen/, June 5, 2020; https://uscode.house.gov/view.xhtml?req=granuleid:USC
-prelim-title8-section1401&num=0&edition=prelim, September 14, 2022.
"Title 8: Aliens and Nationality." The Immigration Nationality Act of 1952 was
amended several times. For a child to be a US citizen from birth (if born to a
US citizen parent and an alien), the residency requirement for the US citizen
parent was changed in 1986 to "five years, at least two" after age fourteen, from
"ten years, at least five" after age fourteen.

19. "Kiviti Family," Immigration Equality, https://immigrationequality.org
/adiel-roee-and-kessem-kiviti/, 2022.

20. "Litigation: Impact," Harvard Law School, https://hls.harvard.edu/dept
/opia/what-is-public-interest-law/public-interest-work-types/impact
-litigation/#:~:text=Impact%20litigation%20is%20brought%20or%20defended
%20typically%20when,organizations%20are%20also%20deeply%20involved%20
in%20policy%20work, 2022. Sometimes only one individual is involved in a
particular case.

21. Aaron C. Morris, interview with Nancy L. Segal, 2022. The Sullivan &
Cromwell law firm maintains offices in New York and Washington, DC, as well

as in cities in Europe, Asia, and Australia. Sullivan & Cromwell LLP, "Lawyers," https://www.sullcrom.com/lawyers, 2022.

22. "Case 2.18-cv-00523," Immigration Equality, https://immigration equality.org/wp-content/uploads/2020/06/Dvash-Banks-Complaint-Filed.pdf, January 22, 2018. As a matter of interest, Alexa M. Lawson-Remer gave birth to twins.

23. Brian Melley, "Gay Couple Sues U.S. for Denying Citizenship to Twin Son," *Los Angeles Times*, January 24, 2018, p. A7.

24. Nancy L. Segal, *Born Together—Reared Apart: The Landmark Minnesota Twin Study* (Cambridge, MA: Harvard University Press, 2012); *Deliberately Divided: Inside the Controversial Study of Twins and Triplets Adopted Apart* (Lanham, MD: Rowman & Littlefield, 2021).

25. Segal, *Born Together—Reared Apart*; *Deliberately Divided*.

26. Nancy L. Segal, *Entwined Lives: Twins and What They Tell Us About Human Behavior* (New York: Plume, 2000).

27. Aaron C. Morris, interview with Nancy L. Segal, 2022.

28. Aaron C. Morris; Kristen Thompson, interviews with Nancy L. Segal, 2022.

29. Jackie Yodashkin, interview with Nancy L. Segal, 2022.

30. Kristen Thompson, e-mail communication to Nancy L. Segal, 2022. Elad collected URLs for every online newspaper and magazine article he discovered about their case. He mentioned sources in Australia, Indonesia, and Italy.

31. Kristin Collins, interview with Nancy L. Segal, 2022.

32. Elad Dvash-Banks, interview with Nancy L. Segal, 2022.

33. Aaron C. Morris, interview with Nancy L. Segal, 2022.

34. Conor Finnegan, "State Dept. Fighting to Deny US Citizenship to Gay Couple's Child," *ABC News*, https://abcnews.go.com/Politics/state-dept -fighting-deny-us-citizenship-gay-couples/story?id=72493795, August 20, 2020.

35. Mervosh, "Democrats Urge Pompeo to End Policy Used to Deny Citizenship to Children of Gay Couples."

36. US Citizenship and Immigration Services (USCIS) defines a child born "in wedlock" in several ways. One way is the marriage between a legal genetic father and a legal non-genetic, non-gestational mother or father. US Citizenship and Immigration Services, "Chapter 3—U.S. Citizens at Birth (INA 301 and 309)," *USCIS Policy Manual*, https://www.uscis.gov /policy-manual/volume-12-part-h-chapter-3, accessed August 2022; Immigration Equality, "New USCIS Policy Acknowledges Marriages of Same-Sex Couples and Their Right to Confer U.S. Birthright Citizenship to Their Children," Immigration Equality (Press Release), https://immigration equality.org/press/press-releases-2/new-uscis-policy-acknowledges-marriages

-of-same-sex-couples-and-their-right-to-confer-u-s-birthright-citizenship-to
-their-children/, August 10, 2021.

37. Ellen Trachman, "USCIS's New Immigration Policy for Families Through Fertility Assistance Is Good, But Not Great," *Above the Law*, https://above thelaw.com/2021/08/usciss-new-immigration-policy-for-families-through -fertility-assistance-is-good-but-not-great/, August 18, 2021. Trachman is an attorney specializing in assisted reproductive technology law.

38. Aaron C. Morris, interview with Nancy L. Segal, 2022.

39. Elad Dvash-Banks, interview with Nancy L. Segal, 2022.

40. Aaron C. Morris, interview with Nancy L. Segal, 2022.

41. Morris noted that the issue of granting or denying citizenship to children born abroad to transnational same-sex couples was identified by Immigration Equality under the Obama administration (2008–2016). He said it is easy to blame Obama; however, it was not really a problem prior to that, because marriage equality did not exist in the United States until 2015. By the time Obama left office, he had become much more overtly pro-equality.

42. Andrew Dvash-Banks, interview with Nancy L. Segal, 2021.

43. Aaron C. Morris, interview with Nancy L. Segal, 2022. "En Banc," *Legal Dictionary*, https://legaldictionary.net/en-banc/, accessed 2022. A case could be petitioned by either side if there are concerns about a decision made by one three-judge panel. The Justice Department under former president Donald Trump took the extraordinary measure of asking the court to do this after they had lost, but the court declined to do so. Aaron C. Morris, interview with Nancy L. Segal, 2022.

44. "Victory! Kessem Kiviti Is Recognized as a U.S. Citizen from Birth by a Federal Judge, and Since the Government Dropped Their Case, She Is a Citizen for Good!" Immigration Equality, https://immigrationequality.org/adiel-roee -and-kessem-kiviti/, October 27, 2020.

45. "History; Locations," In-N-Out Burger, https://www.in-n-out.com /locations, 2022.

CHAPTER 7

1. Sullivan & Cromwell and Immigration Equality, "Complaint-Filed.pdf: Case 2.18-cv-00523, Document 1," https://immigrationequality.org/wp-con tent/uploads/2020/05/Dvash-Banks-Complaint-Filed.pdf, January 22, 2018.

2. Andrew and Elad Dvash-Banks, interviews with Nancy L. Segal, 2022.

3. Amanda Frost, interview with Nancy L. Segal, 2022. Frost teaches in the areas of immigration and citizenship law. Ashley Craythorne, interview with Nancy L. Segal, 2022. Craythorne authored an excellent article on the Dvash-

Banks case before joining the Michigan State Appellate Defender Office; see Ashley D. Craythorne, "Same Sex Equality in Immigration Law: The Case for Birthright Citizenship for Foreign-Born Children of U.S. Citizens in Same-Sex Binational Unions," *Texas Law Review* 97 (2019): 645–71. Meredith Luneack is a staff attorney with the Michigan Immigration Rights Center in Detroit, Michigan.

4. Cristina Rodríguez, interview with Nancy L. Segal, 2022.

5. Sarah Mervosh, "Gay U.S. Couple Sues State Dept. for Denying Their Baby Citizenship," *New York Times*, https://www.nytimes.com/2019/07/23/us/state-department-assisted-reproductive-citizenship.html, July 23, 2019.

6. Larisa Iati, "Federal Agents Seized 6-year-old Elián González at Gunpoint. A Custody Battle Raged for Months," *Washington Post*, https://www.washingtonpost.com/history/2019/11/25/federal-agents-seized-year-old-elin-gonzlez-gunpoint-custody-battle-raged-months/, November 25, 2019. Elián was reunited with his father and returned with him to Cuba.

7. Susan Morgenstern (director), *"I Want to Go Home": Stories from Writers in a Country at War*, New York City, Museum of Jewish Heritage; co-presenters: The Braid and HIAS, July 20, 2022.

8. Alexia Dellner, "How to Embrace a Smash Cake Even If You're a Neat Freak," https://www.purewow.com/family/what-is-a-smash-cake, January 23, 2019.

9. Elad Dvash-Banks, Andrew Dvash-Banks, interviews with Nancy L. Segal, 2022.

10. Laura E. Berk, *Infants, Children and Adolescents*, 9th ed. (Hoboken, NJ: Pearson, 2021).

11. Jackie Yodashkin, interview with Nancy L. Segal, 2022.

12. Jackie Yodashkin, interview with Nancy L. Segal, 2022. Yodashkin now works as an independent organization and strategic communications consultant. https://www.jackieyodashkin.com/, accessed 2022.

13. Elad Dvash-Banks, Andrew Dvash-Banks, interviews with Nancy L. Segal, 2022.

14. Nancy L. Segal, *Twin Mythconceptions: False Beliefs, Fables, and Facts About Twins* (San Diego, CA: Academic Press, 2017).

15. "Welcome to ICOMBO—International Council of Multiple Birth Organizations," ICOMBO, https://icombo.org/, accessed 2022.

16. Jill Diesel, Natalie Sterrett, Sharoda Dasgupta, Jennifer L. Kriss, Vaughn Barry, Kayla Vanden Esschert, Ari Whiteman, et al., "COVID-19 Vaccination Coverage Among Adults—United States, December 14, 2020–May 22, 2021," *Morbidity and Mortality Weekly Report* 70, no. 25 (June 25, 2021): 922–27, https://www.cdc.gov/mmwr/volumes/70/wr/mm7025e1.htm; Centers for Disease Control and Prevention, "CDC Recommends COVID-19 Vaccines for

Young Children," https://www.cdc.gov/media/releases/2022/s0618-children
-vaccine.html, June 18, 2022.

17. Some symptoms of attention-deficit/hyperactivity disorder (ADHD)
include distractibility, impulsivity, and excessive talking. "What Is ADHD,"
Centers for Disease Control and Prevention, https://www.cdc.gov/ncbddd
/adhd/facts.html, accessed 2022.

18. Elizabeth Bryan, "The Impact of Multiple Preterm Births on the Family," *BJOG: An International Journal of Obstetrics & Gynaecology* 110 (2003):
24–28. However, some unaffected twins benefit in selected ways from having a
co-twin with special needs; see Yonat Rum, Shir Genzer, Noam Markovitch,
Jennifer Jenkins, Anat Perry, and Ariel Knafo-Noam, "Are There Positive
Effects of Having a Sibling with Special Needs? Empathy and Prosociality of
Twins of Children with Non-Typical Development," *Child Development* 93,
no. 4 (2022): 1121–28.

19. Maria Garcia, interview with Nancy L. Segal, 2022.

20. Elad Dvash-Banks, interview with Nancy L. Segal, 2022.

21. Nancy L. Segal, *Entwined Lives: Twins and What They Tell Us About Human Behavior* (New York: Plume, 2000); Segal, *Twin Mythconceptions*.

22. Segal, *Twin Mythconceptions*.

23. Andrew Dvash-Banks, Elad Dvash-Banks, interviews with Nancy L.
Segal, 2022.

24. "Reptiles for Kids Birthday Parties and Events: Now Serving All of
Southern California!" Kids Reptile Parties, https://kidsreptileparties.com/, 2021.

25. "LGBTQ Family Fact Sheet," Family Equality Council, www.family
equality.org, June 2020; Avichal Scher, "Gay Fathers, Going It Alone,"
New York Times, https://www.nytimes.com/2018/10/25/nyregion/single-gay
-fathers-through-surrogacy.html, October 25, 2018; David Dodge, "A Family Like Ours: Portraits of Gay Fatherhood," *New York Times*, https://www
.nytimes.com/2021/06/16/well/family/gay-fatherhood-photos.html, June 16,
2021.

26. Ellen C. Perrin, Ellen E. Pinderhughes, Kathryn Mattern, Sean M.
Hurley, and Rachel A. Newman, "Experiences of Children with Gay Fathers,"
Clinical Pediatrics 55, no. 14 (2016): 1305–17; Lisa Rapaport, "Gay Fathers
Face Stigma as Parents," Healthcare and Pharma (*Reuters*), https://www.reuters
.com/article/us-health-lgbt-gay-dads-idUSKCN1P92TS, January 15, 2019;
Jennifer L. Wainright, Stephen T. Russell, and Charlotte J. Patterson, "Psycho-
social Adjustment, School Outcomes, and Romantic Relationships of Adoles-
cents with Same-Sex Parents," *Child Development* 75, no. 6 (2004): 1886–98;
Samantha L. Tornello and Charlotte J. Patterson, "Adult Children of Gay
Fathers: Parent–Child Relationship Quality and Mental Health," *Journal of
Homosexuality* 65, no. 9 (2018): 1152–66; Charlotte Patterson, "Parental Sexual
Orientation, Parental Gender Identity, and the Development of Children," *Ad-*

vances in Child Behavior and Development 63 (2022): 71–102; Susan Golombok, Lucy Blake, Jenna Slutsky, Elizabeth Raffanello, Gabriela D. Roman, and Anke Ehrhardt, "Parenting and the Adjustment of Children Born to Gay Fathers through Surrogacy," *Child Development* 89, no. 4 (2018): 1223–33; Susan Imrie and Susan Golombok, "Impact of New Family Forms on Parenting and Child Development," *Annual Review of Developmental Psychology* 2 (2020): 295–316.

27. Gail K. Bliss and Mary B. Harris, "Teachers' Views of Students with Gay or Lesbian Parents," *International Journal of Sexuality and Gender Studies* 4, no. 2 (1999): 149–71; Charlotte J. Patterson, "Children of Lesbian and Gay Parents," *Current Directions in Psychological Science* 15, no. 5 (2006): 241–44.

28. E. Comeau, "First Test-Tube Baby in U.S. Reflects on the Death of an IVF Pioneer," April 10, 2013. Available from: http://www.boston.com/lifestyle /health/fitness/getmovingblog/2013/04/when_there_are.html; Robin Marantz Henig, "Solving Mysteries of Reproduction Helped Make Parenthood Possible for Millions," *ScienceNews,* June 9, 2021. https://www.sciencenews.org/article /mysteries-reproduction-parenthood-ivf-fertilization#:~:text=In%20the%20 first%20half%20of%20the%2020th%20century%2C,husband%E2%80%99s%20 consent%2C%20was%20illegitimate.%20In%201978%2C%20everything%20 changed.

CHAPTER 8

1. Attorneys for Plaintiffs, "Complaint for Declaratory and Injunctive Relief," *PACER, Case 2:18-cv-00523-JFW-JC,* January 22, 2019. An amended complaint was filed on January 14, 2019.

2. "Allegation Law and Legal Definition," *U.S. Legal.com,* https://definitions .uslegal.com/a/allegation/#:~:text=The%20assertion%2C%20claim%2C%20 declaration%2C%20or%20statement%20of%20a,assertions%20without%20 proof%2C%20until%20they%20can%20be%20proved, 2022.

3. "Count," Legal Information Institute (LII), https://www.law.cornell.edu /wex/count, 2021.

4. The Administrative Procedure Act (APA) is a federal act that governs administrative law procedures. Some additional complaints are included in the legal document that was filed, but those listed in the chapter are key. Legal Information Institute, "Administrative Procedure Act," https://www.law.cornell .edu/wex/administrative_procedure_act, accessed 2022.

5. Some dates have been edited for accuracy, as Andrew suggested I do. In addition, I added several events I deemed important to this case.

6. "Case: *Dvash-Banks v. Tillerson [Dvash-Banks v. Pompeo]," Civil Rights Litigation Clearinghouse,* https://clearinghouse.net/case/16417/?docket_page=1

#docket, updated August 4, 2022; https://clearinghouse.net/case/16417 /?docket_page=2#docket, updated August 4, 2022.

7. Alexa M. Lawson-Remer, interview with Nancy L. Segal, 2022.

8. A "white glove experience" exceeds expectations and may come with an unanticipated surprise. Jim Henderson, "Why Choosing a White Glove Experience Matters," https://williamchuff.com/moving-tips-blog/Why-Choosing-A -White-Glove-Experience-Matters#:~:text=A%20white%20glove%20experi ence%20is%20an%20experience%20that,after%20you%20have%20dropped%20 it%20off%20for%20service, April 1, 2022. The nature of Tillerson's attempt to resolve the matter is considered confidential so cannot be disclosed.

9. Guinness World Records, "First Twins Born in Different Countries," p. 62, *Guinness World Records*, London: Guinness World Records (Vancouver, Canada: Jim Pattison Group, 2015).

10. "Guinness Book of Records Twins Claim Causes Cross-Border Incident," *Shropshire Star*, https://www.shropshirestar.com/news/2016/01/09 /guinness-book-of-records-twins-claim-causes-cross-border-incident/, January 8, 2016.

11. Heidi Gannon, e-mail correspondence to Nancy L. Segal, 2022. The information Heidi provided was based on a conversation with her sister.

12. House of Commons Library, "Who Can Vote in UK Elections?" UK Parliament, https://commonslibrary.parliament.uk/research-briefings/cbp -8985/, 2022; Welsh Government, "Who Can Stand for Election?" *Law Wales*, https://law.gov.wales/constitution-and-government/electoral-law/who-can -stand-election, March 17, 2021.

13. To become a candidate for US president, individuals must be natural-born US citizens, be age thirty-five or older, and have resided in the United States for at least fourteen years. "Requirements to Be U.S. President," *ConstitutionUS.com*, https://constitutionus.com/presidents/requirements-and -qualifications-to-become-us-president/, 2022.

14. Nancy L. Segal, Francisca J. Niculae, Erika N. Becker, and Emmy Y. Shih, "Reared-Apart / Reared-Together Chinese Twins and Virtual Twins: Evolving Research Program and General Intelligence Findings," *Journal of Experimental Child Psychology* 207 (2021): 105106.

15. "FAQ: Child Citizenship Act of 2000," *Travel.State.gov*, https://travel .state.gov/content/travel/en/Intercountry-Adoption/adopt_ref/adoption -FAQs/child-citizenship-act-of-2000.html, accessed 2022.

16. Adoptive parents of children from China and Vietnam; e-mail communications to Nancy L. Segal, 2022.

17. Brian Melley, "Court: Son Born Abroad to Gay Couple is a U.S. Citizen," *Orange County Register* (Associated Press), October 10, 2020, p. 13.

18. The Jewish New Year, Rosh Hashanah, was September 18–20, 2020.

19. I received this reply from Ms. Lawson-Remer's former assistant at Sullivan & Cromwell: "While I understand that this is important, I am not at liberty to give out this information. I do not have anywhere that I can refer you to get this information. Good luck in writing your book."

20. Sue Gelmis, telephone communication with Nancy L. Segal, 2022; court employee, telephone and e-mail communications with Nancy L. Segal, 2022.

21. GLAD, https://www.glad.org/, 2022.

22. "Mary L. Bonauto," GLAD, https://www.glad.org/staff/mary-bonauto/, 2022.

23. "Brief of Amici Curiae GLBTQ Legal Advocates & Defenders and National Center for Lesbian Rights in Support of Plaintiffs-Appellees and Affirmance," GLAD, https://www.glad.org/wp-content/uploads/2019/12/Dvash -Banks_Amicus.pdf, December 19, 2019; GLAD, "*Dvash-Banks v. DOS and Pompeo*," https://www.glad.org/dvash-banks-v-dos-and-pompeo/, 2020; National Center for Lesbian Rights, "Dvash-Banks v. Pompeo (Amicus)," https://www .nclrights.org/our-work/cases/dvash-banks-v-pompeo/, 2020.

24. Ashley Craythorne, interview with Nancy L. Segal, 2022; *Foreign Affairs Manual*, "7 FAM 1100 Appendix E: Birth in Wedlock, of Wedlock, Void and Voidable Marriages," July 8, 2014; *Foreign Affairs Manual*, "8 FAM 301.709 Birth Abroad in Wedlock or Wedlock to a U.S. Citizen Parent and a Non-U.S. Citizen Parent," https://fam.state.gov/search/viewer?format=html&query =1401&links=1401&url=/FAM/08FAM/08FAM030107.html#M301_7_7, June 9, 2022.

25. *Foreign Affairs Manual*, "8 FAM 301.709 Birth Abroad in Wedlock or Wedlock to a U.S. Citizen Parent and a Non-U.S. Citizen Parent," https:// fam.state.gov/search/viewer?format=html&query=1401&links=1401&url =/FAM/08FAM/08FAM030107.html#M301_7_7, June 9, 2022.

26. Aaron C. Morris, e-mail correspondence to Nancy L. Segal, 2022.

27. Kristin Collins, interview with Nancy L. Segal, 2022.

28. Cristina Rodríguez, interview with Nancy L. Segal, 2022.

29. Kristin Collins, interview with Nancy L. Segal, 2022.

30. In the United States, between 2014 and 2016, 64 percent of married same-sex male couples and 65.6 percent of married same-sex female couples were raising a biological child, compared with 95.8 percent of married heterosexual couples. Shoshana K. Goldberg and Kerith J. Conron, "How Many Same-Sex Couples in the U.S. Are Raising Children?" The Williams Institute, July 2018.

31. Stephanie A. Grover, Ziva Shmorgun, Sergey I. Moskovtsev, Ari Baratz, and Clifford L. Librach, "Assisted Reproduction in a Cohort of Same-Sex Male Couples and Single Men," *Reproductive Biomedicine Online* 27, no. 2 (2013): 217–21.

32. "Dvash-Banks" (search term), Westlaw, https://1-next-westlaw-com.lib
-proxy.fullerton.edu/Search/Results.html?query=Dvash-Banks&contentType
=ANALYTICAL&querySubmissionGuid=i0ad740120000018313bc94a9c023
c725&categoryPageUrl=Home%2FSecondarySources%2FLawReviewsJournal
s&searchId=i0ad740120000018313bc94a9c023c725&transitionType=ListView
Type&contextData=(sc.Search), 2022; https://heinonline-org.lib-proxy.fuller
ton.edu/HOL/LuceneSearch?terms=dvash-banks&collection=all&searchtype
=advanced&typea=text&tabfrom=&submit=Go&sendit=&all=true, 2022. I
also identified scholarly work that was not listed in the databases I consulted using the search term "Dvash-Banks," e.g., Douglas NeJaime, "The Constitution
of Parenthood," *Stanford Law Review* 72 (2020): 261–380; it is likely that there
are additional references to the other three cases.

33. Sasha Hochman, "Legal and Biological Borders: Citizenship Consequences for Children of Same-Sex Couples," *Columbia Undergraduate Law Review*, November 7, 2019.

34. Courtney G. Joslin, Douglas NeJaime, Mitchell P. Reich, Reedy C.
Swanson, and Danielle D. Stempel, "Brief for Amici Curiae Family Law Professors in Support of Appellees and Affirmance," Case 19-55517, DktEntry:
31, December 19, 2019. The sixty-five professors who endorsed this document
were part of a listserv that included seventy-five professors interested in family law and were invited to take part. Two other law professors (NeJaime and
Joslin) co-authored the brief.

35. "Definition of *Amicus Curiae*," *Merriam-Webster Dictionary*, https://www.
merriam-webster.com/dictionary/amicus%20curiae, 2022.

36. Joslin et al., "Brief for Amici Curiae Family Law Professors in Support
of Appellees and Affirmance."

37. Nancy L. Segal, *Deliberately Divided: Inside the Controversial Study of Twins
and Triplets Adopted Apart* (Lanham, MD: Rowman & Littlefield, 2021).

38. Courtney Joslin, interview with Nancy L. Segal, 2022.

39. Catherine J. Ross, interview with Nancy L. Segal, 2022.

40. T. Grant Benson, "These Two Baby Boys Are Twins, but an Italian
Court Says They Aren't Brothers," *Breaking911*, https://breaking911.com/two
-baby-boys-twins-italian-court-says-arent-brothers/, January 8, 2017.

CHAPTER 9

1. "Parenting Is Overrated," *Intelligence2 Debates*, October 29, 2019, https://
www.intelligencesquaredus.org/debates/parenting-overrated.

2. Cara J. Kiff, Liliana J. Lengua, and Maureen Zalewski, "Nature and Nurturing: Parenting in the Context of Child Temperament," *Clinical Child and*

Family Psychology Review 14, no. 3 (2011): 251–301; Lisabeth Fisher DiLalla and Matthew R. Jamnik, "The Southern Illinois Twins/Triplets and Siblings Study (SITSS): A Longitudinal Study of Early Child Development," *Twin Research and Human Genetics* 22, no. 6 (2019): 779–82.

3. Kenneth S. Kendler and Jessica H. Baker, "Genetic Influences on Measures of the Environment: A Systematic Review," *Psychological Medicine* 37, no. 5 (2007): 615–26.

4. Andrew Dvash-Banks, interview with Nancy L. Segal, 2023; "Toyota Sports Performance Center," https://www.toyotasportsperformancecenter.com/page/show/6762512-public-skating, 2023.

5. Andrew Dvash-Banks, interview with Nancy L. Segal, 2022.

6. Nick Bishop, interview with Nancy L. Segal, 2022.

7. Andrew Dvash-Banks, interview with Nancy L. Segal, 2022.

8. Laurel Mintz, interview with Nancy L. Segal, 2022.

9. J. Jill Suitor, Megan Gilligan, and Karl Pillemer, "Continuity and Change in Mothers' Favoritism Toward Offspring in Adulthood," *Journal of Marriage and Family* 75, no. 5 (2013): 1229–47. I derived the terms *assortative parenting* and *assortative cross-parenting* from the established term of assortative mating. *Assortative mating* is the non-random pairing of partners who are similar in genetic background and/or observed characteristics; examples include attitudes and values, and verbal intelligence and religious affiliation.

10. Julie Fitness, "Favouritism and Rejection in Families: Black Sheep and Golden-Haired Children," *Proceedings of the Australian Psychology Society* 63 (2004): 63–67.

11. Matthew and Ed Moreira Bahnson, interview with Nancy L. Segal, 2022.

12. HeadGlobal, https://www.headgloballlc.com/, accessed 2022.

13. Daniel Head, Darek Sady, interviews with Nancy L. Segal, 2022.

14. Adrian Willings, "Steam Deck vs. Nintendo Switch vs. Logitech G Cloud Gaming Handheld," *Pocket-lint*, https://www.pocket-lint.com/games/news/162825-steam-deck-vs-nintendo-switch-vs-logitech-g-cloud-gaming-handheld, September 29, 2022. Ann Banks, Elad Dvash-Banks, e-mail correspondence with Nancy L. Segal, 2022.

15. "Diwali in Punjab," Society for the Confluence of Festival of India (SCFI), https://www.diwalifestival.org/diwali-in-punjab.html#:~:text=In%20Punjab%2C%20Diwali%20Festival%20is%20the%20time%20for,victory%20of%20righteousness%20and%20lifting%20of%20spiritual%20darkness, 2022.

16. Nancy L. Segal, "Cooperation, Competition, and Altruism within Twin Sets: A Reappraisal," *Ethology and Sociobiology* 5, no. 3 (1984): 163–77; Nancy L. Segal, Keith A. Chavarria, and Joanne Hoven Stohs, "Twin Research: Evolutionary Perspective on Social Relations," Catherine A. Salmon and Todd K. Shackelford (eds.), *Family Relationships: An Evolutionary Perspective* (New York: Oxford University Press, 2007), 312–33.

17. Pikachu is a fictional species in the Pokémon media franchise.

18. Elad Dvash-Banks, interview with Nancy L. Segal, 2022.

19. Andrew Dvash-Banks, Elad Dvash-Banks, interviews with Nancy L. Segal, 2022.

CHAPTER 10

1. In 2003, the Massachusetts ban on same-sex marriage was ruled unconstitutional. "First Legal Same-Sex Marriage Performed in Massachusetts," This Day in History, https://www.history.com/this-day-in-history/first-legal-same-sex-marriage-performed-in-massachusetts, May 14, 2021. In June 2006, the California Supreme Court ruled that the ban on same-sex marriage was unconstitutional. Same-sex couples were allowed to marry between June and November of 2008; this practice was declared unconstitutional in 2010, a decision sent on appeal to the US Supreme Court. This decision was reversed in 2013. FindLaw, "California Same Sex Marriage and Domestic Partnership Laws," https://www.findlaw.com/state/california-law/california-same-sex-marriage-and-domestic-partnership-laws.html, June 20, 2016. Also see note 9.

2. Eunice Esomonu and Molly Callahan, "Which Books Are Banned, and Where? A State-by-State Guide to Banned Learning in the U.S.," *News at Northeastern*, https://news.northeastern.edu/2022/03/22/banned-books/, March 22, 2022; Amy Watson, "Number of Books Banned in Schools in the United States from July 2021 to March 2022, by State," *Statista*, https://www.statista.com/statistics/1310288/school-book-bans-us-by-state/, July 5, 2022.

3. Devan Cole, "Florida Legislature Passes Bill Prohibiting Some Classroom Instruction About Sexual Orientation and Gender Identity," *CNN.com*, https://www.cnn.com/2022/03/08/politics/florida-dont-say-gay-bill/index.html, March 8, 2022.

4. Ian Prasad Philbrick, "The End of Roe," *New York Times*, https://www.nytimes.com/2022/06/25/briefing/roe-v-wade-struck-down-explained.html, June 25, 2022.

5. Sheryl Gay Stoltenberg, "Thomas's Concurring Opinion Raises Questions About What Rights Might Be Next," *New York Times*, https://www.nytimes.com/2022/06/24/us/clarence-thomas-roe-griswold-lawrence-obergefell.html, June 24, 2022; Silvia Foster-Frau, "LGBTQ Community Braces for Rollback After Abortion Ruling," *Washington Post*, https://www.washingtonpost.com/nation/2022/06/24/abortion-fears-lgbtq-gay-rights/, June 24, 2022.

6. Annie Karni, "Same-Sex Marriage Bill, Considered Dead on Arrival, Gains New Life," *New York Times*, https://www.nytimes.com/2022/07/20/us

/politics/same-sex-marriage-bill-senate.html?referringSource=articleShare, July 20, 2022. However, it does not codify (arrange into a systematic code) the entire Supreme Court decision on *Obergefell v. Hodges*; see Isaac Saul, "The Respect for Marriage Act," *Tangle*, https://www.readtangle.com/respect-for-marriage-act /#:~:text=However%2C%20the%20Respect%20for%20Marriage%20Act%20 does%20not,that%20have%20been%20lawfully%20performed%20in%20 other%20states, July 25, 2022. The bill would repeal the 1996 Defense of Marriage Act that defined marriage as the union between a man and a woman. If the court were to overrule it, the new bill would require states that discontinued issuing marriage licenses to same-sex couples to acknowledge same-sex marriages performed legally in other states. US senator for California, Dianne Feinstein, press release, "Senators Introduce Bipartisan Respect for Marriage Act," https:// www.feinstein.senate.gov/public/index.cfm/2022/7/senators-introduce-bi partisan-respect-for-marriage-act, July 19, 2022.

7. Foster-Frau, "LGBTQ Community Braces for Rollback After Abortion Ruling."

8. In *Griswold v. Connecticut*, the Supreme Court invalidated a Connecticut law that made it a criminal offense to use birth control devices or to advise anyone about their use. John R. Vile, "*Griswold v. Connecticut (*1965)," *The First Amendment Encyclopedia*, https://mtsu.edu/first-amendment/article/579 /griswold-v-connecticut, accessed 2022.

9. In *Lawrence v. Texas*, the US Supreme Court invalidated sodomy law, legalizing same-sex sexual activity in every US state and territory. Krystyna Blokhina Gilkis, "*Lawrence v. Texas*," Cornell Law School—Legal Information Institute, https://www.law.cornell.edu/wex/lawrence_v._texas, September 2018.

10. Prior to 2015, the legality of same-sex marriages was determined at the state level. These states included Massachusetts (the first to do so in 2003), as well as Connecticut, Hawaii, Maine, New Hampshire, New York, Vermont, and Washington. Elaine S. Povich, "Without *Obergefell*, Most States Would Have Same-Sex Marriage Bans," Pew Charitable Trusts, https://www.pewtrusts .org/en/research-and-analysis/blogs/stateline/2022/07/07/without-obergefell -most-states-would-have-same-sex-marriage-bans#:~:text=A%20ruling%20 overturning%20Obergefell%20wouldn%E2%80%99t%2C%20however%2C%20 reverse%20state,Maine%2C%20New%20Hampshire%2C%20New%20 York%2C%20Vermont%20and%20Washington, July 7, 2022.

11. Associated Press, "Supreme Court Overturns *Roe v. Wade*, Allowing States to Ban Abortions," https://www.wtvr.com/news/local-news/supreme -court-overturns-roe-v-wade-june-24-2022, June 24, 2022. The three liberal justices were Stephen Breyer, Sonia Sotomayor, and Elena Kagan. Note: President Joseph R. Biden announced that codifying *Roe v. Wade* would be a priority of his administration if the Democratic Party expanded their control of the Congress following the 2022 midterm elections. Alan Rappeport, "Biden Vows

to Codify Abortion Rights if Democrats Win Midterms," *New York Times*, https://www.nytimes.com/2022/10/18/us/politics/biden-abortion-midterms .html?smid=nytcore-ios-share&referringSource=articleShare, (Section A, p. 14), October 18, 2022.

12. Daniel Head, interview with Nancy L. Segal, 2022.

13. Catherine J. Ross, interview with Nancy L. Segal, 2022.

14. Courtney G. Joslin, interview with Nancy L. Segal, 2022. *Dobbs v. Jackson Women's Health Organization* was the Supreme Court case that overturned *Roe v. Wade*. The decision was made on June 24, 2022.

15. Madeleine Carlisle, "Florida Just Passed the 'Don't Say Gay' Bill. Here's What It Means for Kids," *Time Magazine*, https://time.com/6155905/florida -dont-say-gay-passed/, March 8, 2022; Ann Banks, interview with Nancy L. Segal, 2022.

16. Catherine J. Ross, interview with Nancy L. Segal, 2022. See Antonin Scalia's dissenting opinion: *Lawrence v. Texas*, 539 U.S. 558 (2003) (Scalia, J., dissenting): 589–91. Justice Scalia's opinion is available at https://www.law .cornell.edu/supremecourt/text/539/558.

17. Sasha Hochman, interview with Nancy L. Segal, 2022. I spoke with Hochman just two weeks after the Supreme Court had overturned *Roe v. Wade*.

18. Remy Tumin, "Same-Sex Couple Households in U.S. Surpass One Million," *New York Times* (2022), https://www.nytimes.com/2022/12/02/us /same-sex-households-census.html.

19. Nikki McCann Ramirez, "Senate Passes Bill to Protect Same-Sex Marriage," *New York Times* (2022), https://www.rollingstone.com/politics/politics -news/respect-for-marriage-act-passes-senate-1234631989/; Annie Karni, "Bill to Protect Same-Sex Marriage Rights Clears Congress," *New York Times* (2022), https://www.nytimes.com/2022/12/08/us/politics/same-sex-marriage-con gress.html; Michael D. Shear, "Biden Signs Bill to Protect Same-Sex Marriage Rights," *New York Times* (2022), https://www.nytimes.com/2022/12/13/us /politics/biden-same-sex-marriage-bill.html.

20. Douglas NeJaime, interview with Nancy L. Segal, 2022.

21. Douglas NeJaime and Courtney G. Joslin, "How Parenthood Functions," *Columbia Law Review* (2023); Courtney G. Joslin, interview with Nancy L. Segal, 2022. Also see the Uniform Parentage Act of 1973, updated in 2017 to "ensure the equal treatment of children born to same-sex couples." National Conference of Commissions in Uniforms State Laws, https://www.uniformlaws.org/Higher Logic/System/DownloadDocumentFile.ashx?DocumentFileKey=e4a82c2a -f7cc-b33e-ed68-47ba88c36d92&forceDialog=0, 2017.

22. Roni Caryn Rabin, "An Abortion Ban with Unexpected Consequences for Older Mothers," *New York Times*, October 8, 2022, p. A15; Nancy L. Segal, *Twin Mythconceptions: False Beliefs, Fables, and Facts About Twins* (San Diego, CA: Academic Press, 2017).

23. Shirley McGuire and Lilly Shanahan, "Sibling Experiences in Diverse Family Contexts," *Child Development Perspectives* 4, no. 2 (2019): 72–79.

24. Jill Elaine Hasday, "Siblings in Law," *Vanderbilt Law Review* 65, no. 3 (2012): 897–931.

25. Elad Dvash-Banks, interview with Nancy L. Segal, 2022.

26. The Supreme Court could conceivably overturn the 2015 decision of *Obergefell v. Hodges* that granted marital rights to same-sex couples.

27. Andrew Dvash-Banks, interview with Nancy L. Segal, 2022.

28. Hulu, *Ordinary People*, https://www.rottentomatoes.com/m/ordinary_people, accessed 2022.

Bibliography

PRIMARY SOURCES

Details concerning the specific papers, documents, and individuals I have consulted appear in the endnotes to each chapter.

Legal Documents

Attorneys for Plaintiffs. "Complaint for Declaratory and Injunctive Relief." *Case 2:18-cv-00523-JFW-JC*, January 22, 2019. An amended complaint was filed on January 14, 2019.

"Case: *Dvash-Banks v. Tillerson* [*Dvash-Banks v. Pompeo*]." *Civil Rights Litigation Clearinghouse*, https://clearinghouse.net/case/16417/?docket_page =1#docket, updated August 4, 2022.

Day, Terri N. Letter to Andrew Dvash-Banks, *PACER: Case 2:18-cv-00523-JFW-JC, Document 1-3*, March 2, 2017.

"Excerpts from the Deposition of Andrew Mason Dvash-Banks in Support of Plaintiff's Motion 7," 2019.

"Excerpts from the Deposition of Terri Nathine Frances Day in Support of Plaintiff's Motion for Partial Summary Judgment." *PACER, Case 2:18-cv-00523-JFW-JC, Document 84*, January 19, 2019.

GLAD. "Brief of Amici Curiae GLBTQ Legal Advocates & Defenders and National Center for Lesbian Rights in Support of Plaintiffs-Appellees and Affirmance." https://www.glad.org/wp-content/uploads/2019/12/Dvash -Banks_Amicus.pdf, December 19, 2019.

———. "*Dvash-Banks v. DOS and Pompeo*." https://www.glad.org/dvash-banks -v-dos-and-pompeo/, 2020; National Center for Lesbian Rights, "Dvash-Banks v. Pompeo (Amicus)." https://www.nclrights.org/our-work/cases /dvash-banks-v-pompeo/, 2020.

Hernandez, Carlos. Letter to Congressman Ted Lieu, c/o Ashley Fumiko Dominguez, *PACER, Case 2:18-cv-00523-JFW-JC, Document 10-4,* October 2, 2017.

Immigration Equality. *Case 2:18-cv-00523-JFW-JC.* https://immigration equality.org/wp-content/uploads/2020/06/Dvash-Banks-Complaint-Filed .pdf, January 22, 2018.

Joslin, Courtney G., Douglas NeJaime, Mitchell P. Reich, Reedy C. Swanson, and Danielle D. Stempel. "Brief for Amici Curiae Family Law Professors in Support of Appellees and Affirmance." *Case 19-55517,* DktEntry 31, December 19, 2019.

"Memorandum." *Case 19-55517,* D.C. No. 2:18-cv-00523-JFW-JC, https:// immigrationequality.org/wp-content/uploads/2020/10/DVASH-BANKS -Ethan-ninth-cir-order-10.09.2020.pdf, October 9, 2020.

"Notice of Appeal." *Case 2:18-cv-00523-JFW-JC, Document 133,* May 6, 2019.

Sullivan & Cromwell and Immigration Equality. "Complaint-Filed.pdf: *Case 2.18-cv-00523, Document 1.*" https://immigrationequality.org/wp-content /uploads/2020/05/Dvash-Banks-Complaint-Filed.pdf, January 22, 2018.

"US District Court: Civil Minutes—General." *Case 2:18-cv-00523-JFW-JC, Document 123,* February 21, 2019.

Personal Interviews

Family members, friends, and associates of Andrew and Elad Dvash-Banks; teachers of twins Aiden and Ethan Dvash-Banks

Professionals and students in the fields of psychology, education, law, immigration, citizenship, communications, journalism, and religion

Books

Cox, Adam B., and Christina M. Rodríguez. *The President and Immigration Law* (Oxford, UK: Oxford University Press, 2020).

Hill, Fiona. *There Is Nothing for You Here: Finding Opportunity in the Twenty-First Century* (New York: Mariner Books, 2021).

Issenberg, Sasha. *The Engagement: America's Quarter-Century Struggle Over Same-Sex Marriage* (New York: Penguin Books, 2021).

Soble, Ronald L., and Robert E. Dallos. *The Impossible Dream: The Equity Funding Story—The Fraud of the Century* (New York: G. P. Putnam's Sons, 1975).

Selected Research Studies and Magazine Articles

Dodge, David. " 'A Family Like Ours': Portraits of Gay Fatherhood." *New York Times*, https://www.nytimes.com/2021/06/16/well/family/gay-fatherhood -photos.html, June 16, 2021.

Grover, Stephanie A., Ziva Shmorgun, Sergey I. Moskovtsev, Ari Baratz, and Clifford L. Librach. "Assisted Reproduction in a Cohort of Same-Sex Male Couples and Single Men." *Reproductive Biomedicine Online* 27, no. 2 (2013): 217–21.

National Survey of Family Growth. "Number of Sexual Partners in Lifetime." *Centers for Disease Control and Prevention*, https://www.cdc.gov/nchs/nsfg /key_statistics/n-keystat.htm#numberlifetime, November 8, 2021.

Okamura, Kunihiro, Jun Murotsuki, Mitsuru Iwamoto, Hidetaka Endo, Taka-nori Watanabe, Kazuo Ohashi, and Akira Yajima. "A Probable Case of Superfecundation." *Fetal Diagnosis and Therapy* 7, no. 1 (1992): 17–20.

Rodrigo, Andrea, Mark P. Trotice, Silvio Azaña Gutiérrez, Victor Montalvo Pallés, and Cristina Algarra Goosman. "How Many Eggs Do You Need to Obtain to Perform IVF?" *inviTRA,* https://www.invitra.com/en/number -of-eggs-obtained/, February 21, 2022.

Segal, Nancy L., Jeffrey M. Craig, and Mark P. Umstad. "Challenge to the Assumed Rarity of Heteropaternal Superfecundation: Findings from a Case Report." *Australian Journal of Forensic Sciences* 52, no. 5 (2020): 547–52.

Segal, Nancy L., and Joseph L. Nedelec. "Heteropaternal Twinning: Unique Case of Opposite-Sex Twins with Different Fathers." *Forensic Science International* 327 (2021): 110948.

Segal, Nancy L., Francisca J. Niculae, Erika N. Becker, and Emmy Y. Shih. "Reared-Apart/Reared-Together Chinese Twins and Virtual Twins: Evolving Research Program and General Intelligence Findings." *Journal of Experimental Child Psychology* 207 (2021): 105106.

Soong, Stephen, Ristan M. Greer, Glenn Gardener, Vicki Flenady, and Sailesh Kumar. "Impact of Mode of Delivery after 32 weeks' Gestation on Neonatal Outcome in Dichorionic Diamniotic Twins." *Journal of Obstetrics and Gynaecology Research* 42, no. 4 (2016): 392–98.

Wenk, Robert E., T. Houtz, M. Brooks, and F. A. Chiafari. "How Frequent Is Heteropaternal Superfecundation?" *Acta Geneticae Medicae et Gemellologiae: Twin Research* 41 no. 1 (1992): 43–47.

Yu, Neng, Margot S. Kruskall, Juan J. Yunis, Joan H. M. Knoll, Lynne Uhl, Sharon Alosco, Marina Ohashi, et al. "Disputed Maternity Leading to Identification of Tetragametic Chimerism." *New England Journal of Medicine* 346, no. 20 (2002): 1545–52.

SELECTED SECONDARY SOURCES CITED OR CONSULTED

Adler, Seth. "Inside the Elite Israeli Military Unit 8200." *Cyber Security Hub*, https://www.cshub.com/threat-defense/articles/inside-the-elite-israeli-mili tary-unit-8200, June 11, 2020.

Akin Gump Strauss Hauer & Feld LLP. "Regulatory: Immigration Law and Policy." https://www.akingump.com/en/experience/practices/regulatory /immigration-law-and-policy.html, 2022.

BBC News. "Trump Migrant Separation Policy: Children 'in Cages' in Texas." https://www.bbc.com/news/world-us-canada-44518942, June 18, 2018.

Berk, Laura E. *Infants, Children, and Adolescents*, 9th ed. (Newbury Park, CA: Sage, 2022).

Blixt, Allison. "Will the State Department Stop Discriminating Against My Family?" https://immigrationequality.org/about-us/what-we-do/impact-litigation /will-the-state-department-stop-discriminating-against-my-family/, 2022.

Bryan, Elizabeth. "The Impact of Multiple Preterm Births on the Family." *BJOG: An International Journal of Obstetrics & Gynaecology* 110 (2003): 24–28.

Carter, Bill. "ABC Is Canceling 'Ellen.' " *New York Times*, https://www.nytimes .com/1998/04/25/arts/abc-is-canceling-ellen.html, April 25, 1998.

CJNews. "What Is the Jewish Festival of Purim Otherwise Known As?" *Chicago Jewish News*, https://www.chicagojewishnews.com/what-is-the-jewish -festival-of-purim-otherwise-known-as/, 2022.

Cox, Adam B., and Cristina M. Rodríguez. *The President and Immigration Law* (Oxford: Oxford University Press, 2020).

Craythorne, Ashley D. "Same Sex Equality in Immigration Law: The Case for Birthright Citizenship for Foreign-Born Children of U.S. Citizens in Same-Sex Binational Unions." *Texas Law Review* 97 (2019): 645–71.

Dickow, Cheryl. "Firstborn Sons." *Catholic Exchange*, https://catholic exchange.com/firstborn-sons/#:~:text=First-born%20sons%20have%20 always%20held%20a%20place%20of,mother%E2%80%99s%20 womb%2C%E2%80%9D%20is%20said%20to%20belong%20to%20God, August 17, 2010.

Fiske, Gavriel. "Purim: Part on Hevre." *Jerusalem Post*, https://www.jpost.com /Local-Israel/In-Jerusalem/Purim-Party-on-hevre, March 13, 2008.

Foreign Affairs Manual. "7 FAM 1100 Appendix E: Birth in Wedlock, of Wedlock, Void and Voidable Marriages," July 8, 2014.

———. "8 FAM 301.709 Birth Abroad in Wedlock or Wedlock to a U.S. Citizen Parent and a Non-U.S. Citizen Parent." https://fam.state.gov /search/viewer?format=html&query=1401&links=1401&url=/FAM /08FAM/08FAM030107.html#M301_7_7, June 9, 2022.

Forrest, Kim, "14 Jewish Wedding Traditions and What They Mean." https://www.weddingwire.com/wedding-ideas/jewish-wedding-traditions, June 13, 2018.

Guinness World Records. "First Twins Born in Different Countries," p. 62. *Guinness World Records.* London: Guinness World Records (Vancouver, Canada: Jim Pattison Group, 2015).

Guttman, Nathan. "Pew Level: Meet the Mazorti, Israel's 'Tradition' Tribe." *Forward,* https://forward.com/news/335410/pew-report-meet-the-masorti-israels-traditional-tribe/, 2022.

Hochman, Sasha. "Legal and Biological Borders: Citizenship Consequences for Children of Same-Sex Couples." *Columbia Undergraduate Law Review,* November 7, 2019.

Hvidtjørn, Dorte, Laura Schieve, Diana Schendel, Bo Jacobsson, Claus Sværke, and Poul Thorsen. "Cerebral Palsy, Autism Spectrum Disorders, and Developmental Delay in Children Born After Assisted Conception: A Systematic Review and Meta-Analysis." *Archives of Pediatrics & Adolescent Medicine* 163, no. 1 (2009): 72–83.

IKAR. "What is IKAR?" https://ikar.org/ask/what-is-ikar/, 2022.

Immigration Equality. "Dvash-Banks Family." https://immigrationequality.org/andrew-elad-and-ethan-dvash-banks/, 2018.

———. "Kiviti Family." https://immigrationequality.org/adiel-roee-and-kessem-kiviti/, 2022.

———. "Mize-Gregg Family." https://immigrationequality.org/derek-jonathan-and-simone-mize-gregg/, 2022.

———. Press Release: "Appellate Court Upholds Previous Ruling that Twin Son of Gay Married Couple Born Abroad is U.S. Citizen from Birth." file:///Users/csuftitan/Desktop/Nancy's%20Work/Book%20NEXT/Immigration/Appellate%20Court%20Upholds%20Previous%20Ruling%20That%20Twin%20Son%20of%20Gay%20Married%20Couple%20Born%20Abroad%20is%20U.S.%20Citizen%20from%20Birth%20-%20Immigration%20Equality%20_%20Immigration%20Equality.html, October 9, 2021.

———. Press Release: "Immigration Equality and Sullivan & Cromwell LLP File Two Lawsuits Against U.S. State Department for Discriminating Against Married Same-Sex Couples and Their Children," January 22, 2018.

———. "What We Do." https://immigrationequality.org/about-us/what-we-do/, accessed 2022.

———. "Zaccari-Blixt Family." https://immigrationequality.org/allison-stefania-and-lucas-zaccari-blixt/, accessed 2022.

Legal Information Institute. "Defense of Marriage Act (DOMA). Cornell University, https://www.law.cornell.edu/wex/defense_of_marriage_act_%28doma%29, 2020.

Melley, Brian. "Gay Couple Sues U.S. for Denying Citizenship to Twin Son." *Los Angeles Times*, January 24, 2018, p. A7.

Mervosh, Sarah. "Democrats Urge Pompeo to End Policy Used to Deny Citizenship to Children of Gay Couples." *New York Times,* https://www.ny times.com/2019/06/06/us/citizenship-immigrants-lgbtq.html, June 6, 2019.

———. "Gay U.S. Couple Sues State Dept. for Denying Their Baby Citizenship." *New York Times,* https://www.nytimes.com/2019/07/23/us/state-de partment-assisted-reproductive-citizenship.html, July 23, 2019.

Rosenfeld, Dovid. "Firstborn (Bechor) Privileges." *Aish,* https://aish.com /firstborn-bechor-privileges/, December 2, 2016.

"Sandak." *The Jewish Chronicle.* https://www.thejc.com/judaism/jewish-words /sandak-1.4005, July 18, 2008.

Segal, Nancy L. *Born Together—Reared Apart: The Landmark Minnesota Twin Study* (Cambridge, MA: Harvard University Press, 2012).

———. *Deliberately Divided: Inside the Controversial Study of Twins and Triplets Adopted Apart* (Lanham, MD: Rowman & Littlefield, 2021).

———. *Entwined Lives: Twins and What They Tell Us About Human Behavior* (New York: Plume, 2000).

———. *Twin Mythconceptions: False Beliefs, Fables, and Facts About Twins* (San Diego, CA: Academic Press, 2017).

Tchekmedyian, Alene. "These Twins Were Born 4 Minutes Apart. But Only One is a U.S. Citizen." https://www.latimes.com/local/lanow/la-me-ln-twins -citizenship-20180127-story.html, January 27, 2018.

Trachman, Ellen. "USCIS's New Immigration Policy for Families through Fertility Assistance Is Good, But Not Great." *Above the Law,* https://abovethelaw .com/2021/08/usciss-new-immigration-policy-for-families-through-fertility -assistance-is-good-but-not-great/, August 18, 2021.

US Department of State. "Acquisition of U.S. Citizenship at Birth by a Child Born Abroad." *Bureau of Consular Affairs,* https://travel.state.gov/content/travel /en/legal/travel-legal-considerations/us-citizenship/Acquisition-US-Citizen ship-Child-Born-Abroad.html, accessed June 2022.

———. "FAQ: Child Citizenship Act of 2000." Bureau of Consular Affairs. https://travel.state.gov/content/travel/en/Intercountry-Adoption/adopt _ref/adoption-FAQs/child-citizenship-act-of-2000.html, accessed 2022.

Wainright, Jennifer L., Stephen T. Russell, and Charlotte J. Patterson. "Psychosocial Adjustment, School Outcomes, and Romantic Relationships of Adolescents with Same-Sex Parents." *Child Development* 75, no. 6 (2004): 1886–98.

Yodashkin, Jackie. "Immigration Equality and Sullivan & Cromwell LLP File Two Lawsuits Against U.S. State Department for Discriminating Against Married Same-Sex Couples and Their Children." Immigration Equality, January 22, 2018.

Acknowledgments

$\mathcal{I}$ like saving my words of thanks for the end of a book because writing them is a time to savor the memories of the people who helped me along the way. The contributions of my friends and colleagues were stunning, as were those of the many people I met for the first time who gave so generously of their time and expertise.

Andrew and Elad were the stuff that dreams are made of. They patiently endured hours of Zoom sessions, telephone conversations, and e-mail messages, even after I assured them that "This is the last one!" Both men put me in touch with their family members and friends—across the country and around the world—all of whom were rich sources of information. And in the interest of accuracy and commitment to the project, both Andrew and Elad read the entire book twice prior to its going to press.

Gay Fathers, Twin Sons is my ninth book, and my third completed with the wisdom and guidance of my literary agent, Carol Mann, founder of the Carol Mann Agency in New York City. I was grateful to Carol in 2018 for putting me in the wise hands of Suzanne Staszak-Silva, senior editor at Rowman & Littlefield, for the writing of my 2021 book, *Deliberately Divided*. I am grateful to Carol once again for bringing my idea for the present work to Suzanne's attention, and grateful to Suzanne for taking it on.

My boyfriend, Dr. Craig K. Ihara, professor emeritus in the philosophy department at California State University, Fullerton, brought his extraordinary editorial skills to every chapter. It was interesting, fun, and a little scary as we went over the (often illegible) notes he scribbled into the margins, but his comments were always insightful, perceptive, and helpful. My colleague in the psychology department, Dr. Cheryl Crippen, also cast her discerning eyes on every word I wrote, using easy-to-read tracked changes to enter her probing questions and well-reasoned comments. This is the third book Cheryl has reviewed for me, and I still marvel at the natural talent she brings to the task. Despite her very full teaching schedule, she donated so generously of her limited time.

I owe so much to the legal scholars who understood the importance of their role in this book and spoke with me at length about the case. Many of them put me in touch with their colleagues and forwarded material that added to, and clarified, various aspects of the lawsuit and its outcome.

Andrew's sister and photographer extraordinaire, Ashli Shapiro, sent me hundreds of her stunning photographs, from which I could choose just fifteen to twenty, of Andrew and Elad and their children, taken over the years. Her pictures show the family that the couple built for themselves and their sons, making them all real people for the readers of this book. I am also indebted to graphic designer and identical twin, Kelly Donovan, for processing photographs from other sources. Her artistic magic is evident in this book and in other books I have written over the years.

My graduate students Elizabeth Pratt-Thompson and Rita Guerrero assisted me with this project in so many ways—transcribing interviews, printing papers, and collecting articles. Some people say that professors are only as good as their students, and I endorse that sentiment fully. I also wish to thank the office staff in my department for their clerical assistance, which I relied upon on various occasions.

Saved for the end, but savored just as much, are the thanks due to the lawyers at Immigration Equality and the Sullivan & Cromwell law firm. Their dedication to helping Andrew and Elad, and all couples who crave the freedom to be themselves and raise their children in the best way they know how, is exceptional. We can add to their efforts by following their vital lead.

Index

Note: Page references for figures and tables are italicized.

Books by the Author

Entwined Lives: Twins and What They Tell Us About Human Behavior (2000)
Indivisible by Two: Lives of Extraordinary Twins (2007)
Someone Else's Twin: The True Story of Babies Switched at Birth (2011)
Born Together—Reared Apart: The Landmark Minnesota Twin Study (2012)
Twin Mythconceptions: False Beliefs, Fables, and Facts About Twins (2017)
Accidental Brothers: The Story of Twins Exchanged at Birth and the Power of Nature and Nurture (2018; with co-author Yesika S. Montoya)
Deliberately Divided: Inside the Controversial Study of Twins and Triplets Adopted Apart (2021)

EDITED VOLUMES

Uniting Psychology and Biology: Integrative Perspectives on Human Development (1997; with co-editors Glenn E. Weisfeld and Carol C. Weisfeld)
Twin Research for Everyone: From Biology to Health, Epigenetics, and Psychology (2022; with co-editors Adam D. Tarnoki, David L. Tarnoki, and Jennifer R. Harris)

ANNOTATED PHOTO COLLECTION

Twin Children of the Holocaust: Stolen Childhood and the Will to Survive (2023)

About the Author

Dr. Nancy L. Segal is a professor of psychology and director of the Twin Studies Center at California State University, Fullerton. She has authored seven books, co-edited two volumes, and produced an annotated photograph collection. She has also written over three hundred journal and magazine articles on twins and twin development. Her 2021 book, *Deliberately Divided: Inside the Controversial Study of Twins and Triplets Adopted Apart*, was the subject of a BBC-TV World News documentary, and her book *Born Together—Reared Apart: The Landmark Minnesota Twin Study* won the 2013 William James Book Award from the American Psychological Association. Dr. Segal's research has been featured in the *New York Times*, the *Atlantic Monthly*, and the *Wall Street Journal*. A world-renowned expert on twins, she has appeared on the *Today* show, *Good Morning America*, *Dateline*, *48 Hours*, *The Oprah Winfrey Show*, and National Public Radio. She was a distinguished speaker at TEDxManhattanBeach, in 2017, and has addressed audiences on nearly every continent. Dr. Segal has also served as an expert witness on legal cases involving medical malpractice, injury, and custody of twins.

www.ingramcontent.com/pod-product-compliance
Lightning Source LLC
Chambersburg PA
CBHW031543260326
41914CB00002B/245